4/99

ALSO BY CHARLES FERGUS

The Wingless Crow
Shadow Catcher
A Rough-Shooting Dog
The Upland Equation
Swamp Screamer

SUMMER AT LITTLE LAVA

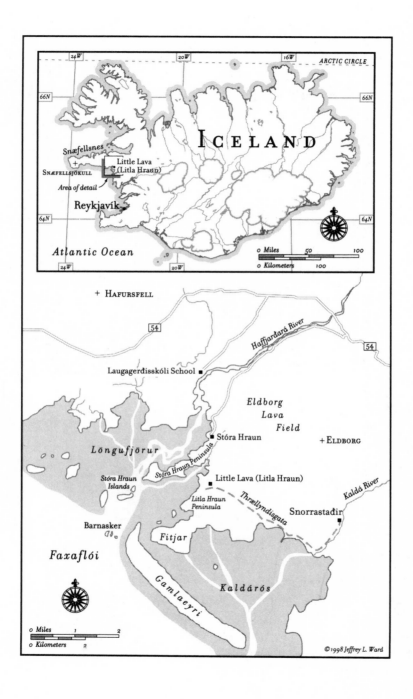

SUMMER AT LITTLE LAVA

A Season at the Edge of the World

CHARLES FERGUS

North Point Press

Farrar, Straus and Giroux

New York

North Point Press
A division of Farrar, Straus and Giroux
19 Union Square West, New York 10003

Copyright © 1998 by Charles Fergus
Illustrations copyright © 1998 by Pétur Baldvinsson
All rights reserved
Distributed in Canada by Douglas & McIntyre Ltd.
Printed in the United States of America
Library of Congress catalog card number: 98-072591
Designed by Jonathan D. Lippincott
First edition, 1998

In memory of
Ruth Foote Fergus
and
Claire Aldona Gallagher

CONTENTS

You have not lived until you have stayed awake a summer's night in Iceland. 　　　　　　　　　—*from an Icelandic poem*

Summer at Little Lava

1 | The Way to Little Lava

Two routes led to Little Lava. The longer one took most of an hour, circling wide through marshy pastureland and traversing a tongue of the lava field that bordered the farm. Now, because the tide was out, I could make a direct approach, straight across the mudflats: twenty minutes' walking.

I tugged on a pair of rubber Wellington boots and slipped my arms through the straps of my pack. Beyond the gravelly spot where I'd parked the car, the ground was sodden; it trembled underfoot. Legs apart to keep my balance, I trod across the spongy turf, then splashed through a shallow pond.

I found myself in a terrain studded with grass-covered hummocks ranging in size from soccer balls to sofa bolsters.

Such hummocks are common throughout rural Iceland. They are called *thúfur*. A *thúfa* arises when water in the soil freezes: the ice, expanding, mounds the soil upward. I clambered over, stumbled between, and lurched through the field of thúfur. Icelanders recognize a form of locomotion called *thúfnagangar*, or "thúfa-walking." It is said that a farmer come to town can be discerned, above and beyond his fusty suitcoat, by the manner in which he clambers, stumbles, and lurches over level pavement.

I came to a teetering halt as, at my feet, a snipe flew up from the grassy crack between two thúfur. *Scape! Scape! Scape!* it cried. It had a long needlelike bill, a russet back, and narrow wings that crooked halfway out their length— wings that whistled as the bird went off twisting and dodging a few feet above the marsh.

I started walking again, headed for the house on its hill.

On the map, the site was marked with an X and the name *Litlahraun* in parentheses. The X and the parentheses meant that the farm was an *eyðibýli*, a deserted place. It would be home for me, my wife, and our son during the summer to come.

In Icelandic, *litla* means "little"; *hraun*, pronounced a throaty "hroin," means "lava" or "lava field."

Little Lava, we called it.

It lay on the coast of Iceland fifty miles north of Reykjavík. It had been a farm for at least six centuries. The last residents had departed just after World War II when, like so many Icelanders, they moved to the city, abandoning the struggle of subsistence farming in favor of weekly paychecks, of electric lights, refrigerators, indoor plumbing, phones, roads—amenities that had never made it across that obstructive marsh.

I had come to Little Lava for my own reasons, my own rewards: solitude, birds on the wing, the healing breath of the wind in my face, and the chance to take the days one at a time, the long bright days of the Northern summer.

The house stood on a green knoll like a big thúfa. The building was small and drab, with unpainted concrete walls. Beyond it stretched a plain of dark lava. To the west lay a gray line: the bay. The house looked like a block of lava tumbled away from the flow, or a box of no particular value washed ashore and stranded by the tide.

It was late May, on the cusp between spring and summer. I had flown to Iceland two weeks ahead of my wife, Nancy, and our son, William. In Reykjavík I had stayed with our friend Thórður, an adept and cosmopolitan fellow in his thirties who makes his living selling long underwear that he imports from Sweden. Thórður lived with his mother and father in their comfortable modern house in a suburb of Reykjavík called Seltjarnarnes.

Icelanders tend toward the literal in their naming of places. Seltjarnarnes means "Seal Pond Peninsula"; Reykjavík is "Smoky Bay," in reference to the steam that early settlers saw rising from the volcanic earth.

At Thórður's parents' house I slept in the guest room, whose windows looked out on Faxaflói Bay. Across the bay, some sixty miles distant, stood the long chain of mountain peaks that formed the spine of Snæfellsnes, "Snow Mountain Peninsula." Little Lava lay where Snæfellsnes attached to the mainland of western Iceland.

In Reykjavík Thórður shepherded me around the city, helping me obtain the government documents that I needed, open a bank account, and buy a car.

I had wanted to go to Little Lava as soon as possible. I filled my backpack with my clothes and some food. I put the pack in the car, along with my collapsible kayak. I drove out of town headed north.

A hundred squelching steps after scaring up the snipe, I roused a pair of more formidable birds: Arctic skuas, about the size of crows, with charcoal backs and pale gray bellies. They came flapping up from the boggy ground and, without hesitating, flew at me. They pumped their long wings. Their webbed feet dangled. *Kee-yow! Kee-yow!* they screamed. I ducked as one of them darted at my face—its wings sounded like a bedsheet ripped in half above my head. Clearly, the skuas had a nest nearby, but I wasn't about to go looking for it, not with those sooty demons hectoring me. I kept on walking, dodging thúfur and ducking skuas. After a while the birds quit harassing me; they flew back and landed on a rock near the car.

We would be passing this way often on our travels to and from Little Lava, and I was glad that these were Arctic skuas and not great skuas. The great skua is a dun-colored brute twice the size of the Arctic skua. Defending its nest, a great skua will glide in silently from behind and club you in the head with its beak or talons. The blow, I'd been told, could knock a man senseless.

The land shelved off about four feet where the marsh met the tide flats. A notch led down to the sand. The exposed boggy banks were of peat, a compressed coffee-colored mass dripping with water and flecked with blackened twigs and rootlets. Peat bogs cover a tenth of Iceland, about half the island's vegetated area. In the past, people burned peat for cooking and to heat their homes. More recently, they have gone about trenching these wetlands, draining them to make pastures and hayfields at the expense of the bog-dwelling birds.

With my first steps onto the flats I sank ankle-deep in mud. Farther out, the greater proportion of sand gave a firmer footing. Twice a day, the tide came and filled the flats. Twice a day, the sea cut off Little Lava from easy access. Now, with the tide out, freshwater stream channels veined the mud-and-sand expanse.

In a burst of orange legs and brown wings, a redshank took to the air, shrieking. Gulls drifted off with more insouciance at my approach. Above the narrow peninsula extending south from Little Lava, a raven flapped and sailed, flapped and sailed.

The clouds knit themselves together, and the wind picked up. The air was chill. I was glad to be wearing a thick wool sweater beneath my parka. Raindrops stung my face. Putting up my hood, I trudged on.

My heart was grieving; my life was full of pain. At times the pain would subside, but it was always there, always waiting, ready to close in again like the rain on this typically fickle Icelandic day.

Nine months earlier, my mother had died. She was

seventy-three years old. She had driven home from a birthday party for her three-year-old grandchild, my brother's daughter. The police believed she had come into her house and surprised a burglar. He picked up a kitchen knife. He backed her into a bedroom. He kept on stabbing until she was dead.

My own house is twenty miles from my mother's house, in central Pennsylvania, and I was the one who found her. Since that day, I had lived with grief, and fear, and hatred for one who could commit such an act: the police had arrested a man within a few days of the killing, a man I knew but slightly, a man who must have been the antithesis of the gentle, wise woman I had loved all my life.

Not long before she died, I told Mom we would be spending the following summer in Iceland. We were sitting at her dining-room table. From the tree-lined street, a breeze blew in through the open windows. William sat on the floor in the living room, playing with some painted wooden blocks that I had played with when I was a boy; Mom had been watching him while I ran some errands in town.

"You'll be there all summer?" She gave me an inquiring look as she set down her red pen. She'd been editing a technical paper for an engineering professor at Penn State University, the school where my father had taught until a few years before his death. For as long as I could remember, Mom had done freelance editing, often for students and faculty for whom English was a second language.

I nodded. "Late May through August. We'll be staying in an abandoned farmhouse. Some friends of Nancy's own it.

No electricity or phone. It's on the coast, and you get there by walking across a marsh at low tide."

"Sounds like your kind of place," Mom said.

Mine, and also my wife's. It was Nancy who had taken us to Iceland in the first place. While doing graduate work at the university, she had become fascinated by the Icelandic sagas, the heroic stories of the land's early settlers written down during the Middle Ages. Together we had visited Iceland three times: once before Will was born, once with him when he was an infant, and once when Mom had taken care of him in our absence. And twice Nancy had gone there on her own, to take guided horseback tours into the deserted volcanic interior and to study the Icelandic language. On those two visits, friends had taken her to Little Lava.

Nancy was enthralled by the culture and the literature of Iceland. I had come to appreciate the country for its wildness, its teeming birdlife, the purity of its air and water, and the grand views opening across the windswept land.

Mom asked me some questions about the house at Little Lava. What kind of shape was it in? Would it keep us warm and dry? I didn't know much about the old farm, having only seen pictures that Nancy had taken. "It'll be a lot better than a tent," I joked. Could we be contacted in case of an emergency? I assured her that, one way or another, a message could be gotten to us.

"What if one of you gets hurt or sick?"

I shrugged; I hadn't figured that out yet. Thórður had advised a cellular phone, but I would not consider one. "It's not like the middle of Alaska," I said. "There's a farm about a mile from the house."

She looked over at Will, still playing with the blocks, building a small house of his own on the floor. "Do you think
he'll like it?"

I shrugged again. I was not at all sure that he would.

She looked at me with level green eyes. "I'll miss you."

I would miss her, too. I was her firstborn. We had always
been close, and we had become even closer after my father
died, of a heart attack, on Christmas Day in 1986.

Memories of that day can still cut me to the core. It was
before Will had been born. Nancy and I had gone over to
my parents' house for Christmas dinner. When we got there,
no one was home, although the lights on the tree were
turned on; then the phone rang. By the end of the day, we
three were sitting together in the living room—Mom,
Nancy, and me. We were numb. I remember that we opened
presents, fumbling with the wrapping paper; I guess it was
a way of distracting ourselves. We were in shock. My dad
was suddenly, irrevocably gone. He had been with us, full
of life, just a day ago. Now we would never see him again.

What could be more bitter, what could be sadder, than to
lose a parent, just like that, on Christmas? I had found out:
to lose a parent through murder.

It was after Dad died that I came to see how much my
mother loved her husband, how deeply his death had hurt
her. Nine years had passed, and Mom still mourned him;
she would be in mourning, I understood, for the rest of her
life. But she also loved life. Life had not ended for her with
my father's death. Slowly she embraced an independence
that she had never before wanted or needed. She expanded
her editing work. She volunteered for the town planning

commission. She served on committees at her church and worked as a liaison with outside service organizations—a day school, the youth service bureau, Narcotics Anonymous— that rented space in the building. She helped the church find an organ builder, decide on the correct model of pipe organ for the sanctuary, and raise the money to buy it.

That afternoon, as we sat at the table in her dining room, I outlined for my mother the book I intended to write. It would be about nature in Iceland and about living in a re- mote, untrammeled place.

There is a book I admire, *The Outermost House* by Henry Beston. Written in the 1920s, it describes a small cottage Bes- ton built on the dunes of Cape Cod, and the time he spent there, observing nature and honoring the passage of the days. I could not have gone to Cape Cod and found the solitude that reigned in Beston's day. In the summer, the Cape is jammed with tourists, many of them equipped with a copy of his long-lasting book. His house, officially proclaimed a Na- tional Literary Landmark, was swept off its foundation and carried out to sea by a storm in the 1970s. I might have tried to find a quiet spot farther up the coast, in Maine or Nova Scotia. But it seemed to me that, at the end of the twentieth century, one needed to migrate farther from the known world, closer to the earth's conceptual rim, to find a truly fugitive setting. Iceland, to my mind, was itself an outermost house of the Western world. And the physical house we called Little Lava—on the far shore of a tidal lagoon, bound by marsh and mountains and ocean and the vast Icelandic sky—seemed to me the quintessential outermost house.

Mom did not share my fondness for wild places. But neither she nor my father had ever discouraged me from back-packing in the Rocky Mountains, canoeing in northern Minnesota, hunting grouse and deer in the rough wooded hills of Pennsylvania. She seemed to understand my need for solitude; that I could think more clearly, breathe more easily, look into my heart more deeply in country that was marginal and lonesome, in a place where the land was stark—reduced to its essence. She did not find anything negative to say about our Iceland plans, even though I could tell from her voice that she'd rather we would not be gone for so long. Perhaps she thought back on the two times when she and my father took my brothers and me to live in Switzerland, where Dad had found work during sabbatical leaves from Penn State. We still talked about our stays in Europe, the things we had seen and done, the people we had met. Mom understood the worth of traveling: how it helped you see things from a new perspective, how it helped you find your place in the world.

And then the bottom fell out of the world for me, when I walked into the back bedroom of her house on that hot September afternoon.

Finally the summer drew near. Friends were surprised when we announced that we would go ahead and live in Ice-land as planned. In truth, it had not been a hard decision. I wanted to get away from home. I wanted to be free from my mother's house—once a focal point of warmth and comfort, now a reminder of cruel, untimely death. I needed a break from my tasks as executor of her estate. I needed to withdraw, for a time, from my brothers and friends, who, through no fault of their own, constantly reminded me of what had hap-pened to Ruth Fergus—of what had happened to us all.

I sensed that Little Lava was a place where I could live simply. Where I could pass the days in peace. Where I could take the first steps into a future that, I hoped, would not be so dimmed with grief and pain.

Crossing the tide flats, I was buffeted by the wind and the rain. I came up to a squarish brown stone. It was about five feet tall. I'd seen it from a distance but hadn't yet inspected it. Cracks fretted the stone. Barnacles studded its surface. Small purple-blue mussels fringed its base, where a narrow ring of clear water pooled in the sand. According to one of my maps, a vegetation and topographic chart issued by the Icelandic government, the rock had a name: Stakkholts-steinn. Stakkholtssteinn was a marker on the boundary be-tween Little Lava and Stóra Hraun, or "Big Lava," so named because it was the larger of the two farms. I had asked Thórður to translate "Stakkholtssteinn." He thought it meant "Stone Near the Sheep Pen in the Woods." Plenty of sheep wandered around near Little Lava, grazing on the open range. But there was not a tree, not a stick of wood in sight, suggesting that the name was very old, from a time when Iceland still had forests of scrubby birch trees.

The rain let up. I took off the pack and leaned it against Stakkholtssteinn. Working the kinks out of my shoulders, I looked around. The clouds had pulled back to reveal sharp-edged mountains.

Closest was Hafursfell, "Goat Mountain," a chunk of rock and scree with a gorge like a knife slit descending from a divot of valley. Where grass grew on Hafursfell's gentler slopes, sheep grazed. The sheep looked like crumbs on a rumpled tablecloth.

An even bigger peak, Kolbeinsstaðafjall, showed canted striations in its rock, reminding me of a layer cake that had fallen on one side.

Between Hafursfell and Kolbeinsstaðafjall lay Hnappa- dalur, or "Knoll Valley," named for the many volcanic for- mations jutting up from the valley floor. The most striking of these was a pair of conical hills whose colors changed strangely with the time of day and the light. Now the hills were the dark rust brown of dried blood.

Beyond the house stood another volcano, Eldborg, "Fire Fortress." Its low truncated cone lay about two miles from Little Lava. Eldborg had spawned the lava field that bucked up hard against the farm's homefield.

I looked westward to the bay, Faxaflói, graying out into the Atlantic. My eyes searched for Snæfellsjökull, "Snow Mountain Glacier," the ice-capped stratovolcano that an- chored the end of Snæfellsnes and gave the peninsula its name. But the clouds were too thick; Snæfellsjökull was not to be seen.

After Mom died, an Icelander living in America sent me a poem written by a well-known Icelandic poet. Nancy trans- lated it. I remembered a line that went something like this: You turn your head and look where there has always been a mountain, and it is no longer there.

I shouldered the pack and started walking. I concentrated on the task of picking my feet up and setting them down in places where they would not skid into a stream or sink into a quagmire or trip over a thúfa. Step, and step again.

I gained the marsh on the far side of the tide flats. A black ewe with yellow eyes stared at me, then turned and ran off briskly through the grass, her white lamb bouncing along behind. One wall of the house was stained dark with rain. Sheep grazed in the homefield, whose stone fences had unraveled in many places. Snipe flew high in the air; they made big circles, climbing up and then tipping steeply downward, their tailfeathers singing out *yu-yu-yu-yu-yu-yu-yu?*—a quizzical, ascending tune.

Climbing to the house, I chanced to look back. The rain-washed flats reflected the glowing gray light that came flooding down from the sky.

Above the flats a bird was approaching. Its long wings beat slowly and steadily. The bird was immense. It was an eagle, a white-tailed sea eagle, the largest bird in Iceland and the rarest. I'd been told that eagles nested near Little Lava, but this was the first one I had seen.

There is an Icelandic saying: "When the eagle flies, all nature is silent." The saying, I realized, must be metaphorical. As the eagle approached the shoreline, a pair of redshanks rose and circled it, screaming. A tern gave a grating cry and feinted at the larger predator, veering aside at the last moment and flitting up whitely to dive again. The eagle passed directly over Little Lava. When it reached the lava heath, cock ptarmigan came flying up, sounding their booming alarm calls.

The eagle paid no heed to the uproar. It flew on, its wings sculling through the air. It crossed the lava field and headed toward Eldborg's cone, where it vanished into the rain.

2 | *P o i s o n   C o l d*

Pétur and I jumped down from the wagon and landed in the mud. The tractor was in up to its transmission. The farmer swung out of the cab, looked the situation over, and said something in Icelandic to Pétur, who replied. The farmer sniffed and shook his head gravely.

It was the seventh of June, a chilly day roofed over with blue sky. The tractor looked small, immobilized there on the tide flats. A passing black-backed gull stopped and lay on the wind; it looked us over in our plight, then dipped a wing and planed off.

Pétur was on hand to help me fix up the house. We had bought boards, plywood, and tarpaper in Reykjavík; these had been trucked north and deposited on the gravel road near Stóra Hraun. I had briefly met the family there, who volunteered their tractor to haul the materials across at low tide. But the tractor had broken down, a state in which it seemed likely to remain for some time. A call was placed to a neighbor, who arrived with his tractor, pulling a red high-sided steel hay wagon. Into the wagon Pétur and I loaded the building supplies, Pétur's toolbox, a folded-up cot with a metal frame and a mattress, and our backpacks laden with food and other sundries.

The farmer addressed Pétur again.

"Is there a shovel at Litla Hraun?" Pétur asked me.

"I think so."

I slogged off through the mud, then went trotting across the gravel toward the homefield. I ran straight into the cold northeast wind that came rushing down Hnappadalur Valley. The wind brought tears to my eyes.

I went into the house and turned right, entering the work-shop. The room was chockful of junk. From the jumble I extracted a shovel with a weathered shank and a rusty blade. I carried the shovel outside and jogged back toward the flats.

Pétur was walking along the shoreline picking up stones. The half brother of an Icelander I knew in the United States, Pétur was in his early thirties, with handsome, regular fea-tures and eyes that were alternately laughing and thoughtful. He was self-employed as an artist, and looked the part, with his hair banded back in a ponytail and a goatee on his chin. He was tall, broad-shouldered, and slim-waisted, with long ropy muscles. When he laughed, a vein pulsed in his fore-head. He moved in bursts of strength and speed.

Pétur was the longtime partner of Anna, whose family owned Little Lava. He had volunteered to fix up the house for us, and we had sent a sum of money to be used in buying materials. But when I'd gotten to Reykjavík I found that Pétur had done nothing to make the house more livable; he hadn't spent any of the money, hadn't even been to Little Lava since our exploratory trip there the previous December. I was not surprised. As agreeable and enthusiastic as Pétur could be, I had found him unfocused and easily distracted. Yet he could do almost anything when he set his mind to it: draw a portrait, sail a boat, remodel a kitchen.

I was now somewhat worried, however, because Pétur and Anna had split up, with Pétur living alone in the apartment they had shared in downtown Reykjavík. And, as I had since my mother's death, I assumed that if something could go wrong, it would. There seemed to be little reason for Pétur to help me, other than the friendship that had grown between us, a friendship that was not old. That, and the special fondness he had for Little Lava: for the starkness of its setting, for the quality of the light.

I looked at the tractor and wondered if we could free it. The tide had turned, and in a couple of hours the lagoon would be awash. I wondered how much it cost to rebuild a tractor engine. Everything was expensive in Iceland, about three times what one would expect to pay back home. I wondered if I would be held responsible if the machine got swamped.

The farmer took the shovel and began digging out around the wheels. The mud was gray and viscous. It was unclear to me why he had chosen this particular route, although at the time I had supposed he knew what he was doing. He had not stopped to confer with the folk at Stóra Hraun, hadn't picked up a resident there, who might have known the crossing. After we loaded the wagon, the farmer drove along a faint road extending south from Stóra Hraun; descended from the peninsula onto the flats; and went boring across toward Little Lava. He slowed, made a wide turn while reconnoitering, then aimed for a small cove and gunned it for shore. With a hundred yards to go, the tractor had bogged down.

The farmer plied the shovel in front of the wheels and behind them. Pétur took over and continued the digging. He attacked the mud, slinging it to one side. I pitched the stones Pétur had gathered into the wells dug fore and aft of the wheels. The stones went *thuck* into the mud and disappeared. My turn with the shovel. Then the farmer took over again and attended to the front wheels.

Finally he climbed back into the cab and put the tractor in gear. The tall ribbed tires spun, caught on the stones, spun, caught, advanced a foot or so, and churned down into the mud again.

The farmer got out. He rubbed his face and muttered something in Icelandic.

I looked out toward the channel. The flats were still dry, but the big stream on our side of the lagoon had swollen markedly. I had picked up a tide table in Reykjavík but had not yet figured out how much of a delay there was, here along the coast north of the capital or inside the lagoon behind its barrier beach.

We dug. We threw in more stones. The farmer went pacing around, looking for a solid bottom. Cold as it was, I was sweating. Pétur said in a low tone, "This guy is not so smart."

So far I was inclined to agree, although I had found that the citizen of Reykjavík will often quickly and unfairly disparage his rural counterpart, even to the point of calling him *heimskur*, the Icelandic word for stupid. Heimskur actually means "homely," in the way that a person who has never traveled may become stunted in his outlook. The slur, I'd been told, was originally used by Vikings—early Icelanders who went out in longships, raiding and plundering far and wide—to describe men who stayed at home.

We dug, and dug some more. We carved out two trenches in front of the tires and paved them with rubble. The farmer got back in the cab and rocked the tractor back and forth. Its engine roaring and belching exhaust, the tractor pulled free. Its wheels flung mud at Pétur and me. The machine turned onto firmer sand and crept toward shore. Soon its wheels were grinding over rocks. Then onto grass. Pétur and I trotted along behind as the farmer motored quickly toward Little Lava.

Once there, we wasted no time in unloading, heaving the boards to one side, leaving the plywood in the grass with the tarpaper rolls on top to hold it down in case the wind rose. It would have been nice to go inside and brew some coffee for ourselves and the farmer, but we all understood the need to get back. I took the shovel in case the tractor got stuck again. This time, however, it crossed without any problems. Pétur and I stood holding on to the wagon sides, our knees flexed to take the shock out of the bumps. The tractor trundled back up the Stóra Hraun Peninsula and, after a quarter-hour, arrived at the farm, where several of the tenants were standing around near the mailbox visiting with some other people sitting in a battered automobile.

I had been unwise in not settling on a fee beforehand. The farmer got out of the tractor and stood there expectantly. Pétur began talking with him. The man looked at the ground. He cocked his head to one side, opened his hands palms up. Finally Pétur placed some bills in his hand. Without looking at the bills, the farmer stuck them into his pocket. Pétur spoke a general goodbye to the people standing about, took my elbow, and steered me onto the dirt track toward Little Lava. *"Takk,"* I said to the farmer, using the Icelandic word for "thanks." He nodded, a bit curtly, and Pétur and I moved off. I realized we had left the shovel leaning against a stack of plastic fertilizer bags near the mailbox; I decided to get it some other day.

We walked quickly to cross before the tide. As we marched across the flats, Pétur explained that the man had requested an exorbitant sum. "He thought you were a rich American." Pétur grinned, showing white, even teeth. "I gave him five thousand." Five thousand *krónur*, or crowns, amounted to a bit less than a hundred dollars; it seemed to me a reasonable amount. Pétur had paid the farmer out of the money I'd sent toward fixing up the house.

Pétur's long legs bore him across the mudflats. Careless of his leather hiking boots, he strode through the rising stream channels. I followed, hoping that the farmer had not been too disappointed and that the people at Stóra Hraun would not think I was a cheapskate. I glanced at the cove where the tractor had bogged down. Deep furrows marred the mud. Through the summer, the tide would smooth out the furrows, but would not erase them. They would remain, exposed twice a day at the ebb.

Abandoned farms like Little Lava dot the coast of Iceland. They are found in grassy valleys leading up to the deserted central highlands; on peninsulas jutting out into the sea; on islands in the fjords. Near Little Lava were scores of similar homesteads, with names like Hömluholt and Moldbrekka and Miðbakki and Kotdalur and Landbrot.

Some of the farms were old, dating back to the Age of Settlement, from around A.D. 870 to 930, when most of the usable land in Iceland was first occupied. Thórður had found a reference to Little Lava in *Fornbréfasafn*, a collection of old Icelandic documents. The farm showed up in a registry of lands leased to peasants by the Catholic Church in 1354. At that time the place was called Seta Hraun or Setuhraun. Thórður interpreted *seta* to mean settled, as a place that had been occupied, plus the familiar appending "hraun" in reference to the lava field. Nancy noted that the word *setur* implied a priest's seat; she wondered if the farm had been a parsonage at one time.

At Little Lava the remains of many structures were scattered about the ten or so acres of the homefield: low walls, stone pens, and curious grass-grown mounds, like outsize thúfur, bespeaking those six centuries, and possibly several more, of human occupation.

Three structures were still identifiable:

A stone-and-turf-walled barn, about the size of a one-car garage, lay slumped in on itself, revealing rotting rafters, one of which was a recycled oar. The grass was still green on the buckled roof. Now the barn was no more than a windbreak for the sheep, whose olive droppings lay scattered about the homefield.

The second structure was also a wreck: a summerhouse begun in the 1960s by Anna's mother, Oddný, and her then-husband, Guðbjartur, and never finished. The wall studs were gray and wind-whittled, the floorboards stove in. The sheep liked the summerhouse, too, sleeping inside it, or shifting from one side to the other to take advantage of the sun and keep shielded from the wind.

The third house was the one we would live in. Begun in the 1940s, it had been abandoned before it was completed. It measured 22 by 27 feet. The surfaces of the concrete walls were embossed with the grain pattern of boards that had held the pour. The roof was asbestos paneling, brittle with age. From the top of each wall a section of roof angled up and in to a short ridgeline punctuated by a concrete chimney.

The house sat on its knoll with a view in every direction. Wind rattled the windows and hissed through cracks around the wooden door. Gray, green, and orange lichens blotched the outside walls. At one eave the concrete rain gutter had spalled off, letting water run down the wall. Where the planes of the roof met, wooden flashing boards had rotted, letting in the rain. The moisture had trickled through sod laid to insulate the attic, staining and bulging the fiberboard ceilings and walls inside the house and rotting the window frames.

Entering through the outer door, one found oneself in a small vestibule that had been paneled with concrete-smeared boards, obviously those used in forming the exterior walls. Nails for hanging up coats had been driven into the boards. A short ladder led up to the attic. The ladder was actually a steep set of stairs; it appeared to have come from a ship, and probably had been found along the shore. Old boards and coils of rope lay on top of the moldy sod in the attic. The sky glinted through the gaps in the roof.

To the right of the vestibule a door led to the workshop, so filled with stuff that one had to turn sideways to enter.

Left of the vestibule another door opened onto a parlor, with old chairs, a bed, and two seaman's chests. From the parlor a door led to the kitchen, long and narrow, with another bed, two tables, shelves, and a rusty cookstove; also a door to the outside, windowless and nailed shut. Off the kitchen, in the north corner of the house, was a small pantry.

That's all there was to Little Lava.

The previous December, Pétur had met me at the hotel in Reykjavík where the bus from the airport drops off arriving passengers. It was a few minutes past eight in the morning. The sky was midnight black. The wind sent the rain billowing across the parking lot. We climbed into Pétur's old Citroën. No, he hadn't had time to get to Little Lava. He explained that he was taking a course in graphic design and had been working like crazy for months, trying to finish his assignments before the term ended at Christmas.

"When I get them done, in a day or so"—Pétur smiled broadly, reached across, and clapped me on the shoulder with a big hand—"then we will go to Litla Hraun."

I would be staying at his apartment in the old city. I had lived in this part of town seven years earlier, in another house about four blocks away; I had spent much of my time taking care of Will, who was then only a few months old, while Nancy did research in the National Library.

Pétur left me at the apartment and hurried off to school. The one-bedroom flat was stiflingly hot—warmed, as are all buildings in Reykjavík, by geothermal heat obtained from subterranean chambers of lava that lie close to the city. I took a nap on a cot in the living room. When I woke around ten, the sky was just growing light. On the other side of the narrow street was a four-story office building: I looked across and saw people working at their desks.

Those days, I was barely functioning. Only three months had passed since my mother's death. A day was not a day: it was shattered bits of time. At night I had trouble sleeping. When I closed my eyes, I saw Mom as I had found her. I saw the man arrested for her murder. I was convinced of his guilt, based on evidence that the police and the prosecutor had shared with me; I considered how I would kill the man, given the chance, and many of my vengeful imaginings were even more brutal and violent than what had been done to my mother. Several times I had dreams in which I encountered the accused murderer, who for some reason was out of jail. In one such dream we were in the basement of a house. He stood there smirking at me, and I understood that he was not in any way remorseful over what he had done, that he didn't expect to be punished; there were others like him, other murderers, also in the house—I managed to jerk myself awake and out of the dream.

Mornings, I didn't want to get out of bed. The late-arriving light and the gray weeping skies didn't help any. The days were only about six hours long; dawn and sunset together seemed to take up three of the six hours. But I made myself get up. I ate breakfast—dried cereal, toast, strong coffee. I washed the dishes. I made up the cot, which had been purchased, Pétur told me, for our eventual use at Little Lava. I waited for Pétur to finish his work at the art institute.

Probably he would have loaned me his car. But since I had never been to Little Lava and didn't know how to get there or where to cross the tide flats or the marsh, I thought it unwise to go on my own.

I occupied myself by running errands: buying maps, checking on the prices and availability of supplies in hardware stores, skimming through books in the National Library. I walked the streets of Reykjavík, past the small turn-of-the-century houses with their neat gardens, their tin-sided walls and brightly painted roofs. I walked about in the cemetery. Looking at the headstones, I was filled with a gnawing grief. The stones bore the names of Icelanders: Ragnar Jónsson. Hallgerður Jakobsdóttir. Bryndís Gunnarsdóttir. Einar Einarsson. Sons, daughters, parents, none of them still in this world.

I read a book I'd brought from home, about sea kayaks,

and considered which type of kayak to get. I had also brought a novel, but my mind could not hold on to characters or plot.

On Bankastræti, the main shopping street, storefronts were filled with fashionable clothes, glittering jewelry, and sleek furniture. Christmas shoppers crowded the sidewalks. The weather had turned cold, and big flakes of snow came drifting down to collect on streetlamps and holiday wreaths. I met a friend for coffee in a bistro. A choir of rosy-faced children came in and sang carols, and the patrons in the shop stopped chatting, put down their cups, and applauded after each song. I told my friend about my intention of living at Little Lava, at Litla Hraun. He grinned. He told me that Litla Hraun was also the name of a federal penitentiary in southern Iceland; on many other occasions when I mentioned the farm's name to Icelanders, they would smile or laugh out loud at the thought of the American writer spending his summer in prison.

In the four o'clock dusk I walked back to Pétur's apartment. I wanted badly to go to Little Lava, to see the place, to assure myself that the farm and its surroundings would be a retreat, a refuge, and not a place of grim confinement. But all I could do was wait.

Finally, at noon one day we drove onto the car ferry in the harbor; the ferry crossing would save a long drive around a fjord that bit inland east of the city. The boat cleared the harbor breakwater, and across the breadth of Faxaflói the cone of Snæfellsjökull came into view. The bay was gray-green, dull, and frigid-looking. Behind us, Reykjavík and the entire Reykjanes Peninsula were cloaked with gray scud. The sun peered through the overcast, pale and unconvincing. We stood on deck for a while, and a crew member noticed us and beckoned us onto the bridge. I was surprised to find that no one was actually piloting the ferry; a computer program was steering the vessel. The captain sat in a swivel chair, drinking coffee while he glanced at a sonar screen and looked out over the water. Pétur talked to him for a while in Icelandic. "Whales," Pétur said to me. "He has to watch out for whales."

We went into the lounge. Passengers were eating hot dogs and sandwiches and reading newspapers. Children watched Disney cartoons on a wall-mounted video set. Pétur bought a newspaper and checked the tide table. He made a wry face. "We'll be getting there close to high tide. Also, it's *stórstreymi*—what is it in English?—the highest tide of the month." He thought for a moment, his brow furrowing. "Spring tide," he said finally.

The ferry slowed, its engines reversed, and it slid into the slip at Akranes. We drove off the gangplank and through the small town; on its outskirts, we headed north.

Along the road, sheep and horses grazed in the withered grass. Gravelly frost-covered mountains rose into a sky filled with pink-bottomed clouds. West beyond Snæfellsjökull, a stripe of yellow light lay along the horizon. We came to an even smaller town called Borgarnes. At the truck stop, as we filled the gas tank, a pair of ravens went past, riding the bitter wind, ronking back and forth to each other. Beyond the town Pétur turned west onto a road that, he said, had been paved for the first time only a few years earlier.

We passed the lava field of the volcano Eldborg. Eldborg looked like a church collection plate turned upside down. On our right, the two ruddy cones guarded the entrance to Hnappadalur Valley. We turned away from the cones and drove down a gravel road alongside a rushing river, the Haffjarðará. We should properly have stopped at Stóra Hraun, but that would have obliged us to have coffee and stay and chat, forcing us to cross in the dark.

Pétur parked the Citroën next to a low tan bluff. The tide was in, covering the flats. My eyes searched for the house and found it. On the far side of the wind-chopped water it stood: stark, tiny, alone.

Pétur wrestled on his heavy pack. I got my own pack onto my back, and Pétur and I both picked up doubled plastic shopping bags, filled with stove coal, in our gloved hands. Nancy had warned me of the rigors of the roundabout crossing, and now I would know them.

We started out hiking to the north, angling away from Little Lava. The wind made our eyes water and our noses run. Underfoot, the soggy pastureland was stiffening, starting to freeze. We had to backtrack repeatedly, to find places where we could jump across the tide-flooded streams. Finally we got around the north end of the marsh and turned south. Now the wind was at our backs, shoving us toward Little Lava.

The tide forced us to the edge of the lava field. We had to climb among the rocks when we encountered streams swollen full to their sources, springs that trickled out at the edge of the lava. We trekked across brittle gray grass and sought sheep trails through the jagged rock. Now and then, from a high point I would catch a glimpse of the house, which did not seem to be getting any closer.

My breathing was ragged. I was sweating. I unzipped my parka and took off my stocking cap. Although a heavy smoker, Pétur was fit, ten years younger than I, and more athletic; he would forge on ahead, then have to wait until I caught up.

The daylight was starting to fade. The clouds were breaking up, and chinks of pale-green sky showed between them. The wind whined in the lava.

We came around a heap of lava, and there stood the house. I followed Pétur as he climbed through the hummocks covering the homefield. On the wrecked building next to the house a scrap of tin was flapping, banging, banging.

Pétur leaned his backpack against the wall. Turning to the entry, he lifted free from its cleats a wooden outer covering, like a shutter. He set the covering aside. He untied a cord holding the inner door shut, turned the knob, and pushed.

Inside, the light was dim. No one had been in the house for months, maybe a year. No one had built a fire or cooked a meal, and the dwelling was the temperature of the ground on which it stood, the rocks that jutted up through the concrete floor. The cold that seizes an abandoned house strikes straight to the soul, and at that moment Little Lava was as cheerless a place as one could imagine.

My heart sank as I contemplated the dingy, cluttered interior. I had somehow imagined it would be cleaner and cheerier, more inviting. Instead, it made me think of a dilapidated old hunting camp. The house smelled of failure, of despair. Or maybe I was only sensing the depth of my own despair.

What was I doing here? It was crazy. This wasn't an adventure, it was an ordeal. I wanted to be away from this bitter hermitage. I wanted with all my heart to be home, in my snug warm house, with Nancy and Will by my side.

But I was at Little Lava. And there was much to do before night fell.

First we checked the spring downhill from the house, on the edge of the lava, and found it murky and full of algae. "The sheep have been in it," Pétur said. He led the way around a low ridge of frozen lava into a grassy bowl out of the wind. In one of the rock walls was a shallow cave with a stone floor and a pool of still, clear water. Dipping with a saucepan, we filled our buckets.

Back to the house. I found a kerosene lamp whose wick was crusty, but not so crusty it wouldn't light. Pétur shredded newspaper, split a board into kindling. He placed paper and kindling in the firebox of the old cast-iron stove, dashed some kerosene onto the pile, and applied a match. It was already cold outside—it felt like the low twenties—and the clearing skies and strengthening wind promised that the temperature would fall even lower. A bed sat at the far end of the kitchen. We brought in a second bed from the parlor and shut the door to enclose ourselves in the one room. When the fire in the range was roaring, Pétur scooped coal onto the flames. He set up a two-burner Primus stove on a grimy table, connecting its hose to a propane canister. He lit the Primus and put on a pot of water. I found a mouse-tattered blanket and cut it into strips; using the screwdriver blade of my knife, I forced the strips into cracks around the windows and the nailed-shut back door to exclude the drafts of cold air.

"*Eitur kalt,*" Pétur said. Then: "Poison cold."

We kept our sweaters on, and our down vests. We drew in close to the stove. I sat on a stool that was the vertebra of a whale. Pétur cooked a meal of fish balls and boiled potatoes. We ate the fish and potatoes along with crackers, cheese, flatbread, and smoked lamb streaked with fat; for dessert, bars of chocolate. We brushed mouse droppings off the mattresses and spread out our sleeping bags. Pétur had a heavy mountaineering bag to keep him warm. I had brought a lightweight bag to use in his apartment, not imagining that the cold would be this intense at Little Lava. I found the three blankets least befouled by mice and spread one of them under my bag and the other two on top of it.

We shoveled coal into the stove. Our breath steamed in the golden light. After a while it became apparent that the stove would not warm the kitchen to a comfortable level. When Pétur tried to shut a baffle in it, to create a longer path for the flame, the handle came off in his hand and the baffle clanked uselessly into the stove's innards. The fire was rushing straight up the chimney. It was heating the air above Little Lava. Inside the house, ice began forming on the windowpanes. Outside, the night was black. The wind moaned, starting out low and building to a howl; slowly it diminished, then rose to a crescendo again.

Útburðarvæl, Petur called it, "the Wail of the Carried-Out Ones": the wailing of the winter wind that echoed the cries of newborn infants who, in pagan times, when famine gripped the land, were carried outside and left to die of exposure because there was not enough food to sustain another soul.

We huddled close to the stove. Pétur boiled more water and brewed a pot of coffee. I let him drink most of it; I hoped it would make him get up early in the morning, and he would then build the fire back up.

Before going to bed I went outside to empty my bladder. The wind almost swept me off the stoop, and I hurried around to the leeward side of the house. The clouds had all blown off, and stars swarmed in the heavens. In the starlight, the mountains of Snæfellsnes shone a ghostly gray. At the end of the peninsula snow-covered Snæfellsjökull glimmered a shade paler than the other peaks in the range. As I watched, a fan of light rose into the blackness above Snæfellsjökull. The light strengthened. It separated into five fingers whose color was a glowing whitish gray like the mountain itself. The fingers of light began moving. They undulated slowly and independently of one another. I found myself holding my breath, listening: it seemed as if the display of aurora borealis was in some way alive, and if I listened hard enough I would hear a low steady breathing or some pure celestial note. I stood there shivering for as long as I could bear it, watching the fingers of light shift and shimmer, the stars as bright and brittle as I had ever seen them. My ears ached. My hands grew numb. The wind shrieked past the house, made the roof scrap bang on the old turf barn.

That night inside my bag I wore all the clothes I had brought, including two pairs of long underwear, wool trousers and shirt, sweater and down vest, cap pulled over my ears, and a scarf around my neck. My breath clouded toward the ceiling. I listened to the wind, the crackling of the coal burning, the faint sifting of ash as it fell through the grates in the stove. Starlight suffused itself into the room. Turning onto my side, I drew my legs up close to my body and slipped my hands between my thighs. I had never felt so empty or so alone. I was in Iceland, in a tiny house on a forbidding coast where the wind roared out of the north, wind that had scoured its way across the Greenland Sea and the Arctic Ocean imprisoned beneath its icecap.

I slept. When I woke, my hip joints ached with cold. The night was still black. The wind wailed. The stove was dead. I wrapped myself into a ball. Pétur lay in the bed next to mine—diagonally, because he was so tall—and I thought about waking him and asking if I could get into his bag with him. I was unsure how he would take such a request; Icelanders have a tradition of sleeping numerous to a bed and probably he would have made room. But I pulled my head down deeper into my own bag and drifted off again.

In the morning, the coffee did its work. Pétur went stumbling out into the howling wind, then came back inside and lit the stove. I lay in bed for another hour. My throat was raw; I felt miserable. When I finally got up, ice was still thick on the windows, through which a reddish light entered. We made oatmeal for breakfast. We drank two pots of coffee.

We fed the ravenous stove. The light slowly brightened inside the house. Going about with a tape measure, we noted the dimensions of the rooms. We inspected the old furniture, trying to decide what could be used during the summer and what should be discarded or stored elsewhere.

We heard a raven croaking and poked our heads out the door and did not see a raven anywhere. Far to the south, the sun rose above the cloud bank still hanging over Reykjavík and sent its pink-gold rays across the lava field, lighting every spire and boulder, casting every cranny into shadow. Eldborg stood low and tawny and solid-looking. The mountains on Snæfellsnes glowed like molten metal.

We bundled up and went outside. The noon sun was an evening sun. It seemed to give off no more warmth than the moon. We hiked down the peninsula. In the wind-flattened grass lay driftwood, old bottles, snarls of rope, colored plastic trawler floats like outsize Christmas ornaments. I scuffed along with my head down. I could hardly see, my eyes were tearing so heavily in the wind. We did not encounter a bird. We met four horses: a bay, a gray, a white, and a black-and-white; short-coupled, big-headed, barrel-chested Icelandic horses. They came up and stared at us. The hair on each horse stood fluffed up like the insulating fur of a bear. Tracks of horses, sheep, and foxes marked the congealed mud. Foam had blown off the lagoon, lodged against rocks, and frozen into fragile-looking lace. Puddles were hard enough to stand on. The sun hung just above the horizon. To the west, Snæfellsjökull glowed pink, then chilled to a dull blue when clouds hid the sun.

We had planned on staying a second day, but the cold was

too much. The stove had consumed almost the entire fifty pounds of coal we had lugged over; and although there was a second bag of coal in the Citroën's trunk, we did not see much point in hauling it across, to barely keep us warm another night.

We stuffed our gear into our packs. We closed up the house and left. By the time we reached the car, the sky was deep purple. The engine finally turned over, cranking and catching on the battery's last amps. In the diminishing light we drove past Stóra Hraun, where the dogs raced out and bit at our dust. We followed the road up the river. Yesterday the river had been tumbling down its valley, foaming over rocks. Now it was frozen from bank to bank.

3 | *T h e   B i s h o p ' s   S p r i n g*

On the afternoon that the tractor carried our supplies to Little Lava, Pétur and I went straight to work. He started in on the windows, replacing rotted sills and fiberboard jambs that moisture had stained and buckled. We painted the wood white: it framed views of the saltmarsh darkening and brightening under clouds and sun, the haystack hump of Hafursfell, and the whole of mountainous Snæfellsnes, with Snæfellsjökull at the peninsula's western end.

Snæfellsjökull is an impressive mountain. It looks like pictures I have seen of Mount Fuji. At its summit is a glacier pierced by wide-set spires of rock; under certain light conditions, the rock formations suggest horns; sometimes they are the eyes of a skate.

In early June, snow still mantled the mountain's upper

half. The base of Snæfellsjökull matched the ocean's blue-gray, so that the peak's snowy portion looked like a white triangle suspended in midair. The mountain seemed almost sentient—brooding, guarding the peninsula, waiting for something to happen. But what? Although guidebooks described the volcano as dormant, an Icelandic geologist had told me, "Someday it will erupt again."

While Pétur trimmed out the windows, I carried armloads of trash out of the workshop. Dry-rotted boards, cork fishnet floats gnawed to pieces by mice, wads of yellowed newspaper, snarls of string, mildewed sheets of plastic, empty kerosene jugs. In an old foundation I built a fire. The wind made the fire roar and sent black smoke chasing down the Litla Hraun Peninsula.

In the unfinished summerhouse next door I found an area where the wooden floor was still intact. There Pétur and I placed the too-short beds with their scarred, splintery frames and musty horsehair mattresses. Not knowing whether Anna's family might regard those items as antiques, we had determined to save them.

We worked all day in the light that did not wane. We ate buttered flatbread and smoked lamb. Around midnight, we put away our tools and paintbrushes. Pétur drank his bedtime coffee. He crawled into his sleeping bag, tied a blue bandanna across his eyes, and was soon snoring.

I lay on the cot in the parlor. I slept for a short while. I woke to the wind rattling the windowpanes, sheep bleating, snipe flighting—and the light, continuous now in this boreal part of the world.

I pulled on my sweater. The house door opened onto the lava field and Eldborg's low cone.

Banks of gunmetal clouds shifted across the pale-blue sky. It was just past two o'clock, and sunrise was not far off. Standing on the stoop, I heard a strange sound from the lava: a mournful yapping yowl, *howp howp howp howwooo*, the last note long and drawn-out. The call came again, sad and wild and wary. It was hard to pinpoint; it seemed to move around from place to place. I looked out across the shadowy rubble and could see nothing out of the ordinary. Actually, there was nothing at all that *was* ordinary in that forbidding, fractured expanse.

The irregular throaty yowls strengthened and diminished. I was fairly certain the calling came from a fox. Long ago, it is said, a witch in Lapland fell in love with an Icelander, who spurned her; in retaliation, the witch sent the fox to Iceland, to eat the birds and rob the nests and kill the sheep and make life just a bit more difficult for the people living on that remote, standoffish isle.

As I listened, the yapping grew fainter. It seemed to move away down the arm of rocky land extending south from Little Lava. The calling died out. And the song of springtime in Iceland continued: wind combing the grass, snipe winnowing, lambs baahing, whimbrels piping their plaintive bubbling tune.

The sun edged out from behind a mountain in the highlands. It lit the clouds a gaudy orange-red. The cones of Hnappadalur—those breast-shaped portals at the valley's mouth—became a rich purple.

The landscape seemed to smolder. The lava field looked as if it might start rumbling and advancing at any moment. Grass stems in the homefield were spears of flame. In the salt marsh, the hardy plants glowed pink and lime, yellow and spruce-green.

Three snipe zigzagged above the house, illuminated against the firmament. A golden plover winged past, singing its mournful *tirr-pee-ooh*. A meadow pipit flew up from the grass, fluttered high in the air, and came rocking down like a diminutive parachutist, all the while twittering sweetly.

Ptarmigan rasped from the lava. Geese gabbled in the marsh. On such a warm, clear morning—or was it night still?—I wondered if the birds and beasts slept at all.

I went back to bed but could not sleep. I thought of my mother. In those days, I thought about her almost all the time; other thoughts seemed mere distractions from the matter that had been forced upon me. Sometimes, to fend off my sorrow, I tried to put her out of my mind. But that made me feel guilty. Why should I banish her? Why should I dishonor my mother by refusing to remember her? What I could not help remembering was my last vision of her.

She lay on her back in her congealed blood. I do not know how long I stared, at her wounds and at her face; perhaps no longer than thirty seconds. And yet an eternity was compressed into that span. My mother, my own mother, was dead, and someone had killed her. I could not go to her, dared not even touch the face of the one who had been so dear to me.

Finally I was able to break free. I turned and stumbled down the hall. I picked Will up and carried him outside. He had come within a few steps of finding her; he had gotten halfway down the hall—calling "Grandma, Grandma"—when something clicked in my mind: the small signs of disarray in the house told me things were very wrong. I called Will back to the kitchen and made him wait there.

Outside, still holding Will, I went down the driveway. Neighbors were coming along on the sidewalk, worried expressions on their faces. I told them Mom was dead. I remember thinking that my life had changed, that I would never be the same person again, that what I had seen and what I must live with had, suddenly and immutably, set me apart. It had changed the way I would look at the world.

Now, thousands of miles removed, I let the horror wash over me as I stared up at the stained brown ceiling in the parlor at Little Lava. It seemed I needed to go through the event, view it in my mind again and again, to accept that it had happened. It can be a writer's curse, to have the sort of imagination that lets him inhabit the mind of another human being. I was in the house. I saw the killing through her eyes. I felt what she felt.

I lay on the cot, listening to the wind sucking past the walls, vibrating the windows in their frames. My sorrow was great.

I wondered if, at some point, when I thought of my mother I would remember her as I had known her. Sitting and reading to Will as she held him in her lap. Cooking a meal in her kitchen, playing the piano, discussing—quietly and firmly, as was her fashion—some point of politics; or watching sports on television, or taking her short toeing-out steps as she walked her dog. Smiling at some memory of our family's life together, smiling her love at me.

I remembered a passage from a novel by the great Icelandic writer Halldór Laxness:

"Who could take your mother away from you? How could your mother leave you? What's more, she is closer to you the older you become and the longer it is since she died."

The day came on. The sun continued its *sólarhringur*, its horseshoe march around the sky. Pétur and I rose and resumed our labors. The sun inched its way across Hnappadalur Valley, whose volcanic cones were a dull, washed-out pink.

Another day of sorting and burning, sawing, hammering, painting. I tried to concentrate on what I was doing. I directed my eyes to observe the way dry-rotted wood flamed and flared up quickly, puffed pale smoke, and became ash; the way white paint sat on rough lumber momentarily before collapsing down into the wood's grain. How the light fell aslant on the concrete floor, whose surface was interrupted by gray-black, foot-polished stones that rose out of bedrock.

We worked as the sun passed the blue shoulder of Kolbeinsstaðafjall. We ate lunch outside with our backs to the house wall, sharing it with a squadron of fat flies that kept buzzing and alighting.

The sun climbed to its southern apogee. It hung above the lava field a double hands' span—about as high as the sun gets in Pennsylvania in November. The light was warm and vibrant and pure; distances seemed infinite. I found it hard getting used to the constant light. The low solar position was also disorienting. Outside at home, I use the sun to estimate the time and to tell directions. Those techniques did not apply in June in Iceland.

In the afternoon I carried the water jugs to the cave in the lava. The cave was a quiet place, offering a respite from the wind that blew so freely. I wondered how many other people had dipped water out of the still, dark pool. Had they rested there, too, looking out at sun or rain or snow? I filled the jugs and took a long drink from one. The water, sweet and cold, made me shiver.

According to Pétur, the spring was called Gvendarbrunnur. It was one of many springs so named in Iceland. Gvendur is a nickname for Guðmundur; Guðmundur Arason was a man of humble birth who, in 1203, became one of two Catholic bishops presiding over Iceland. An advocate of the common people, Guðmundur challenged the power of the chieftains who ruled northern Iceland during that era. He went about with a band of followers, confronting the chieftains and holding them up for food, and sometimes getting into battles with them. He was a great admirer of Thomas à Becket, and had even traveled to Canterbury. It is thought that he wished to become a martyr himself, but the chieftains would not accommodate him; ultimately he ended up under house arrest in Hólar, the seat of his cathedral, where he died in 1237. He is fondly remembered for placing Christian blessings on dangerous mountain passes and banishing evil spirits from bird cliffs where too many egg collectors had fallen to their deaths. While he was blessing one precipice, so the story goes, a voice grumbled out of the rock: "Even the wicked need someplace to live." Guðmundur must have agreed, for from then on he always left a part of each cliff unconsecrated.

Ever since the bishop had blessed it, the spring at Little Lava had remained pure and unfailing. And since it was down in a dim, slippery hole, sheep couldn't get at it.

The afternoon aged. The sun journeyed across Faxaflói. It swung around toward Snæfellsjökull. As the sun drew past the glacier, I could finally tell that it was in descent. The light became softer, with rose and yellow tints. The wind lessened. The sun rolled along, above the peaks of Snæfellsnes, placing them in silhouette. The peninsula was comprised of three separate belts of wild, naked, houseless crags. To the west was the great uplift of Snæfellsjökull, and its associated lava shields and craters. Farther east and closer to us stood Hellgrindur, the "Frames of Death." Ljósufjöll, the "Light Mountains," clustered behind Hafursfell, beyond the flat strip of coastal land.

The sky held its brightness as the sun grazed the mountain summits. It slipped behind Hafursfell, not far from where it would emerge again in two hours. During that time, the sky would not darken.

On the roofed portion of the summerhouse, Pétur and I knelt gingerly on the punky boards that sheathed the rafters. My back ached. My arms were tired. My stomach growled. By giving the summerhouse a new roof, we were creating a storage space for the unusable furniture from the concrete house; also, we were making a sheltered area for a bucket toilet and a place where I could store my kayak when I found the time to assemble it.

Tangerine-colored light filled the sky. It glinted off the water in the lagoon and reflected from the windows of the concrete house. "What we are doing," Pétur said, "is very Icelandic." He stretched out a sheet of tarpaper, took a big-headed nail out of the corner of his mouth, and hammered it through a wooden batten to hold the sheet in place. "It's summer," he said. "It's midnight. We're outside, working on a roof."

That afternoon the temperature had soared into the fifties —unusually warm for June in Iceland. Following the cold snap in December when Pétur and I had shivered at Little Lava, the winter had turned mild, stayed dry, could hardly be termed a winter by Icelandic standards. Spring had come early.

When Nancy and I first visited Iceland in 1986, June was oppressive: day after day of wind-whipped rain, with the temperature struggling to reach the forties. One evening at a farm on the north side of Snæfellsnes, we pitched our tent in the lee of a wall of fertilizer sacks to keep the wind from flattening it; in the morning we crawled out to see the mountains all about covered with new snow. On the heath were bands of golden plovers newly arrived from the south. In the bays, the eider ducks were still courting; they had not yet settled down to the business of nesting. Wood thrushes, snow buntings, and meadow pipits flew about call-ing incessantly, staking out territories and competing for mates.

This year, with winter so short, all the migratory birds had arrived before I did. Most of them had begun nesting, and some had brought off their broods. Crossing the marsh, Pétur and I had surprised a hen merganser with a crew of fluffy brown ducklings who paddled after their mother as she churned around a bend in one of the narrow, deep-cut tidal streams.

I found a meadow pipit's nest, a tiny cup in a thúfa's grassy flank. A ringed plover feigned a broken wing as it tried to lure me away from its nest on the gravelly flats south of the house. On the route to Little Lava, the skuas continued to aggressively defend their nest, which Pétur finally located: two large eggs, olive-colored and blotched with brown, on the flattened top of a thúfa.

A pair of white wagtails had claimed the ruined summer-house. They were sprightly birds with white faces and black caps, and tails that flicked constantly up and down. The wag-tails were offended when we carted the old furniture inside and tarpapered the roof. *"Tchik, tchik,"* they scolded, flitting from perch to perch. Their nest, of woven grass, rested on a horizontal framing member. I climbed up for a look. The cup, lined with sheep's wool, held seven eggs.

By noon of our third day, Pétur and I had made some progress. The workshop was looking more like a room than a boar's nest. In the old summerhouse I installed a toilet, a wooden seat with a hole and a slop bucket beneath. (When it wasn't raining, I planned to step out into the lava.)

Pétur had replaced or repainted all the window trim: it was amazing how this brightened the rooms. He had built a double bed, a simple wooden frame for a pair of mattresses we had brought from Reykjavík. The double bed would go in the kitchen, the cot would remain in the parlor.

We cleaned the floor and brushed a coat of acrylic sealant onto the wavy concrete. We installed new hinges on the outside door and the two operable windows. We were all set to tackle the gaps in the roof when a friend of Pétur's showed up; abruptly Pétur decided to go back to Reykjavík. It was frustrating. Working on the roof was just dangerous and difficult enough that I did not relish doing it by myself. But since the weather had stayed so unexpectedly fair, I was not sure the roof leaked badly enough to warrant immediate repair. It would have to wait until after Nancy and Will arrived; they were due to land in Reykjavík in three days.

Suddenly I missed them terribly. I missed the simple normalcy of having them near me. I felt quite blue as I watched Pétur and his friend grow smaller and smaller, hiking away across the flats.

I fetched water from Gvendarbrunnur. In the kitchen, I made a cup of tea. I tried to read and couldn't string the sentences together. I closed the book. The house was silent around me. The wind whispered. I opened a drawer and got out a knife, a sharp, long-bladed knife with a curved tip; what you'd use to butcher a sheep or a seal. I laid the knife on the table. It was ridiculous. Crazy, to feel threatened in such an isolated place. The murder had reduced me to the state of a frightened child in a dark room.

I would go back to the city the next day. But I would stay at Little Lava long enough to attend an important local event.

I heated water on the Primus and took a sponge bath. I shaved around my beard. I brushed off my pants and put on a plaid wool shirt—my only clean one. Donning my Wellingtons, I tramped down the homefield and started across the lagoon. The mudflats were still exposed, although a glance at the tide table—which I'd tacked to the kitchen wall—had informed me that the tide was rising.

A cool day, with fluffy white clouds that closed ranks now and then to send down veils of rain. When the clouds parted, spokes of sun fell upon distant farmhouses, yellow-green fields, rocky slopes, crenellated cliffs.

I made a big loop around the skuas' nest. They flew to-

ward me, fluttering and scolding, but didn't attack. I got into
our car—a Mitsubishi four-door, ten years old, a rather typical Icelandic vehicle—and crept along on the rutted track.
I passed Stóra Hraun. A wealthy man in Reykjavík owned
Stóra Hraun, so I'd been told, as well as the Haffjarðará, the
salmon river on the farm's western border; the farm was
leased to the family living there. The buildings at Stóra
Hraun needed painting. Abandoned cars and tractors in
various stages of dismemberment littered the fields. The
livestock included a small herd of dairy cows and an inde-
terminate number of sheep. The two collie-type dogs came
out as I passed and chased along behind the car, barking.

I took the gravel road to the highway, turned right on the
blacktop, and exited the main road at the foot of the big
mountain, Kolbeinsstaðafjall. Below the peak stood a small
cream-colored church with a pitched metal roof and a bell
tower.

Someone had recently trimmed the grass around the
headstones in the cemetery. The church was on the farm
Kolbeinsstaðir, or Kolbeinn's Stead; according to a map in
Landnámabók, the Icelandic *Book of Settlements*, Kolbeinn
was an original settler. He or one of his descendants apparently had been a chieftain. When Iceland became Christian
around the year 1000, the churches were situated on the
chieftains' farms, where many of them remain to this day.

Iceland is dotted with small churches like the one at
Kolbeinsstaðir. Three other churches lay within fifteen miles
of Little Lava. All were Lutheran churches; Lutheranism is
the official state religion of Iceland. The priests are civil servants. The churches are used for confirmations, christenings,

weddings, and funerals, rarely if ever for weekly Sunday-morning churchgoing—a practice to which most Icelanders, rural and urban, do not adhere.

The tang of fresh paint filled the sanctuary. The arched ceiling had been painstakingly painted in four different shades of blue. The straight-backed pews, ten on each side of the aisle, had been renewed with bright mustard-yellow paint, with which the maroon cloth seatbacks contrasted prettily.

About thirty people sat in the church. They seemed not unlike the people who live near my home in Pennsylvania —weathered faces, a bit reticent of manner or perhaps only self-contained. Mostly men and women in their forties or older, and a few younger adults with children. Today's Mass would include the confirmation of Jón Thór, thirteen-year-old son of the couple who farmed at Stóra Hraun.

Icelanders use a patronymic naming system, which at one time was the norm throughout Scandinavia but survives today only in Iceland. Jón Thór Kristjánsson sat in the right front pew between his mother, Margrét, and his father, Kristján. Jón Thór was about five feet tall, husky, with a freckled face and a thatch of sandy-colored hair. He was decked out in shiny black shoes, black trousers, and a white robe.

Margrét had invited me to the ceremony. She was a sturdy matron with short-cropped dark hair that had been given a henna tint. Her husband, Kristján, was tall and lanky, with unruly red-blond hair and a rawboned face, usually lit with a shy smile; later I would learn that today was his fiftieth birthday. Others in attendance from Stóra Hraun included

Jón Thór's fifteen-year-old sister Kristín (full name, Kristín Kristjánsdóttir), an outgoing girl, blond, as tall as I was and outweighing me by thirty pounds; and Guðlaug and Sigurveig, known respectively as Lauga and Veiga, Kristján's twin older sisters, also large, ample women.

The priest, in black vestments and a white ruff, droned in Icelandic. He shifted his position, from the lectern, to the altar, to a high wooden pulpit on the sanctuary's right side. His gaze seemed fixed on some distant vision.

I recognized some of the hymns, played on a treadle organ by an elderly woman who wore her long gray hair in two braids pinned in circles behind her head. She was garbed in the national costume, a black dress with a skirt to the ankles, a black vest over a ruffled and embroidered white blouse, and a flat black cap with a silk tassel. The congregation sang in Icelandic. On the hymns I knew, I sang along in English.

The music reminded me of Mom. Church had been an important part of her life. She had been raised a Baptist. She rarely missed a Sunday service for as long as I could remember. She always sat in the same pew, at first with our family, then with my dad, then by herself. On the rare Sundays when Nancy and Will and I drove in from the country, we would sit with her, which made her glow. In the last year of her life, with a new organ in the church, Mom had begun taking lessons from the church organist, learning to play the instrument herself.

We held her memorial service in the church, in State College, Pennsylvania, the town that adjoins Penn State. The mourners filled the sanctuary and the choir loft in back and overflowed into a fellowship room in the basement, where they listened over the sound system. My friends were there. My brothers' friends. My mother's and father's friends, from years and years back, people in whose wrinkled, age-spotted faces the light of life still shone. I wondered if another funeral in that town had ever attracted so many mourners. I think the display of mourning came from two sources: a deep and genuine respect and grief for Ruth and her family; and a sense of affront, that such a murder could have happened in the community. Perhaps the mourners sensed, as I had, that State College was no longer a small town, that it had crossed some vague sort of boundary and become a less humane and a more dangerous place—it was a city now.

On the morning of the memorial service, the police announced they had made an arrest. When my mind started veering in that direction, I pulled it back to Iceland. I looked at the priest and listened to the flow of his chanting. The carved wooden altar, the play of light on the wood. The four shades of blue in the ceiling. The choir of six, as they shakily sang an anthem. I sought comfort, in congregation with country people in a simple church on a plain beneath a tall mountain.

After the ceremony the folk filed out of the Kolbeinsstaðir church. It was raining lightly. The people got into cars and drove to a social hall about a quarter-mile away; I walked there, on a road that divided pasture fields. In the hall, tables had been set with fancy sandwiches, crackers, cheeses, cakes, cookies, and thermoses of coffee. A separate table was piled with gifts for Jón Thór, to which I added a wrapped package containing a small Icelandic-English dictionary.

The guests talked animatedly with one another. They were formally polite with me, nodding and smiling; they could not or would not speak English.

Someone took me by the elbow. "Charles," a voice said, pronouncing it "Chah-hruls," with a strong accent on the first syllable.

It was Margrét.

"The confirmation was beautiful," I said. "Thank you for inviting me."

"We are glad you could come. Your friend Pétur?"

"He went back to Reykjavík," I said. "He asked me to tell you he is sorry he could not be here." This was a bit of a lie, as Pétur had rolled his eyes at the suggestion of attending the ceremony, to which we had both been invited.

Margrét and I chatted for some time. I complimented her on her English, which was quite good. She told me that she had once been married to an American serviceman stationed at Keflavík, the NATO base near Reykjavík. A son from that union was in attendance at the party. Taking me over to meet him, she said, "You must come and see us at Stóra Hraun. If there is anything we can do, you must tell us. We can give you milk and bread. I can wash your clothes. You have nothing, there across the sand."

Outside the social hall, the cars were beaded with rain. The party looked as if it would go on for some time, but I'd had my fill of coffee and cakes and wanted to stretch my legs. And wanted to be by myself. It was strange and discomfiting how I desired company and yet being among people also made me jittery.

I drove back to the highway, turned west, crossed the bridge over the Haffjarðará, and turned right on a road leading into Hnappadalur Valley and toward the westernmost of the two red cones.

The road passed a long basalt cliff about fifty feet high. The stone stood in hexagonal columns. Some of the columns leaned out from the formation; others had tumbled away, gray angular slabs littering the grass between the rock face and the road.

A fox ran across in front of the car. It picked its way between the boulders. The fox's pelt was a patchy blend of white and dark brown, transitional from its all-white winter coat. The fox followed a narrow band of grass that led upward between the stone ramparts. At the top of the cliff it turned and looked at the car. Then it swapped ends and trotted off into the moors beyond.

When I reached the first cone, I parked on the edge of the road. In the rain-washed land were the colors of the church. The maroon of the pew cushions was the naked rubbly rock—technically called scoria—that composed the conical hill Rauðamelskúla Ytri, "Outer Red Gravel Cone." Mustard was the skin of moss that lay in patches on the lava and the thin soil. The four shades of blue appeared in the changeable sky.

A quarter of the way up the slope, the moss gave out. The scoria lay at an angle approaching 45 degrees. Stones the size of walnuts grated and slipped beneath my boots. For every three steps upward, I slid one step back. The pebbles made little landslides that slowed and stopped; larger stones leaped and tumbled down the hill.

Above me, a shadow detached itself from the hill. It was a *svartbakur*—a great black-backed gull. The bird swooped out from the cone, then swung back around toward me. It had a thick body and wings so long they reminded me of a plank. The gull held in the wind, studying me with its yellow eye. A red spot like a dab of blood decorated its lower mandible. The great black-backed gull is the largest gull in Iceland. People try to kill it, because it competes with them for seabird eggs and preys on the eider ducks which are husbanded for their down. This one soared above me, sounded its hoarse barking call, turned, and rode the wind seaward.

On top I found a patch of thin grass spotted with white excrement and scattered with feathers. I looked for a nest but didn't see one. Partway down the slope, ribs of darker gray rock protruded from the scoria, and perhaps a nest was hidden among the slabs. I sat on the gull's lookout, on the ocean side of the summit, out of the cold wind flowing down the valley.

The land spread out before me. Eldborg, its inner crater barely visible, nestled in the middle of its lava field. The gray fractured lava was spotted with yellow-green heathland, with here and there a darker patch of stunted birch. Beaches stretched westward along the southern fringe of Snæfellsnes; the surf left white wrinkles on the orangish-gold sand. Most Icelandic beaches are black sand derived from basalt. The beaches of Snæfellsnes come from crushed seashells. The coast near Little Lava is part of a twenty-mile-long estuarine and tidal-flat system known as Löngufjörur, or "Long Beaches."

Closer to me, Hnappadalur was a tangled wasteland, a heap of lava carved by water and wind. In Reykjavík I had spoken with a geologist, Haukur Jóhannesson, with Náttúrufræðistofnun Íslands, the Icelandic Natural History Museum. Haukur was a tall, friendly fellow in his middle years who had tramped all over Hnappadalur analyzing and mapping the valley's complex volcanic history. He gave me a colorful geologic map he had drawn up of Snæfellsnes, which I pinned to the parlor wall at Little Lava. He told me that the red cones were 2,600 years old, a figure arrived at through radiocarbon dating. The cones consisted of a glass-basaltic lava whose surface planes reflected light, so that from one direction the cones might look red, while from another direction they might appear brown.

Hnappadalur held two large lakes that had been gouged out by glaciers. Palagonite tuff hills and low peaks formed by subglacial eruptions. Another volcano in the valley was Gullborg, "Gold Fortress," a three-humped formation tinged golden by its cloak of moss. Farms with green pastures were tucked in among the lava flows. The salmon river Haffjarðará hugged the western edges of the Gullborg and Eldborg lava fields as it wended its way to the tide flats and drained into Faxaflói Bay.

The lowlands south of Eldborg are known as Mýrar, the Marshes; on that verdant flatness, small and large ponds and coiling streams reflected the sky. Valleys rose to the east, enclosed by steep mountains. My binoculars revealed the town of Borgarnes to the south, the buildings dwarfed by snow-patched peaks. Across Faxaflói, faint behind a sea haze, were the geometric forms of Reykjavík; I picked out the white Esso oil tanks on the harbor breakwater and tall apartment buildings on the waterfront. Keilir, another cone-shaped volcano halfway between Reykjavík and Keflavík, stood out plainly in the lava field sprawling south and west of the city.

Faxaflói was immense, unsheltered, an arm of the ocean. Today it was calm. I had heard two interpretations of its name. One was "Bay of Manes": *fax* signifies a horse's mane, and the bay, when stormy, sports white manes across its breadth. *Landnámabók*, the *Book of Settlements*, written in the 1100s, states that the bay is named for a Hebridean called Faxi. Faxi—perhaps he had a mane of hair—was a crew member on a ship captained by the Viking Flóki Vilgerðarson, one of the discoverers of Iceland. Sailing from the Shetland Islands around the year 860, Flóki made landfall in the south of Iceland and traveled west along the coast. As Flóki's longship sailed around Reykjanes Peninsula and the bay yawned before them, Faxi is supposed to have said: "It must be a big country we've found; the rivers are big enough."

With the binoculars I was able to pick out Little Lava, like a grain of salt, the merest speck on the sweep of land and water. The tide had risen, a flat bright sheet covering the mudflats. I would be taking the long way back.

4 | *Bad Mood Path*

On June 11, I met Nancy and Will at the airport. I was relieved to be with them; I hugged them both, and held on, and didn't want to let go.

"How are you and Pétur coming with the house?" Nancy asked.

I told her how much we'd gotten done. "It's not a palace," I said with a grin. "Or a tent."

We spent a few days in Reykjavík while they recovered from jet lag. We stayed again in the home of Thórður and his parents. The house is a beautiful modern design, two stories, unpainted slabs of concrete anchored to a rocky hill; sort of an expanded, urbane version of Little Lava. From the kitchen and dining room we could watch ships sailing in and out of the harbor. There were fishing boats, container vessels, the ferry *Akraborg*, and a visiting naval frigate flying the French tricolor.

Thórður was his usual self, gently sardonic and eagerly helpful. His parents, Grétar and Guðný, were generous and hospitable, as we have found most Icelanders instinctively tend to be.

One evening we were sitting having coffee in the living room. The day had been fair; the light was low and serene. Across Faxaflói, the line of sawtooth mountains led the eye down Snæfellsnes to where Snæfellsjökull stood up as a featureless blue triangle against the coral sky.

"I envy you," Guðný said. She is a handsome woman, with a round face, high cheekbones, and short hair. Like most Icelanders of her generation, she was born elsewhere in the country and came to Reykjavík later—"got onto the pavement," as the saying goes. She looked out across the bay to the far peninsula. "To spend a summer in a place like that," she mused, "with nothing that you must do. It is like being a child again."

"Will you visit us?" I asked.

She smiled. "Of course."

Nancy and I were anxious to get to Little Lava. Will, on the other hand, would have been quite content to have stayed in the city, playing games on Thórður's computer and swimming in the heated pool, where the water bubbled in imitation geysers and children shrieked and laughed as they scooted down a tall water slide.

He was complaining a little as we drove the Mitsubishi onto the *Akraborg*, but he soon settled down in front of the video screen in the lounge. Nancy and I went up on deck. We watched as the mountains ringing Faxaflói shifted slowly past. Many of the peaks were still spotted with snow: because it had been such a dry spring, the usual rains had not come to melt away the snowpack. Eider ducks peppered the water near islands and skerries. Cargo ships passed, en route to the harbor. The ferry headed for Akranes, where the tall chimney of a cement plant let off a streamer of smoke that did not smudge the air as much as it pointed out, through its singularity, the near-absence of industrial pollution.

We drove off the ferry, took the main street through town, and were soon headed north.

This would be a short visit to Little Lava, to appraise the work Pétur and I had done and decide what was needed to properly outfit the house. Having already been to Little Lava, Nancy knew what to expect. Will did not. I could tell he was apprehensive about living in a house without electricity and running water. I had kidded him about it, mentioning that at least he wouldn't have to take a bath very often—something he didn't like doing at home.

Living without electricity did not daunt me. For three years after I built our house in the mountains, Nancy and I had lived unconnected to the grid. We had a generator, which was switched on occasionally to power tools and the vacuum cleaner, and to pump water. Our refrigerator ran on propane. Evenings, we read by propane and kerosene lamps. I remembered the simplicity of those first three years of our

life together. I looked forward to recapturing it at Little
Lava.

We stopped at Stóra Hraun for introductions. Margrét
brought out coffee, bread, cucumbers, and tomatoes: it is an
Icelandic custom of long standing to feed any visitor who
shows up on the doorstep. She told us *"Gjöriði svo vel,"*
which seemed to mean something like "Please eat a lot." To
this day I have not figured out if it is an insult to decline an
offer of coffee; however, what is a fine and a laudable tradition can sometimes conflict with ferry schedules and the
rising tide. At Stóra Hraun we drank our coffee and ate
the sliced cucumbers and the small hard tomatoes grown in
the Icelanders' geothermally heated greenhouses.

We got out my maps and heard stories about the local
area, with Nancy, Margrét, and Margrét's teenaged daughter
Kristín leading the exchange in a mix of Icelandic and English. Icelanders were always impressed that Nancy could
speak their language, a complicated tongue with gender-
bearing nouns and changeable case endings. Nancy tells me
that she accepts the fact that she is butchering the grammar
and forges on ahead.

Kristín got out a book, published in Iceland in 1954, about
the United States; the pride she took in translating a passage
about our home state turned to embarrassment when she
had to describe Pittsburgh as "a dirty, ugly city."

Margrét repeated her offer to wash our clothes. She

wrapped up some cake for us to take along, and some of her rich dark rye bread. By the time we left the house, the tide was high and we had to make the long crossing. I had been back and forth to Little Lava on various errands at least ten times, several of them requiring the indirect route, and I was still trying to figure out the best path.

Wearing our packs, we had to backtrack when confronted with stream channels that were too wide for Will to jump across. We stopped to examine the coarse grasses in the marsh. Moss and lichens covering the rocks. Birds that started up, calling shrilly or fleeing furtively at our approach. We squirmed through a wire fence, its barbs tufted with sheep's wool. We stopped often to let Will rest, and pull his socks up inside his boots, and collect rocks and feathers. He carried a daypack with a few light items, including a plastic bag filled with Lego blocks. I had found an old broom handle at Little Lava, and he used it as a staff to keep his balance.

That evening we made a meal of sliced vegetables and *hangikjöt*, or smoked lamb, between buttered slices of flatbread. The best hangikjöt, it is said, is cured with the smoke from burning sheep manure. Afterward, we walked south down the peninsula, taking in the views of the mountains, some naked and others grass-clad, all skirted with fans of eroded rock; the volcanoes of differing sizes and shapes; and the lava field, like a huge asphalt parking lot broken into pieces and shoved around by some Promethean bulldozer.

I walked holding hands with Nancy. "It's good to be back," she said. "Back together, and back at Little Lava." We watched our son, a thin, wiry boy under a baseball cap, as he turned over chunks of driftwood, examined glass bottles, rocks, seaweed, and trawler floats. He called to us about each new discovery, and we duly inspected it and, more often than not, ended up carrying it.

With my family about me, I could sense the tension falling away, like ice cracking off a bush in springtime when a thaw warms it and the wind shakes it.

It felt good to have the summer before us. To be in a place where no telephone could summon us, where the sun marched conspicuous around the sky, where birds went about their tasks, where the sea came and went as it had ever done—where complexity, strife, and trouble seemed far away.

By morning the wind had shifted to the southwest, bringing fog and clouds. After breakfast we donned raingear and went outside. I had spent so much time working that I'd not yet begun exploring in the lava. Nor had I hiked out onto the tide flats or taken the time to assemble my kayak, let alone paddle it around within the estuary. All of these things I looked forward to hungrily.

A trail commenced in the lava just east of our house. It was called Thrællyndisgata, which, according to one of our Icelandic friends, meant something like "Way of the Mind of a Slave." Or, as Pétur had put it, looking out across the heaped-up, contorted rock with its sharp edges and sudden declivities and precariously balanced slabs: "Bad Mood Path."

If you were a thrall and had to follow that route while

herding sheep or traveling from farm to farm, it would certainly put you in a bad mood. Maybe a slave's mind was thought to wander in the manner of Thrællyndisgata, which fell off into shallow creases, turned through brush that scraped at shanks and hands, and meandered from one stone cairn to the next. Or perhaps the trail's name pointed out the difference between free men, who had horses and could ride swiftly across the tide-exposed sands of Löngufjörur, and slaves on foot, who had to poke along through the lava.

The path was beaten dirt. Beside it grew low clusters of heather, crowberry, and trailing blueberry plants whose stems were spangled with tiny bell-shaped pink flowers. Gray-green moss covered the pitted rocks, and the fine silvery branchlets of reindeer moss spread across the ground. Wild thyme had sunk its roots into small cracks in the lava. The thyme had bright-green leaves and pretty lavender flowers; rolled between one's fingers, the leaves gave off a spicy scent.

Thrællyndisgata led over rounded humps of lava where no plants grew. It dipped into hollows thicketed with gnarled birch trees and runty rowan trees and creeping junipers hiding from the wind.

"William," Nancy called, "what do you do if you get lost in a forest in Iceland?"

He grinned. He already knew the punch line to that one: "Stand up!"

Normal Icelandic weather had reasserted itself. Rain, blown by the wind so that it spattered against the rocks and rattled in the brush. A brief lull, during which the clouds thinned and the sun peered faintly through the overcast.

Then the clouds massing again, rank upon rank of them marching in over the bay, the rain pelting down; then an eye of blue overhead and a sudden dazzle of sunshine that vanished in a slow wink, followed by gusts and another hard shower.

When the rain let up we could see one cairn, and sometimes two, on the trail ahead of us. When the rain fell hard, we were reduced to trudging along staring at the path, then looking up, startled, when we encountered the next mound of rocks.

Some of the cairns were waist-high, some taller than a man. Beneath their cloaks of lichen and moss, the rocks had been fitted together carefully. Throughout Iceland, cairns mark the way: over mountain passes, across the moonscape of the interior, through the frequent lava wastes. Travelers have used the paths for centuries. When a snowstorm overtook a wayfarer, a row of cairns could save a life. Cairns were sometimes called "bone women," or beggar women. A passerby might stop, take a sheep bone out of his saddlebag or cloak pocket, suck out the marrow, then write a ribald verse on a scrap of paper—stick it in the bone, place it in the cairn for the next traveler's amusement. Bernard Scudder, an Englishman living in Iceland, has translated one such poem:

> *Many men from my lips took*
> *a pleasure only rarely found.*
> *Every vicar and holy book*
> *I vow to wrap my legs around.*

We reached a tall cairn that was plainly visible from the house on a clear day. Now it loomed up hoary in the mist. No sheep bones had been filed among its stones, although we had passed a few such moldering on the trail's edge— probably a ewe that had fallen into a crack and had its remains scattered by ravens and foxes.

A sudden whirring made us look up. A chunky brown bird sailed away across a serrated ridge: a ptarmigan.

Seeing the bird reminded me of my friend Heiðar, with whom I had hunted ptarmigan—*rjúpa*, in Icelandic—eight years earlier. It was during a trip I'd taken to a remote region in northwest Iceland called the Vestfirðir, or West Fjords. Heiðar was a market hunter. He had with him a beautiful yellow Labrador retriever, a young bitch named Nóra. He told me that he killed ptarmigan by the hundreds each autumn and sold them to restaurants and to people wanting to prepare the traditional Icelandic Christmas dinner of roast rjúpa. The few birds I shot I added to his bag. In return, he told me about our prey.

Lagopus mutus, the rock ptarmigan, inhabits Greenland, northern Canada, Alaska, Siberia, and Scandinavia. The species is closely related to grouse, quail, and pheasants. Most such chickenlike fowl are short-range fliers, but the rjúpa is different—as I had learned when I shot at one and missed, and watched it fly across a broad valley, power its way up a mountain, and, a pinprick in my vision, alight in a boulder field on the ridge. According to Heiðar, flocks of ptarmigan regularly move ten miles or farther, shifting from one feeding ground to another. They eat berries and the buds and leaves of birch. Each evening when we got back to the farm,

Heiðar would hang our birds by the neck inside a shed; juice from birch buds in their crops would trickle down over the birds' breasts, giving the meat a minty taste.

In the heath along Thrællyndisgata, a second rjúpa jumped onto a rock fifty yards away. We all focused our binoculars. A male: his white breast showed up brightly. With a loud call that sounded like a belch, the rjúpa leaped from his perch and flew into the air. Fifty feet he rose, then a hundred; he slowed, spread his wings, and cupped them, and, continuing to proclaim his odd crepitant song, floated back to earth. He landed on another boulder and stood with his head erect, wings drooping, and tail spread.

In winter, both male and female ptarmigan turn white. In spring, as the snow melts, the birds begin to molt, their white plumage replaced by a mottled brown that paints them into a landscape of heather and lichen-flecked rock. By late May, the peak of the mating season, the female's molt is complete, her camouflage perfected. For another month the male's breast remains a bright, attention-grabbing white. Gyrfalcons, the main predators of ptarmigan, zero in on the males, killing up to a third of them, while the biologically more valuable females—already fertilized by their mates— sneak off and nest.

Leaving the cock rjúpa to oversee his territory, we hiked on.

A swale in the lava contained a puzzling section of trail: two parallel stone walls, laid knee-high, with rocky fill between them. The segment of improved trail was about thirty feet long. Who had fixed this part of the path? And why had they bothered, with the rest of Thrællyndisgata so winding and treacherous? It was like driving down a country lane and coming onto a four-lane interstate that lasted for a tenth of a mile.

On the far side of the swale, Thrællyndisgata resumed its rocky, tricky meander. It led us through two sorts of lava: pahoehoe lava and aa lava. The terms are Hawaiian in origin. Iceland, like Hawaii, sits on a mid-oceanic ridge where two plates of the earth's crust are slowly pulling apart. Lava comes welling up through the rift.

In Icelandic, pahoehoe lava is *helluhraun*, or "smooth lava." When helluhraun flows along on the ground, its skin congeals before its mass cools and solidifies. Sometimes the flow looks like ropes laid parallel to and touching one another. Or it hardens into pillow shapes, or wrinkles like an elephant's skin. Once the surface cools, the lava may continue to flow in tunnels beneath the crust. Gas pockets can develop in the tunnels; after the flow hardens, the pockets remain as chambers and caves. It can be worth your life to cross a lava field solo. Step on a thin ceiling above a chamber and you may break through and fall in. Fifteen feet down, you find yourself looking up at the sky through a small hole. Often the chambers are shaped like kettles, with sides that curve inward as they near the surface. If you cannot climb out, you starve to death and your bones are never found.

Aa lava is *apalhraun* in Icelandic, "block lava." Chemically it is identical to helluhraun. Apalhraun emerges from fissures in flows that are thirty to one hundred feet thick. During an eruption the front of the lava mass, covered with slag and rough debris, creeps and grinds slowly forward. Chunks that break loose from the advancing front are steam-rollered beneath the mass. Once solidified, apalhraun is rougher and harder to negotiate than helluhraun. Its sharp edges cut shoe leather and chew away boot soles. The stones shift underfoot, tumbling the careless walker, snapping bones, lacerating skin.

The trail passed dales and ridges, whaleback rises, spires as high as houses. In the changing light the lava took on a weird appearance. We called out the shapes: shark fins, cockscombs, castle turrets, grave markers, crouching cats. Icelanders used to believe—and some still believe, or at least feel it prudent not to disbelieve—that magical beings such as *álfar*, or elves, and *huldufólk*, or hidden folk, inhabit lava fields. In times past, thieves and outcasts hid in the wastes, sheltering in caves, drinking from springs, eating berries and pilfered sheep.

We stopped in a copse of shoulder-high birch, old trees with trunks as thick as my thigh. A robinlike bird with a brown back and reddish sides flew off through the branches. It was a *skógarthröstur*, or "wood thrush," known as a redwing in Britain, where the species also breeds. The thrush lit on the ground and scampered behind a rock outcropping.

We climbed up out of the birches. The rain had settled to a drifting mist. The fog was lifting. Eldborg showed a deep purplish-blue. Clouds hung on its rim. Behind the volcano, sunlight flashed gold-green against the steep stratified flanks of Kolbeinsstaðafjall. In front of us, the line of cairns continued across the lava, marking the route to a neighboring farm. I wondered what the land had looked like when people began building those bone women. A few more trees, perhaps; little else would have changed since then.

Will rapped on a stone with his stick. The sound echoed back from the lava. We heard a thin warbling *trui-trui* from a hidden redwing. From the top of a ridge a hundred yards off the trail came a sudden whuff-whuffing of wings.

The eagle beat its way into the air. It called out, a harsh *klee klee klee*. Its beak was hooked and massive. Its wings looked improbably long and as broad as doors; at their ends, black feathers spread like fingertips. The bird sailed over our heads. Its short, wedge-shaped tail was a luminous white. Its beak and feet were butter-yellow. Another eagle lifted from the lava. It, too, gave out a high-pitched hollow cackling as it flew in our direction.

The eagles circled above us, scolding loudly. We knew they had to have a nest nearby. It was a strange feeling, to be the object of the attention of such imperious birds. Not wanting to disturb the eagles further, we withdrew and headed back toward Little Lava.

That evening, rain beat against the house. Outside, seen through the blurry glass, sheep grazed stoically in the milky light. The wind blew the rain across the lava field in sheets.

In the middle of the night, Nancy and I wakened to the sound of water dripping. It was falling from the ceiling onto the middle of our bed. We took up the mattresses and the down sleeping robe and, going into the parlor where Will slept, bedded on the floor.

5 | *Sea Eagles*

In the city, in a mall department store, we bought dish towels, throw rugs, and pillows. Guðný gave us some old pillowcases. At the Saturday flea market, held in a warehouse near the wharf, we found flatware, mismatched plates, kitchen utensils, an iron frying pan, a porcelain teapot, and a dish-drying rack. From a vendor I purchased a large metal canister with a secure lid: sunk into the murky spring near the house, it would make a refrigerator of sorts.

I had been to the flea market before.

In 1994, Nancy spent two weeks in Reykjavík taking a language course at the university. One evening at the municipal swimming pool, a large, craggy-faced Icelander attached himself to her; he followed her home on the city bus, conspired to run into her about town, and gave her love poems he had written to her. In English, of course. His most ambitious rhyme involved "Nancy," "fancy," and "necromancy." Some of the poems he declaimed in the men's dressing room at the pool. An Icelandic friend of ours named Venni overheard the poems and figured he knew the "Nancy" they extolled. With another friend, he confronted the poet and persuaded him that his attentions were not wanted.

In December 1995, while killing time in the city waiting for Pétur to finish his art projects so that we could go to Little Lava, I went to the dockside flea market with Venni. As we drifted past the tables, Venni stopped. He pointed out the man who had written the poems to Nancy. The poet had a booth from which he was selling used books, including some editions of the Icelandic sagas. In the sagas, the writing of love poems to another man's wife provides an excellent spark for setting off a blood feud.

Venni spoke to the poet, whose smile faltered when I was introduced as the husband of the acclaimed Nancy. In those days, in the aftermath of my mother's death, I was feeling rather grim. A fight would not have been completely unwelcome. I told the poet that Nancy had kept his poems and showed them to me. I said that sometimes, when we wanted to have a good laugh, we read them aloud. The poet pursed his lips. He looked down and began rearranging the books on his table. I did not feel particularly proud of myself. Venni grinned and elbowed me as we moved on to the next stall.

.   .   .

Reykjavík is a clean, attractive city with a small-town atmo-
spere. More than 160,000 Icelanders live in the metropolis
and several adjoining towns. I have heard Icelanders say,
"There is Reykjavík and there is Iceland." The population of
all Iceland is 270,000—about as many people as live in New-
ark, New Jersey, or St. Paul, Minnesota, or Anaheim, Cali-
fornia. There are many times more birds in Iceland than
people. The population of the puffin, *Fratercula arctica*, is
estimated at 10 to 12 million. The eider duck, *Somateria
mollissima*, at 400,000 to 600,000.

Iceland lies in the North Atlantic 600 miles west of Norway, 500 miles northwest of Scotland, and 200 miles southeast of Greenland. Reykjavík, in the southwestern quadrant
of the country, is at 64° north latitude—roughly as far north
as Nome, Alaska.

Iceland is about the size of Ohio, although its shape is
more complex. It reminds me of a sea monster, with a bul-
bous body, a crested head rising in the northwest, and two
arms reaching out westward, the Reykjanes and Snæfellsnes
peninsulas.

Its high latitude and maritime setting might lead one to
assume that Iceland would have a "dull, Lenten, Northern
clyme," as one early observer noted. Iceland can indeed
show a cold and forbidding face. But it is a contradictory
place, where summer can burst forth in warmth and bril-
liance, and where winter, although long and dark, is not as
extreme as the island's name implies.

The tempering influence is a tongue of ocean water called

the Irminger Current, named for a Danish naval officer who conducted hydrographic studies in the region in the 1850s. The Irminger Current is an arm of the Gulf Stream, the most powerful current in the global ocean, a gyre of warm water whose course to this day remains incompletely understood. The Gulf Stream comes up past Florida, passes Nova Scotia and Newfoundland, and angles northeastward across the Atlantic. The Irminger Current splits off from the Gulf Stream near the Faroe Islands and bends back north and west, brushing Iceland's coast. The Irminger Current is warm but by no means tropical: even in summer, the waters off Iceland get no warmer than 50 degrees.

While in the city I went to see one of the authors of my bird book, *Guide to the Birds of Iceland*.

Kristinn Skarphéðinsson works for the Icelandic Natural History Museum, the same institution that employs Haukur Jóhannesson, who had told me about the geology of Hnappadalur Valley. The museum is housed in a nondescript concrete building near Hlemmur, a busy bus terminal in the central city. Kristinn was using a copy machine when I arrived. He invited me into his office. He was tall, blocky through the hips, with a young-looking face and a thatch of graying sandy hair brushed skyward. He had earned a doctoral degree in wildlife biology at the University of Wisconsin. He was a bit guarded toward me at first, especially when I started asking about eagles, but he warmed up after learning we had a friend in common, a professor at Penn State with whom he had gone to graduate school. She had studied chickadees; Kristinn had done his research on ravens, returning to Iceland for fieldwork each summer. I thought that Kristinn's reaction to me was typically Icelandic: This stranger is linked to a friend of mine, so I'll trust him. Besides, he might be useful.

Unlike some Icelanders who study abroad, Kristinn had gone back to his native land, which was a fitting place for an ornithologist. I had read the following passage in my copy of *Guide to the Birds of Iceland*:

> Few areas in the world of similar size contain as great a variety and combination of bird habitats as Iceland: mountainous country with areas of vegetation extending up to the glaciers; wetlands with tundra vegetation and sand dunes; moorland crossed by valleys and heather-covered heaths; sand-flats with bare rocks and cliffs; stony soil with sparse vegetation; valleys leading off fjords and bordered by steep cliffs with scree at their base; moorland covered with hummocks; scrub and forest; lava fields with and without vegetation; mudflats and river deltas; coastal sand dunes covered with lyme-grass; lakes with islets, both in the lowlands and the highlands; sand beaches, pebble beaches, and erosion banks; offshore islands; nesting cliffs (some 10 km in length and up to 500 m high, homes to thousands of birds); farmland, forestry plantations and domestic gardens.

Kristinn explained that, as a government ornithologist, he was collecting data for a distribution atlas of Iceland's breeding birds. He was studying the migratory wading birds that gathered on the extensive mudflats in southwestern Iceland, including those of Löngufjörur, near Little Lava. And he was keeping tabs on the population of the *haförn*, the white-tailed sea eagle.

"There are around 140 eagles in Iceland," he told me in impeccable English. "That includes about forty breeding pairs, up from a low of ten pairs in the 1960s."

I mentioned the eagles we had seen along Thrællyndis-gata; I said I suspected they had a nest.

"Yes," Kristinn said. "To the north of the trail, on a small stack at the edge of the rough lava. That's a traditional nesting spot, although this is the first time in nine years that it's been used." He leaned back in his chair and looked at me. "You're lucky. Two breeding pairs have territories near where you're living. Both pairs nested this spring." Recently, he had flown in an airplane over the area, checking for nests. "The other nest is on a small island in Löngufjörur," he volunteered.

The white-tailed sea eagle is *Haliaeetus albicilla*, the European congener of the North American bald eagle, *Haliaeetus leucocephalus*. When Iceland was settled, the island may have supported 200 to 300 pairs. By the end of the nineteenth century, a campaign of persecution had nearly wiped out the great birds. In the belief that eagles were killing sheep and eider ducks, farmers shot them. Strychnine baits put out for foxes poisoned eagles as well. By the early

1900s, the only place in Iceland where eagles remained were the rugged Vestfirðir, the West Fjords—the head of the sea monster I saw when I looked at the map, in Iceland's extreme northwest.

In 1913 Iceland bestowed formal protection on the sea eagle, the first nation in the world to do so. *Haliaeetus albicilla* was once found in Britain and throughout Europe and northern Asia. Today it survives in Iceland, Greenland, and in parts of Japan, China, Russia, Iran, Turkey, the Balkans, Austria, Germany, and Scandinavia. Coastal Norway is home to about half the entire Western European population, estimated at a thousand pairs.

Strychnine was outlawed in Iceland in the 1960s, and since then, Kristinn said, the eagle population has been coming back, although at a slow rate. Not until age five or six do eagles select mates. Depending on the abundance of food in their territories, they may not start breeding until age ten. They do not always breed each year, and when they do, the female lays only one egg or, at the most, two. Not all the eggs hatch. Not all the hatchlings survive. Bad weather can kill them, or lack of food. They succumb to accidents while learning to fly. Some never become adept at catching prey.

Kristinn was familiar with Little Lava and its surroundings. He had hiked around the area while studying the migratory birds that stopped on the mudflats in spring and fall, on their way to breeding and wintering grounds elsewhere. "You've missed them this year," he said, "but the red knots flood those mudflats in the spring." The red knot is a chunky, chestnut-colored shorebird named for its call, a hoarse *nut*. Knots leave their wintering grounds in Britain and western Europe, fly to southwestern Iceland, replenish their body fat by gorging on invertebrates in the mudflats, and wing onward to breeding grounds in Greenland and Arctic Canada. "You'll see them coming back through in August," Kristinn said, "but they won't be as colorful then."

He estimated that around thirty species of birds nested near Little Lava—in the lava heath, along the edges of ponds, in the marsh, and on offshore islands.

Seals lived along the coast. Foxes were abundant, despite the efforts of gun-toting farmers. A truly beautiful place, Kristinn said, although the weather could be trying, with lots of wind and rain. He spoke of mountain passes channeling the wind and intensifying it, and said there were places on Snæfellsnes where cars were regularly blown off the road— "That's mainly in the winter, though," he said. I should be careful when hiking in the lava and on the mudflats, where the tide could come in with astonishing swiftness. "Talk to some of the farmers, tell them what you're doing," he said. "If you run into trouble with your kayak, they may be able to help you. Watch out for *straumur*—strong currents around the islands near the salmon river's mouth. People have drowned there."

It turned out that Kristinn even knew our house; he was in the habit of stopping and having a look inside it whenever he hiked out on the peninsula past Little Lava.

"It will be good to see smoke coming from the chimney," he said.

.   .   .

In an old edition of the *Journal of American Folk-Lore* I
found an article, "Icelandic Beast and Bird Lore," by the
Canadian-born Arctic explorer and anthropologist Vilhjálmur
Stefánsson, who was of Icelandic descent.

It is believed that an eagle will sit by a stream for hours
on end, waiting for a salmon to swim past close enough that
the eagle can seize it using the talons of one foot while holding on to the bank with the other foot. If the salmon proves
too heavy for the eagle to wrest from the water, the bird is
in a fix, because when an eagle's talons strike home, they
cannot be unclenched. Nothing can bring a person better
luck than to find an eagle in such a dilemma and free it.

Should a man place some gold in an eagles' nest, one of
the pair of eggs therein will hatch into a stone of consider-
able virtue and the other one into a dragon. The stone has
the power to make its possessor invisible and to deliver any
woman easily of child. The dragon is fierce and strong, able
to carry off two-year-old colts.

If a man lays his head on a pillow containing an eagle
feather, on the next day he can be deceived and easily taken
advantage of.

The Return of the Sea Eagle, by John A. Love, published
in England in 1983, revealed to me the physical magnifi-
cence of *Haliaeetus albicilla*.

Eagles have sharp vision. Their eyes are large, about an
inch in diameter, or slightly larger than those of the average
human. So ample are an eagle's eyes that they are directed

both frontally and sideways in the skull. This arrangement permits binocular stereoscopic vision to the fore, vital for sighting prey at a distance, and peripheral vision to each side, useful in detecting motion.

Its great wings let an eagle soar efficiently and carry heavy loads, as when hauling prey out of the water and back to the nest. The wingspan is two and a half meters, or around eight feet.

The upper mandible of an eagle's beak, four inches long, is used to pierce and tear; in most cases the actual killing of prey is accomplished with the needle-sharp talons of the feet. When an eagle strikes a bird or a fish, the impact of the collision triggers a bone-and-tendon arrangement that causes the talons to lock shut. Thick feathering on the legs protects an eagle against the thrashing of prey. The bottoms of an eagle's feet are covered with spicules of horny flesh, the better to grip its kill.

An eagle will soar along above the water's surface, shoot out one or both feet, and snag a fish. Most fish that eagles catch weigh from one to six pounds. Eagles themselves weigh from eight to fourteen pounds. In Iceland, eagles prey on ocean catfish and lumpsuckers. Sometimes they take cod, although usually cod lie too far beneath the water's surface. It can happen that an eagle latches on to a fish too large to be overpowered; the fish dives, taking the bird with it. In the Orkney Islands a halibut was once caught with an eagle's feet still embedded in its back, the rest of the bird having rotted off. In Greenland in the 1970s, a Danish ornithologist photographed a sea eagle, its talons sunk in a fish too heavy to be lifted, rowing itself to shore, using its wings as oars.

Strategically placing the sun at its back, an eagle will fly toward resting gulls or ducks. It may single out an eider in the water and repeatedly stoop on it. Each time the eagle attacks, the duck dives. One would think a duck could keep on diving indefinitely, but it gets tired out. A Russian biologist counted the times an eagle had to stoop before it exhausted and killed an eider. Seven attacks. Twelve. A German observer reported up to sixty-five attacks made over periods of from thirty-five to forty-five minutes. Male eiders are often selected, perhaps because their white bodies are conspicuous when underwater.

In Iceland, Kristinn Skarphéðinsson told me, eagles kill many fulmars. The fulmar is a petrel, a pelagic bird of the open ocean that comes in to the land only to nest and raise its young. The Icelandic word for fulmar is *fýll*, or "stinker." The English name "fulmar" means essentially the same thing, "foul gull," the *mar* coming from the Old Norse word for gull. Both names refer to the fulmar's habit of vomiting an evil-smelling slurry onto any creature that menaces it. On a lake in southern Iceland I once found a black-backed gull that had run afoul of a fulmar. The gull's feathers were smeared together, as if by tar; the bird flopped and cried piteously as it tried to get away, beating the water with its ruined wings.

According to Kristinn, eagles have a way of killing fulmars without exposing themselves to the vomit. "They do it on the wing," he told me. "The eagle is a faster flier than the fulmar. Fulmars nest high up on the cliffs, and the adults go out to sea to get food for their nestlings. An eagle will fly above a fulmar, so that he is aimed out in front, in the direction that the fulmar is going—" He brought one of his hands angling down suddenly onto the other. "The fulmar has no opportunity to use its defense."

Kristinn guessed that the eagles living around Little Lava fed mainly on fulmars and fish. It was a rich habitat, he said, otherwise two pairs would not be nesting so close together.

He informed me of a new regulation protecting Iceland's eagles: "No one is allowed within 500 meters of a nest." He watched me with blue eyes that were placid and penetrating. "However, it would be all right if you kept track of those nests for me. Don't go near them for at least a couple more weeks. By then, the young will have grown most of their feathers. Choose a good warm day, not a rainy one, so they don't get chilled when the adult leaves the nest. Let me know how things go. Maybe you could use the phone at Stóra Hraun.

"Later on, I'll be banding the eaglets," he said. "You can watch if you want."

6 | *Settling In*

After my mother died, my eyes could not shed tears. It seemed that weeping would be a natural thing for an aggrieved son to do. But even though I would have welcomed being able to cry, my tears would not flow.

I was crying on the inside, while remaining composed, even stoic, on the outside. Sometimes I found it hard to draw a full breath. My outlook was bleak. I couldn't get comfortable around strangers. When I was among people, as in a town, I always watched my back; I did this even in Reykjavík, where violent crime is almost nonexistent. I felt distanced from my friends, ejected from the world of peaceful day-to-day living. I practically stopped making love to Nancy—although when I was alone, as I was on occasion at Little Lava, it might be that the only way I could relax enough to fall asleep was to release myself with my hand.

My eyes did not shed tears. So instead, my brain shed thoughts. I forgot things I had said or done. I lost track of plans and commitments. What terrified me most was the inability to hold on to my thoughts, to muster concentration sufficient to write, or even to read books.

In Pennsylvania I had been seeing a counselor; it was a relief to have someone to talk to who was neither a stranger nor a friend. I told him how much I wished I could break down and cry. He told me that crying required a total letting go of one's defenses. My mind, having witnessed brutality, having confronted evil, would not let my body lower its guard.

While I was still in Pennsylvania, I was in town one evening, and on my way home I found myself turning into Mom's neighborhood. It was dark outside. Winter, snow on the lawns. I drove past the neatly kept houses, many of them owned by people who worked at Penn State. I turned onto Hillcrest, Mom's street.

A light was on in the house, in the back room, what we'd always called the family room. The bedroom where Mom had died, in the opposite end of the house, was dark. The front windows of the house were lit with a pale, indirect glow. A car sat parked in the carport—not hers. I was renting out the house; so far, I hadn't been able to sell it because of what had happened there.

I stopped the car. Everything looked the same as it had when Mom was alive, except that there were sticks, small tree branches brought down by an ice storm, littering the front yard.

Suddenly a thought came to my mind: I wish I could fall a long way and somebody would catch me. Tears filled my eyes, but as always, something took hold of me on the inside, and I couldn't let go. *Somebody to catch me.* That somebody, I knew, was my mom. But she was no longer here, she was far away from me, she was part of the long unscrolling of lives—once singular and vibrant, now historical and remembered—that had temporarily coalesced in me.

I took a deep breath. I put the car in gear and drove home.

We were still in the capital on our provisioning trip. From Thórður's house in Seltjarnarnes, I telephoned Pétur. He was ready to get out of the city, all fired up to go back to Little Lava and finish fixing up the house. We set a time to meet that evening. We would pick him up at his apartment, catch the last ferry, and drive north.

"Not tonight," Nancy said as I was hanging up the phone. "It will be high tide when we get to Stóra Hraun. You can't expect Will to make the hike around the marsh that late at night."

I called Pétur back. We would pick him up in the morning. He agreed to the change, although he sounded disappointed.

The next morning we went to his apartment. No one answered when I buzzed his flat. Instead of hurrying to the docks and catching the ferry without him, we decided to wait. We walked downtown and looked in the shops. We had tea and pastries in a bakery. We went back and checked the apartment again: no Pétur. As the hours passed, we tried without success to reach either him or Anna—who, although she and Pétur had separated, was the person with whom he would have left a message.

"He must have gone out drinking," I said in disgust to Nancy, as for the dozenth time I jammed my thumb down on the buzzer on the wall of the apartment building. "He went to the bars last night and never made it home." I kicked at the door, found that it was open a crack. I went in and climbed the stairs. I knocked on Pétur's door. No answer. "*Goddamn.*" I made a fist and pounded on the wood. A woman opened a door across the hall, stared at me, and closed the door again. I clumped back downstairs.

Nancy tried to cool me down. When that didn't work, she basically ignored my griping. Will was pleased with the delay, since we ended up at a children's fair held in a drizzling rain at a park near Pétur's flat. I fretted and bitched the day away. How like an Icelander to promise something, then back out when an opportunity to go drinking presented itself.

"Look," Nancy said, "let's just go on to Little Lava. Maybe he'll show up later."

First thing the next morning we headed for the *Akraborg*. With their usual officious impatience, the ferry workers waved our car on board, into cheek-to-jowl parking with the other cars and trucks. An hour later we drove off the boat at Akranes. After another hour, the cone of Eldborg came into view.

When we pulled into the customary spot by the low cliff, we parked next to a small gray sedan. I thought I recognized it: Anna's old Fiat. Looking across the tide flats, we saw a human figure crouched on the roof of the house.

We hastened across the flats, toting food and clean laundry and leaving behind in the trunk the rugs and other household items to be carried over later. As we neared the homefield, Pétur saw us. He straightened and waved a tar-blackened paintbrush. He was wearing a brimmed hat of mine; also a dust mask, as protection against asbestos fibers that might be stirred up by working on the roof.

I climbed up the ladder, another piece of ship's stock that I'd found washed ashore. Pétur grinned, lit a cigarette, and told me what he'd done since arriving. He had installed a sink—it drained to the outside, through a hole in the concrete floor—so that we could get rid of dirty dishwater without having to step outside and fling it. He had cemented new firebrick into the stove. And he'd started on the roof repairs: new corner boards covered with tarpaper and further sealed against the elements with roofing cement.

Impatient as the time had approached for the ferry's evening departure, Pétur had borrowed Anna's car, since his own had broken down again. With the furnishings and materials he was hauling—including a mirror he had framed with rough wood and a sink he'd taken out of his own apartment (he intended to remodel his kitchen at some future date, although he hadn't purchased a replacement sink yet)

—he figured our car would be too small for all of us plus the load. "Didn't Anna phone you?" he asked.

I shook my head. I explained how we'd gone to his place in the morning, then hung around town. I was a fool and an ingrate. I wondered if I would ever regain my old balance, which, as I recalled it, included an ability to shrug off disappointments and to trust other people.

"Do you have any food?" Pétur asked. "I ate what I could find, it wasn't much."

We had promised to bring the groceries. "Now you'll be well fed," I told him.

We both laughed, and the air was fully cleared. I propped my elbows on the concrete chimney. The view from the roof was superb. I listened as Pétur described the fox he had seen in the lava, the eagle that had soared above the house. And I cocked an ear to the immense stillness, broken only by the whispering of the wind.

Grasses waved gently in the homefield. The mountains east of Hnappadalur Valley looked like great sleeping beasts. The prow of Kolbeinsstaðafjall glowed as if lit by an internal fire. Checking on Eldborg and Snæfellsjökull, I found them in their true and proper positions.

I spotted the tall cairn along Þrællyndisgata, near where we'd roused the nesting eagles. To the west Faxaflói lay as calm as I'd yet seen it, laving against a low barrier island and a rock skerry like a serrated black tooth, where the salmon river debouched into the bay. The tide was sheeting in over the flats; I was reminded that among the tasks I needed to accomplish was finding the stream channels and fixing them in my mind, so that when I went hiking and the tide turned, I could get back safely.

Pétur ground out his cigarette, put his dust mask back on, and lifted a brace and bit. I positioned a mask over my mouth and nose, picked up a hammer. From inside the house came the sounds of pots and pans. Will came out and called up to us, telling us that supper would be ready soon.

A raven glided across the marsh, a moving wedge of black. A tern passed in its airy, bouncing flight. Gulls on unknown missions rowed across the sky. A snipe dithered down the air—Icelanders know the bird as *hrossagaukur*, "horse cuckoo," because the sound it makes when diving resembles a steed whickering.

It was good to be back. Already Little Lava felt like home.

We did another round of cleaning: dusting, sweeping, scouring. Old bottles, cans, and other junk that couldn't be burned were bundled into trash bags, to be carried across the marsh and deposited in a bin at a turnout along the road.

We decorated our new windowsills with treasures found close about: raven feathers, tan and white shorebirds' plumes, glossy bits of lava, egg-sized chunks of pumice. Purple mussel shells. A seal's jawbone with a curving canine tooth. Old green-glass fishnet floats, like the ones Nancy had seen for sale in an antique shop in Reykjavík. We hung a horseshoe on the wall, placed a weathered oar on nails above a window. In the kitchen someone else had hung up a tope hook, a massive barbed hook weighted with lead, used to catch shark; also bits of brass horse harness and carved wooden pieces from a loom. A photograph of Anna's mother Oddný—young and pretty, in a white nurse's uniform and peaked cap—looked down from a shelf. Oddný had been born at Little Lava.

Nancy mouseproofed a small cabinet and filled it with food. The grocery in Borgarnes—part of a rural cooperative that sold everything from fenceposts to fishing lures to magazines about American movie stars—offered a decent selection of groceries. Prices were three and four times what we were used to back home, but we had learned that in Iceland one should refrain from reading price tags and go ahead and fill the cart.

We bought oranges imported from Spain, kiwis from New Zealand, apples from the state of Washington. Small, starchy, flavorful Icelandic potatoes. Fresh bread. Russian jam. Butter, cheese, milk, and *skyr*, a traditional Icelandic dairy product similar to yogurt. Smoked lamb and lamb pâté. A carton of ten eggs cost 245 krónur, or thirty cents each. Kellogg's Corn Flakes, McVitie's Digestive Biscuits, Gunnar's Mayonnaise. We laid in a supply of *harðfiskur*, or dried fish; smeared with *smjör* (butter), it made a palatable snack.

In the sheep-fouled spring near the house, I mucked out a flat spot for the metal canister. The water seemed cold enough to keep perishables for at least several days. I put eggs and cheese and milk inside the container and placed a rock on the lid.

In the parlor we set up a kerosene heater, which I'd hauled back to Reykjavík in May to be cleaned and adjusted.

Pétur took the kerosene jug outside, filled his mouth with fuel, and spewed it out in a stream past a burning brand. Orange flames billowed from his lips. Will considered this a most amazing feat. Pétur had learned it at a carnival in Jamaica, where he and Anna had spent a winter several years back. Will played soccer with Pétur, using a flaccid ball found in the shop, with old oars stuck in the ground for goal posts.

Determined to sleep outside, Pétur carried his sleeping bag down to the edge of the small bight where the tractor had bogged down. He straggled in the next morning looking bleary-eyed and witch-ridden, importuning us for coffee.

During the night that had never darkened, the birds had kept him awake. Redshanks scolded him. Oystercatchers harangued him. The snipe flew about, making their eerie bubbling sound. Sheep came and inspected him, then ran off, their hooves pounding. Foxes barked. In the middle of the night he awoke to an unholy din. He saw a fox trotting past with a redshank in its mouth. The dead bird's mate was flying along above the fox's head, crying incessantly. The fox passed downwind, a few yards from Pétur's sleeping bag. It hit his scent stream, dropped the redshank, and went sprinting off across the sand.

Before he went back to the city, Pétur insisted that I assemble the kayak and let him try it. He could barely fold his long legs inside the hull. I showed him how to use the double-ended paddles. I gave the boat a push, and off he went, paddling toward the Stóra Hraun Islands, and in the time that I watched, maybe ten minutes, I saw him progress from uncertainty to a fair mastery of the craft.

Pétur was an experienced blue-water sailor, and I wasn't worried when he didn't come back for a long time. He returned after the tide had ebbed, striding along in one of the stream channels and tugging the kayak by its bow line like a man walking a reluctant dog. I splashed out to meet him. He grinned and handed me the rope. "It's perfect for Löng-ufjörur!"

We fed him a big supper, and that evening we saw him off across the marsh. He would come back, he said, and bring Anna with him, and maybe Oddný as well. He looked forward to returning to Little Lava for many years to come; the house, he insisted, was an ideal artist's retreat.

The house suited us as well; it was ideal for writers.

Alone now, we began to settle in. We were ready to stay for weeks, with only an occasional trip out to buy food, to make the acquaintance of other folk living nearby, and to visit the local school, Laugagerðisskóli, to take showers and swim in the geothermally heated swimming pool there—the *laug* in its name signified a hot spring. We could see the school across the marsh and beyond the salmon river. It was three stories tall, a concrete box with a lower wing to one side. In summer, with the children home on the farms, the school was used as a tourist hotel. It was three miles away as the raven flew, but by the gravel road, which followed the river and angled back to the highway, about twelve miles' travel.

I looked forward to spending time with Will. We had tried

to get our niece Claire, Nancy's sister's daughter, to come along with us and watch Will while Nancy and I did our respective things—Nancy wanted to write and ride horseback, while I planned to hike, fish, and watch birds. But Claire had decided to go to France with her high-school French club.

I figured that Will would be content to bury his nose in a book and do a lot of playing with Lego blocks. And when we managed to get him outside, he'd enjoy himself.

In the morning we put on our backpacks and scavenged for wood along the tide line. We found short lengths of two-by-fours. Slats from crates, with numbers and words like GLASGOW and PORTUGAL stenciled on them. Will discovered what had apparently been a Christmas tree, a crisp skeletal thing that must have been tossed overboard from a cruise ship the year before. We picked up surf-scoured branches. Cast high on the shore were huge trunks of trees, gray and barkless, neatly sawn across at their butts. Icelanders believe the trees that make landfall on their shores float in from Norway and Siberia. In the past, landowners would turn any such wood into lumber, a precious commodity in a place where trees are stunted and few.

Back at the house we bucked the wood into stove lengths. We split the larger chunks with an ax and ranked the wood in the workshop and the pantry. That evening we built a fire in the stove.

For chairs we had the old whalebone stool and a couple

of sturdy crates. We had bought three cheap plastic chairs in Reykjavík, one of which promptly broke when sat on for the first time. There were two tables: one in the kitchen, overlooking the marsh, and another larger one in the parlor, next to the window facing the lava field. We stored Will's books, games, and toys in the two old sea chests, rectangular wooden boxes with compartmented lids. In times past, fishermen kept their food and belongings in such chests and used them as rowing benches in open boats.

In the night, a storm blew in off Faxaflói. The wind moaned down the chimney. It drove rain against the walls. I woke up in the grainy midnight light.

I was all tensed up, from some dream I could not now remember. I lay back into the mattress and tried to relax by taking slow, deep breaths. I listened, and could not hear water dripping in the house. I turned toward Nancy and fitted my body against hers, my chest against her back, my face in her hair. I smelled her familiar scent.

The house was snug and secure around us. It was harsh and primitive, but it was blessed shelter. I remembered how I had felt on that night in December, in this same room with Pétur, when the wind shrieked and tore past the house and I lay cold and alone in bed. Six months had passed. Perhaps, I thought, I was moving again. Moving forward, proceeding from one drab room into the next. Walking through the chambers of my grief and pain, walking back toward the light of life.

7 | *Long Beaches*

Rain and clouds shrank the world. Grass was greening, stems shooting up—though now they were bowed down under plump beads of water.

I got the shovel, which I'd fetched back from Stóra Hraun. With its shaft across my shoulder I walked downhill from the house. I crossed the marsh, paused at the edge of the tide flats, and, holding the shovel across my body for balance, jumped down into the "sucky mud," as Will and Nancy had dubbed the slick, slippery band around the perimeter of the flats.

I pulled free from the mud and headed toward Stakkholtssteinn. The rain was a mizzling drift that dampened my face.

I'd had another dream the night before. It was a dream I had had more than once. I was walking to my mother's house, trudging along on the sidewalk through her neighborhood. Now the houses there belonged to old people; they were shuttered and silent, where before they had rung with the voices of children. I walked up the driveway and let myself into Mom's kitchen. She greeted me. We clasped each other without saying anything. All was somber, all was sad. She knew she was dead, and I knew she was dead. We were together, mother and son, with a weary sadness between us, both of us understanding that she could not stay for very long. In my dream, I had cried. But when I woke the pillow was dry.

I crossed toward Stakkholtssteinn. The sand, wet and firm, was stippled with what appeared to be burrows: small holes so densely clustered that only a few inches separated one from the next, a field of habitations stretching away for hundreds of yards.

Each burrow had two openings. One of the openings was marked by coils of cast-out sand, while the other, six or seven inches away, formed a small funnel-shaped depression from which water would bubble when I placed my boot near it and set my weight down.

I plunged in the shovel. It made a rasping, shearing sound. I turned a bladeful of sand.

A worm was revealed: as thick as my index finger and about six inches long. It wriggled sluggishly. Its red segmented body was tufted with two lines of short hairs.

As the tide rises, the lugworm thrusts its head out of the

sand to feed; when the tide recedes, the creature withdraws into the safety of its burrow. The worm gulps in water and sand grains, passing them through the tube of its body and digesting bacteria and organic matter. It expels the cleansed sand back onto the floor of the lagoon.

Continuing to dig, I uncovered a thin-shelled clam. Clams and lugworms, I knew, could be used as fish bait. But today I was in a mood to explore, not go fishing.

On a stony point nearby, purple-blue mussels coated the lower ledges; when the tide was in, the ledges were underwater. I turned over a rock. In the puddle beneath it, small translucent organisms wriggled along on their sides until they sank back into the slurry of sand. In America such creatures are called scuds.

I had read a paper, in English, in an Icelandic science journal I'd found at Thórður's house. When biologists surveyed the invertebrate fauna of two tidal mudflats in southwestern Iceland, they had found all the creatures I had already noted that morning, plus vast numbers of midge larvae. Midges are flying insects, most species of which do not bite people but are great nuisances nonetheless, flying into your ears, eyes, nose, and mouth.

According to the scientists, smaller birds such as dunlins and sandpipers eat the midge larvae, snails, and young mussels, which, before mooring themselves to rocks and becoming encased in thick shells, crawl about on vegetation of the intertidal zone. Larger shorebirds like oystercatchers and black-tailed godwits concentrate on lugworms, which they grub out of the sand using their long, sturdy bills.

I stashed the shovel back on shore, tramping its blade into the ground so that the handle stuck up in the air. I walked out on the flats, breathing in the odors: salt and sand, vegetation and decay.

It was an open, airy place, clean despite an assortment of plastic crud from the fishing industry—as well as the more welcome driftwood—that lay tossed up on shore by winter's gales. I never found any evidence of pollution, as from crude oil or chemicals, on Löngufjörur. Birds fed on the flats almost continuously: the suite of different-sized shorebirds, numerous species of gulls, and an occasional skua and raven. The tide flats reminded me of some vast sprawling organism, immobile and disposed to breathe at a rate much slower than that of the creatures taking sustenance from its skin. Each day the flats took two breaths: incoming tide, outgoing tide; water surging in, water ebbing out.

While we were in Reykjavík, Thórður had translated a story he'd found about Löngufjörur, or Long Beaches, in a book, *Landið Thitt Ísland—Your Country, Iceland.*

A man known as Tobbi—short for Tobías—farmed during the 1600s along Löngufjörur, possibly at Skógarnes, whose house and barn we could see as tiny rectangles far off across the lagoon. Tobbi was known as a poet. One day a group of travelers asked him where they could safely cross over the sands. At work in his smithy, making a tool or repairing some article of iron, Tobbi answered them with a verse:

My work is going very slowly in the smithy,
Even though I'm clattering.
You should aim for Eldborg,
Under the hammer of Thor.

The travelers set off toward Eldborg. Perhaps they dawdled, crossing the sands. The tide rose and caught them, and they drowned. After that, Tobbi lost his ability to compose poetry and could bring forth only gibberish. He became known as Æra-Tobbi, "Crazy Toby."

The tide flats belonged to both land and sea, and I treated them with respect. It was clear that one could be marooned by the rapid pincer movement of two flooding channels. Living on the fringe of Löngufjörur, needing to walk across the mudflats when we returned to the outside world, kept us well aware of the tides. We planned our days around them.

In Iceland, as most everywhere else, two tides occur each day, spaced twelve hours and twenty-five minutes apart. Gravity exerted by the moon, and to a lesser extent by the sun, causes the tide to rise and fall. When the moon is full, its orbit places it on the far side of the earth, away from the sun; when the moon is new, it lies between the earth and the sun. During both the full moon and the new moon, when all three celestial bodies are in alignment, the tides are at their highest. Such tides are called spring tides; the Icelandic *stórstreymi*. When sun, Earth, and moon form a right angle to one another, the gravitational pull of the sun partially cancels that of the moon, and the tides are at their lowest: neap tide, or *smástreymi*.

The tides change continually, the time of high and low tide advancing almost an hour each day, with two spring tides and two neap tides arriving every month.

During stórstreymi, a headland below the house became an island. Grass got covered over with water in many places. On the day of the spring tide, and for several days before and after, Little Lava would become almost completely cut off during high tide; the only way to it was through the lava via a long and tedious detour. It made us feel secure, knowing we would not have visitors—although on the other hand, we looked forward to friends coming to see us, even though none had come calling since Pétur left.

The spring tide flooded the lagoon and swelled out of it. Stream channels in the bog went from five feet to five yards wide. Flowers formerly on the streambanks could be seen waving faintly in the current several feet under. Stakkholtssteinn disappeared completely. The water came to the very edge of the homefield.

One evening during stórstreymi, Nancy called for Will and me to come and bring our binoculars. A ewe and her two lambs were trapped on a patch of pasture that had become an island. We watched from the heights of the homefield as the sheep stood huddled on their islet—perhaps they could have swum to dry land had they wanted to. Fifteen minutes passed, and the tide reduced the animals' refuge to an area the size of a coffee table. Then they appeared to be standing on the surface of the water. We discussed a possible rescue, but decided to bide our time. The water rose no higher. The sheep were stranded for about four hours until the tide finally fell and freed them.

. . . .

I walked across the sand.

The misting rain had ceased. The air was growing chilly. The bases of the mountains were a cold smoky blue, their tops still locked in cloud. To my left, Litla Hraun Peninsula extended southwest from the house; it was where we generally went to collect driftwood. On the peninsula, the wind-eroded soil was strewn with volcanic rocks: small white crystals, gray slag, and tan, thumb-sized chunks of pumice, blown out of Eldborg or some other vent in Hnappadalur Valley. A few sedge-rimmed ponds dotted the land, and sheep trails crisscrossed it. There were also rectangular ponds, which I was certain had resulted from the digging of peat.

The peninsula ended in a headland of squarish, heaped-up rocks. From there one looked out on two promontories, Skeley ("Shell Island") and Selhöfði ("Seal Head"), rising from the sand. They became islands at high tide.

Beyond Skeley and Selhöfði stood the channel-marking rocks known as Barnasker, or "Children's Skerry," because, so said our neighbors at Stóra Hraun, the bodies of two drowned bairns had once washed ashore there.

From the end of the Litla Hraun Peninsula, the mainland curved back to a marshy area called Krókar, meaning "Crooks" or "Bends." A stream winding out of Krókar joined one of the larger channels draining the lagoon.

Past Krókar the land extended south again, first as a stretch of rough lava and then as a low marshy peninsula, Fitjar ("Water Meadows"), which had once been a holding of Little Lava and which Anna's mother had sold to Snorrastaðir, the farm across the lava. Fitjar was said to be prime pasture for horses and sheep, and hay could be scythed there.

According to my map, on Fitjar there was a rock called Stelpusteinn, "Girl's Stone." Many large rocks littered the shore there, and I could not tell which one might be Stelpusteinn. The folk at Stóra Hraun told us it commemorated a former resident of Little Lava, a young girl who, while out herding sheep, had drowned when the tide caught her. And when had this drowning taken place? When had the children washed up on Barnasker? In times past, they said, their shrugs implying the passage of centuries.

Beyond Fitjar lay a quarter-mile of mudflats that flooded completely only during spring tide. Beyond the mudflats the barrier beach of Gamlaeyri shielded Löngufjörur from the Atlantic surf. Gamlaeyri meant something like "Old Sand-spit"; its name seemed to imply that the island had at one time been connected to the mainland.

I set my sights on Barnasker and laid tracks across the sand. Two terns spotted me and came winging, to flutter above my head and scold. No other sound in nature seems quite so freighted with outrage as the screaming of a tern. When it believes you are trespassing on its territory or menacing its nest or young, this small white bird becomes fearsome out of all proportion to its size. The call is a rasping shriek. It has in it the warning sizzle of live electricity. The cry can be represented as *kreeee*. The bird's name in Icelandic is *kría*.

I assumed that no tern would place its nest on a tide flat

that went six feet underwater twice daily, and that these two birds simply did not like my face. They hung in the air ten feet above me, taking turns diving at my head. I put up my hood. Their slender wings smacked against the fabric. This was not an onslaught of the most ardent sort, to which I had been subjected in other parts of Iceland. A truly enraged Arctic tern tries to open your scalp with its beak. It defecates on you. Get too near a nesting colony and waves of terns take to the air. You feel a degree of panic, seeing and hearing the white legions rising to attack. People who must walk past tern colonies usually hold sticks above their heads, decoying the birds into elevating the focus of their attacks.

The terns stayed with me as I walked, rending the air with their wrathful cries, expressing in no uncertain terms what they thought of the two-legged intruder. I looked for a shell or a stone to shy at them; I could find none. I contented myself with studying the birds, as handsome as they were ill-tempered. The plumage of a tern is mostly white, with blue-gray tints to the upper surfaces. It has a black cap, black-tipped wing primaries, and a vermilion bill. In the air the bird tucks its red feet up into its breast feathers, stream-lining its body and yielding a clean, trim appearance, all curves and attenuations. The twin points of the tail form a deep V. The long narrow wings, crooked halfway out, are as translucent as snow.

After the terns lost interest in me and flew off, I came to a place where two freshwater channels merged. The stream on my right came in from the northeast, its upper reaches trickling out of the marsh between Stóra Hraun and Little Lava. The channel on my left came in from the southwest

past the island Selhöfði, Seal Head. The map gave this second channel three sources: the marshes of Fitjar, the area
known as Krókar, and the flats along the western edge of
the peninsula trending south from Little Lava. The two
channels looked to be knee-deep. Where they joined, the
flow was waist-deep. One would not want to blunder into
such a ditch on the rising tide.

Downstream from this confluence the new stream soon
poured itself into the salmon river, the Haffjarðará ("Sea-
Fjord River"), a broad, powerful flow that came muscling in
from the far side of the Stóra Hraun Peninsula. There the
water was far too deep and swift for me to even think of
entering.

I took off my boots and socks, rolled my pants above my
knees, and waded the channel off Seal Head, holding a boot
in each hand. The water was cold and clear, the current
pushy but not threatening, and the sand bottom gave a good
footing. On the far side I sat on my parka. I scuffed my feet
dry with my socks and put my boots back on.

The Seal Head channel was the dividing line. If I crossed
it and tarried too long, and the tide came sneaking in, re-
versing the channel and deepening it, I would be cut off
from the direct route back. However, I saw that I could
regain dry land south of Little Lava, even on a rising tide,
by circling around Seal Head and cutting across one of the
feeder streams. If the tide was too advanced even for that,
I could climb onto Seal Head and wait the three or four
hours until the water ebbed enough that I could again cross.
Or I could retreat to Gamlaeyri and strike off southeastward
for a mile or so, until I came to the mucky flats—the ones

that didn't go under, except at stórstreymi—and then make my way to Fitjar. Although it looked marshy and tedious to walk on, Fitjar connected directly to the lava field.

During the three hours on either side of dead low tide, crossing would be simple. Since it was midsummer, darkness would not complicate an effort to reach the mainland. If I kept my head and didn't take chances, I had no reason to fear getting caught by the tide.

The floor of the lagoon grew less muddy and increasingly sandy the farther I walked. The mountains had emerged from the gloom, dark and cold-looking, as if they'd been dredged up out of the sea.

Wet, the sand was a dark honey color. Contrasting with the golden sand was an admixture of black sand. The two elements, shell and basalt, having different weights, had been sorted into patterns by the tide. Patterns like the grain in a piece of wood: stripes of repeating gold and black, next to areas where the two colors marbled together.

In places the sand was as flat as paper. Elsewhere it was covered with bumps. Ribs, one after another, went rippling along for yard upon yard. In the brindled sands were low places filled with larger shell fragments—ivory, peach, ma-hogany, blackish-purple, colors of sunset and storm.

Here the Haffjarðará River was half a mile across. It flowed around the two Stórahraunseyjar, the Stóra Hraun Islands. Each island was narrow, several hundred yards long, and oriented parallel to the river's flow. The islands were rimmed with rock and carpeted with luxuriant grass, showing that sheep had not been pastured on them for some time. Beyond them rose higher, sandier Suðurey, or "South Island."

A seal stuck its head out of the river and stared at me. Its eyes were black holes in its bright-sheened head. It submerged slowly, then periscoped up again, pale and dripping, farther along. As I walked, the creature kept pace alongside me.

Cries of terns, oystercatchers, and gulls filled the air. Sandpipers sped past on blurring wings. Six geese flew over in a line. Eiders powered past just above the river's surface, big, fast, solid-bodied ducks, in bands of six and ten and twenty.

According to the map, I had reached the northern tip of Gamlaeyri, a place called Toppar, or "Tops." The Tops in question seemed to be a clutch of sand-blasted rocks, like a gang of outlaws squatting on the dunes a few feet above the sea. Among the rocks were tar-smeared wooden spars and scraps of nylon rope.

At Toppar, the elements came together: sand, sea, river, rock. Freshwater flow met surf in a bickering disputation. Salt spray freshened the air. Waves struck and boomed, creamed against wrack-fringed rocks; foam blossomed and dissolved. Dozens of eiders bobbed in the confused water around Barnasker, their heads all seemingly turned in my direction. The water in the channel rose up, sloshing and swirling. It subsided, only to come foaming upward again, lurching sideways in a swiping motion that made my land-lubber's stomach tighten.

It was no place to venture in a kayak.

In the river, eiders were swimming away from me, worriedly looking back, first over one shoulder and then the other. On the skerry stood shags, their black leathery wings upraised for drying; they looked like demons guarding the mouth of some watery, frothing hell.

I turned south on Gamlaeyri. I had collected several maps of the Löngufjörur area, and the shape of Gamlaeyri was different on every one. It was a strip of sand that yielded to the winter storms, was replenished during the calm of summer, molded and remolded itself to accommodate time and tide.

I struck out down the strand. On my right, the ceaseless dash and murmur of breakers; on my left, the silent flats.

Nine months had passed since that unfathomable day. In all that time, I had not been myself. I would look in the mirror and be startled at the face that stared back at me. I wondered if I would ever again behold my own countenance without gazing into eyes that were pinched with grief.

I was finding it hard to be the observant writer, the interested naturalist. I did not care so much about the intricacies of the natural world as it surged and ebbed and called and flew around me; I no longer desired to learn about this particular organism and how it related to some other organism or to some system of organisms. I wanted simply to be in nature, to let it flow over me, like the tide that washed in upon Löngufjörur's sands. I remembered a line from the

Cape Cod journals of Henry Thoreau: "Where is all your knowledge gone to? It evaporates completely, for it has no depth."

At Little Lava I needed to be aware of my surroundings less in an intellectual than in a pragmatic way: Don't fall into a crack in the lava. Don't get caught by the tide. Keep off rough seas and out of grasping currents. Watch and smell and listen, and, occupied by the messages of the senses, let time work its healing.

What helped me most was to walk. To spend steps by the thousands, so that when I finally came to a stop, my legs still twitched and tingled, goaded by the nerves' commands.

I walked, and remembered. I let my rage burn. I would look at a rock in the lagoon and think not of the beauty of that chunk of the planet, or the small creatures that must cling to it, or the purity of its setting, but of chaining the man to it, the man who had killed my mother. Chaining him to the rock at low tide and letting the sea drown him.

Walking, I would waken as from a dream and realize I had been thinking of my mother, her life, the injustice of her murder, and my own inability to prevent her death, my inability to foresee the awful event that would take her away in terror and in pain. I was helpless to sidestep those thoughts as the miles of sand scrolled beneath my boots. Perhaps I did not want to dodge those thoughts. Perhaps my mind needed to collide with them to finally get past them.

I had seen swans on high, heard oystercatchers chirruping and redshanks squawking, felt the thud of the waves followed by a hushing sound as they sank into the sand. I no-

ticed those things subliminally, if at all, as I grappled with
my grief and with the immensity of the act of murder, set
against the insignificance, the transience, of one human life.

As I made my way down Gamlaeyri, gulls straggled past
overhead. A shag labored along just above the water, flying
so low that its black body and pumping wings were hidden
by the waves' pale crests.

I found a puffin washed ashore dead. All that remained
were the keel-shaped breastbone, a few sodden black feathers clinging to the wings, and the head. The bill was large
and triangular. In life, it would have been decorated with
vivid panels of blue, yellow, and red; now the colors were
faint and washed out.

Farther on lay another dead bird, a fulmar. Its bill looked
as if it had been fitted together out of carefully machined
segments. Two tubes stretched along the bill's top surface,
each ending in a small round opening. The fulmar belongs
to a group of seabirds known as the tube noses. A tube nose
does not require fresh water to drink. After the bird drinks
of the brine, its body screens out the salt and expels it, in
crystalline form, through the tubes of its nose.

Humans are less well adapted to life on the sea. In Iceland, in times past, each spring the men of a region would
gather on the coast to fish. They would sell their catch or
trade it for other necessities and lay in a supply of dried fish
for their families. Men from inland farms might journey
many days to the coast; some of them crossed Iceland com-

pletely, riding horseback or walking on trails through the wastes of the interior, traversing cold rivers, passing volcanoes and the mute, looming glaciers.

The men fished from open boats: four-oared, six-oared, eight-oared. They wore waterproof suits made of sheepskin treated with cod-liver oil. They fished for cod, halibut, haddock, whiting, ling, catfish, and plaice. The cod was most important. It was known by a hundred names, differing according to the region of the country and the condition of the fish, whether small or large or thin or fat or carrying roe. People ate the whole codfish, including the head. Every part of the cod's head had a name. Muscles, cartilage, and skin were eaten, the bones picked so clean that not a scrap of flesh remained.

The fishermen launched their boats from small harbors, rowing out into bays and the ocean. Other larger vessels were there as well, from England, Spain, Denmark, and France. The Icelandic fishery was renowned throughout Europe. From their open boats the Icelanders let down hand lines with dozens of hooks. They put lugworms, clams, and mussels on the hooks to entice the fish to bite. They used "red bait": birds' flesh, seals' intestines, trout and sheep innards.

Tramping along, kicking up sand that the wind blew away, I spied the wreck from a distance. Five minutes' walking brought me to it.

The wooden skeleton lay half-covered with sand. The hull was twenty paces in length. All that remained of it were the keel and some ribs, and an iron spike whittled thin by the salt wind. An Icelandic boat, too short to be a real ocean-going vessel. How many other wrecks, I wondered, lay beneath Gamlaeyri's sands? How many fishermen's bones and seafarers' skulls?

The last *bóndi*, or farmer, at Little Lava was Oddný's father, Sigurður Benjamín Jónsson. Every spring he would go fishing for three weeks, sailing in an eight-oared boat out of a small bay a few miles up the coast. Benjamín, as he was known, had been born at Little Lava. He was one of eleven children, of whom eight died before reaching adulthood. His father, Jón, had also farmed and fished at Little Lava, and had done everything Benjamín did, except that Jón stayed there all his life. One time he and a group of men rode out onto Gamlaeyri to gather driftwood, for fuel and for cutting into boards. Jón said that the ghosts of drowned sailors so disturbed them that the party could not remain on the island. They gathered their horses and struck their tents and hurried home across the sands.

8 | In Northern Waters

To learn how to kayak in Iceland, I had gone to Florida. I wanted to familiarize myself with the sea kayak I had bought, in water that was warmer than 50° Fahrenheit; in water where, if I capsized, I would not start shedding body heat immediately and lose sensation in my limbs and slide off into hypothermia and drown. More than one of my friends, and also Nancy, said I was crazy for taking a sea kayak to Iceland. Nigel Foster thought it a splendid idea.

I met him at a marina in Jupiter, Florida, on the Atlantic coast. A few miles east of us, the Gulf Stream swept silently northward, bound for Iceland, as I was. Foster was a rangy, agile Englishman in his mid-forties, with long hair, a shaggy beard, and startled-looking blue eyes. As we talked, it became clear that Foster's life revolved around sea kayaks. He designed and sold kayaks. He wrote books and articles about them. He was certified by the British Canoe Union as a sea kayaking instructor. He had kayaked in Newfoundland, the Faroe Islands, the Lofoten Islands of Norway, and along the Scottish coast. When Foster was twenty-four years old, he and a companion became the first people to paddle in kayaks all the way around Iceland.

I stayed right at the marina, in a motel room that, I was told, had been a brothel during the Second World War. At night I sweltered in my bed. In the day, on the water, Foster showed me how to handle my boat. He taught me different strokes, to propel the craft, turn it, and steady it in wind and swell. He made me do one self-rescue after another. After dumping the kayak upside down, I was expected to yank off my spray skirt (a waterproof apron that covered the gap between me and the boat) and tumble out of the kayak, forward instead of backward so my shins wouldn't hang up on the cockpit coaming. I would come bobbing to the surface, borne up by my life vest. Quickly I would right the kayak by reaching across the hull and flipping the boat toward me, all the while keeping hold of my paddle. Then I had to throw a leg onto the back deck of the craft, squirm along on my belly until my head was forward of the cockpit, boost myself up, and plunk my backside down in the seat. Afterward, I could tuck my legs back inside.

Thirty seconds. Easy enough in calm water, a bit tougher in the wake of passing cabin cruisers and speedboats, and quite difficult when I was worn out after hours of paddling.

Foster advised me to wear a waterproof dry suit in case I did take a ducking in the unforgiving North Atlantic; if I

couldn't get back in the boat right away, the suit would buy
me a few more minutes. He helped me work out an equip-
ment list, and a means of securing the necessary gear inside
my kayak and on its deck, including a spare paddle, a compass, a repair kit, and an exposure bag—a nylon sack I could
crawl into if I washed up on shore somewhere.

Foster told me about his own trip around Iceland. He and
a friend, Geoff Hunter, arrived on Iceland's east coast via
ferry boat from the Faroe Islands in June 1977. Their first
view of Iceland revealed snowy mountains, gray seas, and
lowering clouds. From the town where the ferry stopped,
Foster and Hunter commenced their journey in a clockwise
direction. The circumnavigation would take them nine and
a half weeks. They paddled fiberglass kayaks that Foster had
designed and built himself.

The two kayakers were awed by the immense white dome
of Vatnajökull glacier: at 3,240 square miles, it is larger than
all the glaciers in Europe and Scandinavia combined.

Foster and Hunter paddled past the Skeiðarársandur, mile
after mile of gray-black sand and stream-braided gravel
where no humans live. In a fog, they were nearly run
down by a fishing trawler. They stopped at Ingólfshöfði, or
Ingólfur's Head, where Iceland's first permanent settler, a
Norwegian named Ingólfur Arnarson, came ashore in the
summer of 874. At that time, the headland was backed by a
fjord and an expanse of rolling grassy fields; today the fields
are buried under sand and the fjord is full of gravel carried
down from the highlands by swift glacial rivers.

Nights, Foster and Hunter slept on shore in a tent. When
the weather was really bad, the men beached their kayaks

and cooked and slept in the shipwreck shelters that dot the southern coast, a treacherous shore where many larger vessels have run aground. The shelters are outfitted with tables, benches, beds, a paraffin lamp, survival rations, a first-aid kit, and a Bible. Before the huts were built, ships' crews were sometimes found huddled together on the sands, dead: they had survived the wrecking of their boats only to die of exposure on the windswept shore.

Windbound for six days, Foster and Hunter hiked inland to a farm, where they were taken in and fed; in turn, they helped their hosts get the hay harvest in. Under way again, they were hailed at sea by the crew of a fishing boat, who offered them coffee. The fishermen waited until the trawler sank into a deep trough next to the kayaks, then passed the steaming cups. Other fishing boats gave the travelers freshly caught cod.

"This was right after the cod war between England and Iceland," Foster said—when Iceland, worried about the depletion of its fishing stocks, had pushed out its fisheries limits from fifty to two hundred miles, and when Icelandic coast-guard gunboats went around cutting the trawl lines of trespassing vessels.

One morning Foster spied the square shape of what he took to be another rescue hut. "After we landed, we found that the 'hut' was a whale skull. Two curving jawbones about eighteen feet long extended forward from the skull. We sat on the jawbones and ate lunch."

After rounding the Reykjanes Peninsula, Foster and Hunter followed the curve of Faxaflói Bay, with Reykjavík passing to starboard. Where the coast bent around to the west again, the waves were breaking regularly and evenly on beaches of golden sand. The kayakers stopped to play; they would surf down a wave just ahead of the break, then pivot their kayaks, slice through the wave, and scoot out into deeper water. When Foster told me this story, I shuddered.

They paddled around the tip of Snæfellsnes, past the snowy cone of Snæfellsjökull. On an island in Breiðafjörður, or Broad Fjord, snow fell on them in midsummer. A dolphin surfaced slowly between the kayaks, had a look at them, and sank down again as quietly as it had risen. The travelers did not see any killer whales, which are present in the waters around Iceland.

On the days that they paddled, Foster and Hunter averaged thirty miles. "The soles fell off our boots," Foster said, "and we tied them back on with fishing line." They augmented their supply of dried food with eider ducks, surreptitiously caught and cooked. They ate puffin, fulmar, and herring gull. Recalling the fulmar, Foster told me, "The meat is oily, but the taste is quite pleasant."

On the north coast, in a raging sea, Foster kept company with a dainty little bird with a ruddy patch on its neck; the bird, about the size of a newly hatched chicken, was spinning around in circles on the water, feeding casually in the troughs between the monster swells. Foster wanted to meet the lighthouse keeper at Hornbjarg in the West Fjords, a man named Jóhann, said to have the largest private library in Iceland. The seas were bashing the shore in ten-foot waves, creaming over the rocks near the base of the light-house—"one of those days," said Foster, "when you're living off your nerves."

To find a landing place at first seemed impossible. "Then we saw a person waving from a clifftop. Hand signals guided us through the rocks to a cove. The signaler turned out to be a pretty young woman—the lighthouse keeper's niece. She told us that the day before, the keeper was lifted off the cliff in a harness beneath a helicopter and put on board an Icelandic coast-guard gunboat. While he was in Reykjavík on holiday, the lighthouse would be repainted."

In the lighthouse keeper's library, Foster opened a book on Icelandic birds. He found the little ball of fluff he had seen spinning so nonchalantly between the waves: a red-necked phalarope. In Icelandic, *Óðinshani,* "Odin's hen."

After instructing me for five days, Foster said I was ready for northern waters. Together we went over my maps. I told Foster I mainly wanted to use my kayak to explore within the tidal lagoon. He agreed that I should do most of my paddling behind the barrier island, within the relative calm of Löngufjörur. But he also said I should make at least one voyage on the open ocean, up or down the coast; that I should set aside my qualms and try to achieve a little more than I thought I was capable of achieving, because that was how one encountered the greatest and most transcendent experiences in life.

My kayak was a modern translation of the skin boats used for millennia by native peoples of Greenland and northern Canada. It was not a long, skinny, rigid-plastic craft of the sort that Nigel Foster uses and designs. Rather, it was a "collapsible kayak," a classification that made the boat sound less reliable than it was. Broken down, the kayak fit into a backpack. It could be checked as baggage on an airplane. One assembled it by piecing together sections of aluminum tubing, then stretching a fabric skin over the frame and inflating a pair of internal air bladders to give the structure buoyancy and rigidity. The skin consisted of a heavy nylon on the deck and, from the gunwales down, a waterproof synthetic rubber. The boat was supposed to flex in the swell, to give with the waves in the manner of an Eskimo craft.

The long, narrow kayaks that Foster favors are designed to go streaking along over the water. I tried one in Florida. I couldn't keep it upright. Theoretically, this sort of craft can be righted easily if it turns over, using a maneuver called an "Eskimo roll," in which the paddler gives a sudden jerk to his body while pushing himself back upright with his paddle. If all goes the way it is supposed to, the paddler is never faced with the task of getting out of his kayak and then getting back into it. My boat was more stable than Foster's racy designs. It wouldn't tip over as readily, but if it did, I hadn't a hope of doing an Eskimo roll. I trusted in my natural timidity and prayed I wouldn't capsize.

I had ordered the kayak in red, so that it could be spotted more easily in case of a mishap. I had bought a dry suit, in an egregious modern color, bright blue verging on purple. Over the dry suit was fitted the nylon spray skirt; the skirt cinched around my torso near my armpits and extended down to the cockpit's coaming, to which it was secured by a length of shock cord like a big rubber band.

Inside the hull, I sat on a small sling seat and wedged my

feet against braces attached to the aluminum frame. The boat was thirteen feet long and weighed thirty-five pounds. It drew six inches of water. When I sat in it, my head was two feet above the water level.

I took the kayak out for the first time on a calm evening. A fleece of clouds rested on the mountains of Snæfellsnes. In Hnappadalur Valley, the two red cones stood like glowing pyres in front of a dark cloudbank. Elsewhere the sky was a lambent color seemingly composed of equal parts of blue and gold light.

I carried the kayak to the bight a quarter-mile from the house, where the tractor had bogged down almost a month earlier. I set the boat in the shallows with its stern resting on the muddy bottom. I put on my life vest and got into the boat and secured the spray skirt. I shoved off from shore.

The double-bladed paddle dipped and circled. Water dripped from the blade tips, catching the gentle light. I paddled across the submerged mudflats. I felt very tentative at first, although after a while I began to remember the strokes and balancings and shiftings that Foster had taught me.

The retreating tide drew the kayak along. Beneath me, shells on the lagoon's sandy bottom looked like nebulae in the night sky. Beyond the green-topped Stóra Hraun Islands, Barnasker stood black and jagged above the surf. Beyond Barnasker and across the bay, Snæfellsjökull glimmered with the intensity of the full moon in an afternoon sky; above the glacier hung the pale sliver of the setting moon itself.

A pair of black-backed gulls went lazing past, calling to one another in muted tones. They looked mild, almost ethereal, in the gloaming. As a corrective against seeing them as beneficent birds, I recalled the time when I watched, from the deck of a ferry, as a blackback strafed a brood of newly hatched eider ducklings swimming in the ocean, hauled one out of the water, and gulped it down without missing a wingbeat.

A dunlin, a tiny, freckle-breasted sandpiper, streaked past the kayak a paddle's length away. It turned around in midair and came back. It dipped back and forth in front of the bow, one close arc after another. For a while I thought it would land on the deck, but finally it went winging off across the lagoon.

A tern fluttered along above my wake. It seemed not to recognize me as a human, attached as I was to the fish-shaped hull; it did not even scold. The bird watched the water gurgling behind the kayak. It sideslipped into a dive, hit the water with a splash. It came up with a twisting fish clamped in its bill. Beating its long wings, it lifted itself into the air and flew off.

I entered the stream channel, whose flow joined with the tide. I felt a slow, steady pull. At the end of the peninsula, the water had fallen sufficiently to expose the wrack-draped rocks. The rocks were black and shining. I paddled across the channel and rounded the peninsula. There the current of the Haffjarðará took hold of the boat. The river was submerged in the lagoon, but its power was easy to feel. Angling my bow slightly upstream, I paddled harder; in a few minutes, the water eased as I left the hidden current.

In the western part of the lagoon lay several small islands, too far away to reach on the falling tide. The islands, low, flat, and green, looked as if they were suspended above the silvery water. One of them, I wasn't sure which, was Bæjarey, "Farm Island." At one time there was a church on Bæjarey. According to our neighbors at Stóra Hraun, some people sailing home from church one Sunday drowned when their boat sank. Our neighbors were not sure when the tragedy had taken place. Nancy found a reference to the incident in a book. The drowning happened on the day after Christmas, 1562. Four centuries later and people were still talking about it.

Now there were no buildings on Bæjarey. The island belonged to the farm Hausthús, or "Autumn House," whose pale walls I could just glimpse across the lagoon. All that remained on Bæjarey was an eider colony, which meant I must steer clear of it, at least until the hens brought off their broods. Eiders are strictly protected under Icelandic law— which was why Foster and Hunter had to eat them on the sly. In Iceland, farmers encourage eiders to nest on their land, and later they harvest the down that the females pluck from their breasts to line their nests.

A dozen eider drakes snuck away from me through the gap between the Stóra Hraun Islands. They swam quickly and steadily, their blocky bodies low in the water.

I had noticed more eider ducks around Little Lava than any other kind of bird. Most of those I had seen were drakes; by now the females were nesting on tended islands like Bæjarey, or on the grassy spit of land that extended from Suðurey toward Barnasker, or elsewhere in nooks and crannies of the shoreline. Scientists recognize a concept called "biomass," which stands for the total weight of all organisms in a particular habitat or area. It seemed to me that more biomass was tied up in the bodies of eider ducks than in any other higher life form on Löngufjörur.

The drake eider looks like a dandy in his formal attire: the snowy back, breast, and neck vivid against the black sides and belly. As with the ptarmigan, the hen is in complete contrast: a mottled camouflage brown. In the spring, the male eider swims close to his mate, driving off any other ducks that might interfere with her feeding. After she has built up a layer of body fat, the hen picks out a nest site, a slight depression protected by rocks or overarching grasses, or a roofed hutch provided by a farmer. She lines her nest with down. She lays eggs, three or four of them. Her mate departs to join with other males and unmated birds on food-rich sections of the coast. The hen sets her clutch for a month. She doesn't bother with feeding, living off her fat. She crouches, frozen in place when ravens and gulls soar overhead.

I reached the calm zone where the water eddied near the Stóra Hraun Islands. The islands' sides were sheer and rocky, about twenty feet high. I did not see any eiders there; probably their steepness precluded the islands as nesting sites.

The grassy tops were dotted with yellow and white flowers. Succulent stalks of angelica pushed up above the other greenery. Rounding the outer of the two islands, I again encountered the salmon river. The kayak slid sideways. The boat lined up with the current and floated stern first, downstream.

I took a few testing strokes. I found that I could move slowly but steadily against the current. I felt sure I could return against the combined tide and river flow.

Tilting the kayak into a turn, I pointed the bow toward Barnasker. The lagoon was draining rapidly. All the water was heading for the channel, about three hundred yards wide at its narrowest point. As the current carried me along, I kept turning the boat about and checking to be sure I could still paddle against the flow. I did not want to be borne out of the lagoon, swept like a chip into the maelstrom where the river met the bay.

On the river's shining surface, eiders dipped and fed. An eider uses its wings and feet to swim down to where fish school and mussels cling to rocks. As I drifted closer, the ducks swam away from me, making low moaning calls.

I began to worry about getting too far down the channel. I turned around, ruddering with the paddle and letting the current push the stern about. I commenced paddling. With each stroke I bent forward and planted the paddle in the water, then swiveled at the waist, using the muscles in my back to draw the boat forward.

I was sweating inside the dry suit. The suit was waterproof, and I felt as if I were in a steam bath. I considered not wearing the suit the next time out, but the water dripping from the paddle onto my hands was cold enough to banish that notion.

I worked my way up the channel. The Stóra Hraun Islands

crept past on my left. I came to the northeast end of the island nearest the peninsula. On the island's prow a large creature was crouched.

The eagle raised its head. It looked at me with its dark, steely eye. I worked the paddle hard to hold myself in place. In the dim midnight light the bird was almost black. It lowered its bill and tore at something on the rock. It raised its head again, stretching its hackled neck. Immense wings flapped as the eagle lifted into the air, a fish clutched in its talons.

The eagle flew toward the dark distant barnacle that was Eldborg. Fighting the tide, I followed in its wake.

9 | *Fire Fortress*

Back in December, with Iceland in the grip of winter's frost, facing the long darkness to come, Pétur had talked of summer. "Strange things happen," he told me. "In the summer light you become hyperactive—you want to paint the house, go sailing, go hiking, fix the car, cut the hay, make love—it doesn't matter what time it is, you want to be doing all those things, you want to be doing everything."

Now the light of high summer dominated the land. The light filled the sky the whole day round. The solstice arrived, another day without a night—a day when stones in Iceland are said to come floating up to the surface of ponds, when seals hunch their way onto land, shed their flippers and skins, and take on human form and dance.

I tried to let the summer lift me up. Good weather and

bad, I hiked in the lava and on the sand flats; I paddled in the lagoon.

On a typical day Nancy and I might rise around seven, having stayed up late the evening before, and also perhaps having gone out to enjoy the most peaceful and inspiring time of all: when the sun came tracking out from behind the mountains in the northeast. Will was slow to get moving in the morning—in those quiet hours, Nancy often read while I tended to my notebooks. Once he was up and fed, Will usually annoyed us by lobbying to stay in the house and play cards, or be read to. If the weather was foul, Nancy would oblige him, and they would sit together on the bed in the kitchen, with a fire in the stove and the comforter on their laps. He particularly liked it when Nancy read aloud from the sagas; the gorier the battle scenes, the better. Will didn't have the stamina for our long walks, and often we didn't have the patience to potter along at his speed. Sometimes I would linger in the vicinity of the house and keep an eye on him while Nancy did a longer hike, and sometimes she would free me by overseeing our stay-at-home son.

When we could get him outside (either by coaxing or ordering him), he usually had a good time, as I had expected he would. He and I strolled down the peninsula looking for bright stones. We wandered through the homefield and the marsh, identifying plants using a botanical guide. We found buttercups, thrift, fleshy stitchwort, hairy stonecrop, common sorrel. Moss campion, the Icelanders' *lambagras*, or "lamb's grass," green pincushiony tussocks bristling with tiny pink flowers. Alpine mouse-ear. Alpine bistort. Alpine cinquefoil. Dandelions.

Every five or six days we drove to Borgarnes for groceries. Every couple of weeks, Margrét of Stóra Hraun did our wash. She always returned it all neatly folded, even down to the underwear and socks. Margrét's motives were altruistic and thus typical of rural Icelanders. Also, she understood that in one way or another she would be repaid. She did not hesitate to ask me to remember her, when I went home at summer's end, by sending her cassette tapes of the American country music she adored. Hank Williams was okay, and Hank Snow, music from many years past. And she would like some Charley Pride. She stood very close to me and said, in a confidential tone, "I just *lahhhve* that man." She placed one hand on my shoulder and laid her other hand above her heart. "His music touches me here." She put her face even closer to mine. I tried not to pull back. "He is the dark one," she said, referring to the fact that Charley Pride is a black man.

One day we crossed the flats, started the car, and drove past Stóra Hraun. We chose not to stop for the inevitable coffee, because we had a full slate of plans: we wanted to introduce ourselves at Snorrastaðir, the farm across the lava, and then climb Eldborg.

We took the gravel road toward the highway. On our left, the mudflats of Löngufjörur shone like a freshly swabbed deck. Redshanks crouched on fenceposts; they screamed at the car as it passed their hidden nests, then flapped into the air and chased after it, bombarding us with their shrill, ringing cries. A ptarmigan flushed from the edge of the road. White wings flashing, it made a beeline across a hayfield, headed for the lava. Swans poked up their long white necks from the grassy slopes that fell away to the fissure down which the salmon river came brawling.

A sheep stood in the road. In the summer sheep in Iceland usually look unkempt, and this ewe was no exception. Her fleece hung from her back like a tattered, ill-fitting coat. Her rear end was stained brown. She lumbered off the road, her skinny shanks flashing, only to clamber back onto the gravel after the car had passed.

"Stop," Nancy said.

I braked to a halt.

"A lamb back there—it's in trouble."

I turned the car around, careful not to get the wheels off the berm. I drove back the way we had come. Again the ewe yielded the road without dashing off in panic as the half-wild creatures usually do. The ewe came back to the roadbed, walked one way, turned abruptly, and highstepped in the opposite direction.

The lamb was in the ditch off the south berm. Its body was submerged. Its head tilted up, with only its nose, eyes, and crown poking above the water. The lamb was on the far side of the ditch. I had on my rubber boots, and I found a place where I could step across. All Icelandic sheep have horns, even the ewes and the lambs; this lamb, nice and husky, had three-inch stubs that made excellent handles. I hauled the lamb sloshing onto the bank. It was covered with green scum. Its legs were limp, and it made a grunting sound and ground its teeth together. The cold water had almost killed it.

We drove back to Stóra Hraun, where they were making *rabbabarasulta*, rhubarb jam. Kristján was off working in the fields, and Margrét had taken the car to Borgarnes. Teenaged Kristín was summoned and came sleepily out of the back room. Nancy explained the situation to her in a mix of Icelandic and English. Kristín and her aunt Veiga, one of the older twins, began talking excitedly. Veiga fetched a blanket. Back into the car. With our hefty passengers in the rear seat, William sandwiched between them, I had to drive slowly to avoid leaving our exhaust system on the road.

The lamb had not moved. The ewe looked at all the humans disembarking from the car and took off running. The lamb was still grunting and grinding its teeth. I was persuaded to jump the ditch again, clasp the lamb to my chest, and totter back across. Somehow I made the transit without falling in or filling my boots with water. The lamb was bundled into the blanket and placed on the floorboards of the car below the front passenger seat. Veiga sat there, rubbing the lamb with the blanket, as we drove back to the house. The drainage ditch lay on open rangeland, so it could have been anybody's lamb, but the beast turned out to be from the Stóra Hraun flock, determinable from the notches cut in its ears. It belonged to the absent Margrét, who owned its mother. (Apparently each person at Stóra Hraun had one or more personal sheep.)

Naturally, they wanted to thank us with coffee. If you kill a sheep with your automobile in Iceland, you are liable to pay the farmer for the animal; probably the transaction will be concluded over coffee, cake, cucumber, tomatoes.

We managed to beg off. We drove out to the main road and followed its eastering curve around Eldborg and the lava field. At the end of a mile-long lane, below the volcano, lay Snorrastaðir, where we were greeted, ushered inside with great ceremony, and asked to sit down and partake of coffee.

Snorrastaðir means Snorri's Stead. (Snorri is a not-uncommon Icelandic man's name.) The Kaldá, or Cold River, flowed through the farm. The river was swift and narrow, with trout in it. There were cow, sheep, and horse barns at Snorrastaðir, tractor sheds, and two houses: an older structure built in the traditional series of parallel peaked roofs and a newer house, one-story, made of poured concrete. The farmer at Snorrastaðir was Haukur; his wife was Ingibjörg. They looked to be in their sixties. They lived in the newer one-story house, and Haukur's daughter and son-in-law and their two children lived in the peaked-roof house. Ingibjörg was thin, friendly, and soft-spoken. She seated us at a table laden with bread, butter, cheeses, tomatoes, cucumbers, sweet rolls, two kinds of cake, a pitcher of fresh milk, and a flagon of coffee. Haukur sat down with us, along with a young boy and an old man who seemed to be hired hands. With smiles and nods from our hosts, we set to.

Haukur was short, wiry, bald-headed, with a trimmed gray beard showing remnants of blond. Blue eyes danced in a visage made pink by the wind and freckled by the sun. His voice was deep and authoritative. He drank his coffee through a sugar cube held between his teeth. He put down the cup, filled his pipe with tobacco, tamped it in with a grimy thumb, and lit it.

We knew a few things about Haukur. He was a prosperous farmer. An accomplished horse breeder and rider, he often led horseback groups across the sands, guiding the tourists who came with their mounts on the traditional route up the coast. He owned most of the land around Little Lava, which had been sold to him by Oddný and her family, who were related to him, although we were never able to figure out exactly how.

Haukur's English was limited, and Nancy was thrust into the breach again. He spoke slowly and clearly, and I picked up enough words so that sometimes I understood what was being said.

Over the years I have been reassured by many Icelanders that there is no point in my trying to learn their language. I did my best to memorize the complicated vowel sounds, so that at least I could pronounce words correctly. But to actually converse in Icelandic seemed impossible. In Icelandic, or Íslenska, nouns and pronouns possess a gender and may have different forms depending on how they are used in a sentence. The word "who," for example, has twenty-four forms. Verbs are dative or accusative. Although I could recognize a few Icelandic words, I could not string them into sentences.

A large percentage of every conversation in Icelandic consists of the word *já*, meaning "yes" and standardly pronounced *yow*, although there are ways of enunciating the word, stretching it out, biting it off, or gulping it during a sharp intake of breath, to indicate agreement (of varying degrees), approval, astonishment, dissent, doubt. Several times in the kitchen at Snorrastaðir I felt confident in adding my own já's to the chorus. With all the já's flying this way and that, it sounded like a pack of dogs barking.

Haukur could not have been more accommodating. Of course we could hike on his land—although we should watch out for cracks and caves in the lava. I could fish in the streams near Little Lava. "I would be pleased," he said in English. Then, in Icelandic, he added that he hoped I would catch a salmon in the Haffjarðará, where it widened before flowing into the bay. I could not legally fish farther up the river, where the rights were not his to give. But near the mouth, Haukur owned the rights to fish from his side of the stream—rights that he and Oddný had confirmed through a lawsuit. Of course, fishing the channel would be difficult; the current was strong, and I could get there only at low tide.

He had many questions for us. Where were we getting our water? Ah yes, the spring in the cave, Gvendarbrunnur —jájájájá, excellent water, and no matter how dry the summer, the spring never failed. Did we know that Bishop Guðmundur had blessed that very spring, so many centuries ago, during his flight through western Iceland? And how many foxes had we seen? Were we warm enough in the house? He knew that Nancy was a horsewoman. Did she want to go for a ride across the sands someday? Had we seen any eagles yet? He nodded when we told him of the nest along Þrællyndisgata. Then he announced with obvious pride that *three* pairs of eagles were nesting on his land.

There was the nest we had found, a second one on a small island in the tidal lagoon, and a third nest somewhere in the lava near Eldborg—Haukur had not found its exact location.

I mentioned, with Nancy interpreting, that the ornithologist Kristinn Skarphéðinsson had told me about the first two breeding pairs but had said nothing about a third pair. Three pairs, Haukur asserted, holding up three fingers. Three nests.

Haukur asked if we had read the stories about Hnappadalur and Eldborg in *Landnámabók*, the *Book of Settlements*—and indeed we had.

Landnámabók states that a man named Grímur arrived in Iceland from Norway (it doesn't say when, but presumably in the late 800s or early 900s, when immigration was in full swing) and established a temporary residence in the north. In the autumn he went fishing with his farmhands, taking along his young son, Thórir, who lay in the boat's bow inside a sealskin bag cinched at the neck. Grímur managed to hook a merman and, when he got the creature to the surface, asked him, "What can you tell us about our futures? Where in Iceland ought we to settle?" The merman replied, "There's no point in my making prophesies about you, but that boy in the sealskin bag, he'll settle and claim land where your mare Skálm lies down under her load." Later Grímur went out fishing again, leaving the boy behind; his boat capsized and he drowned.

In the spring Grímur's widow, Bergdís, took Thórir and

traveled west across the moors. The mare Skálm went ahead of them but never lay down. They settled in temporarily for the winter, and by the next summer they were on the move again, headed south. Skálm was still in the lead, and coming down from the moors, just as they reached "two red-colored sand dunes," Skálm lay down under her load. Bergdís claimed land in the vicinity, "from the mountains and down to the sea," as was the custom. The red-colored sand dunes are the ruddy volcanic cones at the mouth of Hnappadalur.

Thórir Grímsson was given the name Sel-Thórir, or Seal Thórir. He became a successful farmer and a respected chieftain. After he had grown old and blind, he went out of his house one evening and found a huge evil-looking man rowing an iron boat into Kaldárós, the estuary of the Kaldá River, which ran through Haukur's farm. The giant strode to a farm called Hrip ("Basket") and started digging near the sheep pen. According to *Landnámabók*: "During the night there was an eruption, and that's how the lava field at Borg started. The farm stood where the mountain is now."

The path led from Haukur's farmyard across a pasture and into a glade of head-high birch trees. The wintergreen smell of the leaves filled the air. The trees gave out where the slaggy upthrust of Eldborg's cone commenced. An English traveler, Frederick Metcalfe, wrote in his book *The Oxonian in Iceland*, published in 1861: "Behold that black tower shaped like the chimney of a blasting furnace; standing so black and sharp athwart the sky. That is Eldborg, or 'Castle of Fire.' "

"Look, Dad." Will pointed with his walking stick.

Four ravens sat on a cairn beside the trail. Their indifference to our approach suggested they were young birds newly fledged.

The ravens had glittering black eyes, heavy black beaks, shaggy black throats, and black wings folded against their black sides. Stoic and immobile, they sat as if the experience of squatting in a nest for the first month of their lives had equipped them with a patience that would allow them to perch on the cairn for the next month.

The Icelandic word for raven is *hrafn*, pronounced *hrop(n)*, the *n* being swallowed for the most part. It is said that ravens hold assemblies every spring and autumn. At the spring get-together, they agree on how they will behave over the summer. At the autumn assembly they pair up, each pair claiming a particular farm for the coming year. The Norse god Odin had a pair of ravens who flew throughout the world and then landed on his shoulders and told him what they'd seen. When the Viking explorer Flóki Vilgerðarson sailed from the Shetland Islands in the ninth century, looking for the big island rumored to lie to the north, he took three ravens with him. After sailing for several days, Flóki released the first raven. It flew back toward Scotland. He freed the second raven; it circled in the air and returned to the ship. The third raven flew straight ahead from the bow, and Flóki followed it. In that direction he discovered Iceland.

We walked toward the ravens sitting on the cairn at the

foot of Eldborg. The ebony birds swiveled their heads this way and that, without ever seeming to look directly at us. They stropped their bills on the cairn. Perhaps they hoped we would vanish if they refused to acknowledge our presence. We got to within a few feet of them before the ravens took off in a flurry of wings. They scattered, two of them heading off into the lava field to the north, and the other two gliding toward Snorrastaðir.

There is an Icelandic folk belief that if a raven flies in the same direction as a man is journeying, and flies low and on his right side, the trip will turn out well. If the raven flies in the opposite direction, or high in the air, then the traveler should turn around and go home and say his prayers. It seemed that here we could take our pick of the omens.

Will was in the lead. His boots sent down trickles of cinders. Where the trail grew steep, I put my hand on the seat of his pants and boosted him upward.

Eldborg turned out to be not as tall as it appeared from Little Lava. The cone was made up of porous sharp-edged rock in many colors: maroon, rust-brown, blue-gray, and a shiny vitrified black with a greenish sheen. The trail switch-backed through the brittle lava to the rim, a band of unconsolidated material about twelve feet across.

The crater fell away at our feet. At the bottom, seventy-five yards down, moss covered the gravel and patches of birch trees fingered up the south-facing slope. In the mid-1700s, two pioneering Icelandic naturalists, Eggert Ólafsson and Bjarni Pálsson, used a cord to measure Eldborg's diameter. They found its greatest width to be 636 Danish feet. A Scot, Ebenezer Henderson, traveled around Iceland in the early 1800s handing out Bibles. In a book that told of his adventures, Henderson related how he had climbed down into Eldborg "by means of a rude defile on the southeast side." I noticed that the path was still present in the crumbly wall almost two centuries later. "When at the bottom," Henderson wrote, "we had a most august view of the clouds."

We stood in the wind on Eldborg's rim.

Nancy raised her binoculars. "I can see Little Lava."

I got my binoculars out. I found the roofs of Stóra Hraun. Sheep dotted the grazing land around the farm. I looked westward and picked out our house on the lava's edge.

The sun was a white disk behind thin clouds. At the end of the peninsula, the snowy cap of Snæfellsjökull seemed to melt upward into the heavens. A hidden raven filled Eldborg's bowl with its croaking. Level with us, snipe danced through the air above the volcano's shoulders.

The geologist Haukur Jóhannesson had told me that Eldborg last erupted between 5,000 and 8,000 years ago. At that time, the sea level was lower than it is today, something that could be inferred from the way the Eldborg lava runs straight into the bay. Where hot lava encounters the sea, Haukur said, its leading edge cools, deflecting the flow to one side or the other. The Eldborg lava is submerged beneath Faxaflói.

Eldborg is a "spatter ring crater" and is presented as the type specimen of that sort of volcano in *Geology of Iceland* by Thorleifur Einarsson, a text which Haukur had recommended to me. A spatter ring crater arises when extremely thin, liquid lava erupts from a circular vent or a short fissure.

"Probably the vent was mostly closed when Eldborg was

erupting," Haukur told me. "Lava pulsated in the crater and came spilling out again and again. You can trace the separate layers all around the rim. Each layer is about one centimeter thick." The geologist discounted the widely held notion that Eldborg is extinct. "The region is still volcanically active. The next eruption could take place just about anywhere in Hnappadalur."

He asked if I'd read the story in *Landnámabók* about the giant causing the emergence of Eldborg. He told me that the eruption mentioned in the annals had indeed taken place during the era of settlement, but that the lava had issued from Gullborg, another vent in the valley. As the centuries passed, people came to associate the eruption with Eldborg, for the reason that Eldborg is so conspicuous. Said the geologist, "It looks more like what a volcano is supposed to look like."

10 | *Homefield*

With the sky so light, it was hard to call an end to the day, and often I stayed up late. There was always something to do, a walk down the peninsula, a hike into the heath, or simply a chance to sit on a driftwood log, listening to the birds singing, smelling the wind or rain, watching clouds grow and dwindle in the sky, facing across the bay toward Snæfellsjökull or its unseen presence.

Nancy and I got into the habit of waking at night and going out to watch the sunrise. We would tiptoe past Will in his sleeping bag in the parlor, let ourselves out the door, and stand in the strengthening light. Guðný, Thórður's mother, had written a sentence, a line from a poem, in my notebook: *Thú hefur ekki lifað, fyrr en thú hefur vakað um sumarnótt á Íslandi*: You have not lived until you have stayed awake a summer's night in Iceland.

We would watch the sun rise, then go back inside and burrow into the warmth of the bed and drift off to sleep.

One night Nancy shook me awake. "Bring your binoculars," she said.

I joined her on the stoop. The sky was pale pink, striped with long lavender clouds; the pink was its brightest over Hnappadalur Valley. A small round cloud, of a darker shade, hung above Eldborg, as if the crater had released a puff of smoke.

A dual sense of calm and expectancy filled the air. Between the house and the lava, three stocky long-maned horses stood with their heads down, dozing. Sheep lay in twos and threes, ruminating peacefully, lumps of white and black and brown among the grass-covered mounds that had once housed humans and their livestock.

Nancy pointed toward the rock overhang beneath which we dumped our garbage: potato peelings, spoiled milk, eggshells, moldy cheese. Also dead mice, caught in traps bought at the co-op in Borgarnes. (There seemed to be no end to the rodents, who fouled the tabletops, gnawed on the cupboard door, went skittering along above the ceiling, breaking the peace of night.)

I focused my binoculars on the shadowy spot below the overhang.

The fox was black. It rummaged head-down in the garbage. No wonder the mice were always gone when we went out to discard the latest catch.

When the fox came out into the open, mahogany tints

shone in its fur. It had small triangular ears, slender black legs, and pale eyes. It looked at us for a moment before crossing the homefield.

The fox ran down into the marshy pasturage, causing sheep to lift their heads. It darted into a ditch and popped up again on the far bank. Nose held high, it turned into the wind. Tirelessly the fox loped along on the downwind edge of the stream channel. First one and then a second pair of redshanks rose from the grass and circled above the hunting canine. The wind brought to our ears the birds' shrill complaints, but we were too far away to tell whether the fox had killed.

The sky brightened to a keen golden yellow. Clouds near the horizon were fiery red. The sun emerged from behind the mountain. The running fox turned blood red. In the marsh, the fluffy heads of flowers became a dazzling pink. On the mute mysterious mounds in the homefield, grass scissored. The mounds, casting thirty-foot shadows, seemed risen up to double their height.

I counted nine mounds at Little Lava that seemed the result of human activity. We tried to identify what sort of functions the structures might have served. We talked to Veiga at Stóra Hraun, who had lived in the area all her life. One day a farmer friend of ours, Hjörtur Hinriksson, showed up, accompanied by four of his seven children; he had finished the morning milking at his farm, Helgafell, on the north side of Snæfellsnes, and driven over the mountains. Nancy had been alerted to his impending visit by a handwritten note that the folk at Stóra Hraun had placed under the car's windshield wiper. I was off hiking at the time and didn't get to see Hjörtur and his family; Nancy and Will met them at Stóra Hraun and escorted them across at low tide.

Will, Nancy told me later, was almost delirious at being with other children. He and Hjörtur's twins, Óskar and Ósk, a boy and a girl a year older than he, ran all through the homefield. The twins couldn't speak English, and Will didn't know Icelandic, but their language was the common one of children at play.

Hjörtur has a son named Hinrik, who was not with him that day; and he has a father, Hinrik, and a grandfather Hjörtur. Hjörtur Hinriksson, Hinrik Hjartarson, Hjörtur Hinriksson—the patronymic chain linking one generation to the next.

The ruins interested Hjörtur greatly. Downslope from the house, toward the marsh but still within the homefield, was a sizable structure, its walls tumbled in and its roof long since collapsed. The sheep barn, Hjörtur said immediately. He pointed out the twin raised mangers, built out of lava rock, one running down the middle of each of the two parallel communal stalls. Hay would have been placed on the mangers for the sheep.

According to Oddný—whom we would finally meet in Reykjavík at summer's end—the unfinished summerhouse stood on the site of the old turf house where she and her sister Ástriður, or Ásta, were born, and where the two girls and their parents had lived until the concrete house was built.

The collapsed building between the abortive summer-house and the concrete house we lived in, broken by time and weather, bristling with rusty nails, with the rotting-oar rafter and the piece of tin that had banged in the wind until I broke it off: that was the cow barn.

The large foundation where I'd burned the junk from the workshop, between the concrete house and the lava field, was a hay barn.

On the edge of the lava Will had discovered a large natural corral, a cleft in the rock with a grassy floor, steep walls, and one small opening. During shearing, sheep would have been kept in this enclosure, called a *rétt*.

A small rock rectangle topping a hill on the way to the spring was perhaps a pen in which ewes were milked. A round hummock might have been a fold for holding the lambs while the farmer milked their mothers. A small unobtrusive lump near the house was possibly a smoke-house. A mound north of the house could have been the smithy.

One day we were visited by our Reykjavík hosts, Grétar and Guðný. They were on their way home from northern Iceland, where they have a small farm on which they have planted thousands of birch and larch trees. Grétar is a soils scientist for the Icelandic government, and it is his goal to someday have a forest on his land. As a gift, we had given him a beautiful edition, illustrated with woodcuts, of Jean Giono's story *The Man Who Planted Trees*.

We spotted the pair coming far across the marsh, got the binoculars out, and identified our callers. We met them at the edge of the homefield. We showed them all around Little Lava, and they loved it, extolling particularly the views of Eldborg and Snæfellsjökull. Guðný had brought fresh bread and a kite for Will. They would not stay for very long; I could tell they were nervous about getting back before the tide rose. We only just managed to hold them long enough for coffee—a pittance compared to their ever-ready hospitality.

Another time Thórður, their son, showed up with his girl-friend, Arna. They came on a cloudy evening, with the skies spitting rain. It happened that I was out in my kayak at the time. Nancy and Will took Thórður and Arna for a walk on Thrællyndisgata, and from a distance they glimpsed the eagles.

They returned to the homefield, or *tún*. Stone walls, made of lava rock, bounded the tún on the north and south, the eastern boundary being the lava field itself. To the west lay the marsh, where the homefield perimeter had at one time been closed off with a barbed-wire fence; now many of the posts were rotted away and the rusty wire sagged on the ground. The walls and the fence divided the tún from the rough sheep-grazing. In the old days, Thórður said, there would have been no fence; in summer a child from the farm would have been assigned the task of guarding the boundary all night long, keeping out livestock.

The homefield was the key to surviving the winter. Its turf was carefully manured; its hay was scythed and raked, collected and baled, and stored under roof. In bad years, when sea ice drifted in upon Iceland from the north, and hung around the island into the spring and even the summer, the hay harvest could fail. Then beasts and people starved. In a normal year, drift ice approaches no closer than 100 miles from northwestern Iceland. The ice has not been a problem during this century of mild winters and rising temperatures; but no one knows when it will come again.

It was Thórður who had found the earliest reference to Little Lava in a *máldagi*, or property registry, of the Catholic Church, dated 1354. The farm appeared in subsequent registries for the years 1367, 1397, and 1575.

The *Jarðabók*, or *Book of Farms*, of 1709 describes in its thirteen volumes all the farms in Iceland at that time. Grétar had a reprint edition in his library. Once when we were visiting, he looked up Litla Hraun and translated the following information for me:

In 1709 the tenant farmer at Little Lava was one Eríkur Jónsson. Profits from the farm went to support the priest at Kolbeinsstaðir. The livestock consisted of six cows, two heifers, a bull, and a calf whose sex was not listed; sixty ewes, twenty-five gelded rams two years old or older, and thirty-seven gelded yearling rams; and four horses and a pair of fillies. The fertilized homefield produced fodder for four cows, twenty lambs, and one horse. The rest of the animals had to be turned loose for grazing, even in winter. "There is an old saying," Grétar told me, "*Sett á Guð og gaddinn. It means 'to survive on God and the frost.'*"

According to the *Jarðabók*, in 1709 there was still some forest on the farm, allowing for charcoal-making, although the wooded area was diminishing. Peat was plentiful, land for cutting turf was scarce. The farm offered good seal hunting and excellent prospects for driftwood. It lacked a shell beach for mussels and clams. Rowing from the beach was difficult, because the water was often shallow over a long distance. Dangers to livestock included the swiftly rising tide, and pits and crevices in the lava. Finally, the summary noted that it was a long way to church, and travel was difficult owing to the extensive lava fields and bogs.

Thórður suggested that Little Lava might have been an offshoot of Stóra Hraun. He theorized that a slave, granted his freedom, had been settled on the more remote holding. Originally, slaves had been brought from Ireland and Scotland by Vikings and migrating Norse farmers. Slavery as an institution was never formally abolished in Iceland; it simply died out. By the year 1000, farmers were learning that it made better economic sense to free a thrall and rent some land to him, rather than house and feed him year-round. Thórður saw Stóra Hraun as the manor, Litla Hraun the croft. Perhaps the croft was a thousand years old.

On the evening when they visited, Thórður and Arna would not stay the night. It was late, almost midnight, when Nancy, Will, and I stood on the stoop, said goodbye to our friends, and turned to go back inside.

"No," Thórður said. "You must walk your guests partway home." He grinned at our puzzlement. "Come on." He beckoned for us to follow him. He had us escort him and Arna to the homefield's edge. "That way your visitors won't take the luck away from Litla Hraun," he said.

.   .   .

People had always gone to Iceland: priests and merchants and rovers and relatives of the folk who had settled there. Starting in the eighteenth century, Iceland became a destination for a different set of travelers: tourists. Accounts of Icelandic expeditions were written in English, French, German, Dutch, Italian, Czech, and Serbo-Croatian. Many of the adventurers came from England. Sir Richard Francis Burton, translator of *The Arabian Nights* and a British explorer and diplomat, visited Iceland in 1872 at the age of fifty-one. In trying to explain the lure of the country, Burton identified a condition he called "Iceland on the brain." Visitors to Iceland were impressed, Burton wrote, by "everything and everybody" in this "most difficult and expensive country in the world," where they could feast their eyes on "scenes of thrilling horror, of majestic grandeur, and of heavenly beauty."

The travelers' accounts present a picture of ordinary life in Iceland in the 1700s and 1800s. Many of them were written in a somewhat belittling tone, others were not.

> While examining some fissures, we found the remains of a woman who had been lost about a year before, and of whom there had hitherto been no tidings. Her clothes and bones were lying scattered about; the bones of one leg remained in the stocking. It is probable that she had missed the path during a thick shower of snow, and had fallen over the precipice, where her body was torn to pieces by eagles

and foxes (from *Travels in Iceland* by Sir George Steuart Mackenzie, a Scottish mineralogist who toured Iceland in 1810).

The byre we now visited was a good specimen of Icelandic domestic architecture. From three sides it presented the appearance of a confused cluster of turf mounds. Among these, two are conspicuous, one for having a chimney formed of a barrel with both ends knocked out, the other for being longer than all the rest, and for having two or three glass panes inserted at intervals in the turf. The former is that of the kitchen, the latter of the [*baðstofa*], or sleeping apartment. On the fourth side of the house is the front, consisting of a series of wooden gables between thick turf walls. (The Reverend Sabine Baring-Gould, a Devonshire parson, arrived in Iceland in 1862. Later he became a novelist, a writer of hymns, including the well-known "Onward, Christian Soldiers," and author of the treatise *Were-Wolves and Their Natural History*.)

Mackenzie again, and I would be surprised if at one time there was not a house, a *torfbær*, at Little Lava like the one he described:

The thick turf walls, the earthen floors kept continually damp and filthy, the personal uncleanliness of the inhabitants, all unite in causing a smell insupportable to a stranger . . . There is no mode of ven-

tilating any part of the house; and as twenty people
sometimes eat and sleep in the same apartment, very
pungent vapours are added in no small quantity to
the plentiful effluvia proceeding from fish, bags of oil,
skins, &c.

The mounds turned out to be nothing more than
the grass roofs of the house and offices, and the banks
and dykes but circumvallations around the plot of
most carefully cleaned meadow, called the [tún],
which always surrounds every Icelandic farm. The
word [tún] is evidently identical with our own Irish
town-land, the Cornish *town*, and the Scotch *toon*,
terms which, in their local signification, do not mean
a congregation of streets and buildings, but the yard,
and spaces of grass immediately adjoining a single
house." (In 1856 Lord Dufferin, whose full name was
Frederick Temple Hamilton-Temple Blackwood,
sailed to Iceland in his private schooner yacht, *Foam*.
Later he became Viceroy of India and supervised the
British Empire's annexation of Burma.)

At midnight . . . we stopped at a small cottage
called [*Skálabrekka*]. All, of course, was shut; but we
followed Captain Von Scheel, who scaled the walls,
and each of us endeavoured to find some window or
hole in the roof, through which we might rouse some
of the inhabitants . . . The salutation [the Captain]
made use of was [*Hér sé Guð*], "May God be in this
place!" which, after he had repeated it near a dozen

of times, was answered with [*Drottinn blessi thig*], "The Lord bless thee" (Ebenezer Henderson, the Bible distributor who climbed down into Eldborg, from his account published in 1814).

When J. Ross Browne, an American who traveled in Iceland in the 1860s, first laid eyes on a stretch of land covered with thúfur, he mistook them for "the remains of cultivated fields—probably potato hills."

"To get drowned, to break your neck or your limbs, to be maimed, to be boiled alive, or, at the least to be prostrated with rheumatism, are quite in the cards" (Frederick Metcalfe, *The Oxonian in Iceland*, 1861).

"The country is very solitary" (Elizabeth Jane Oswald).

"The scene before us was exceedingly dismal" (Mackenzie).

"The scene before us looked inexpressibly desolate" (Pliny Miles).

"The general aspect of the country is the most rugged and dreary imaginable" (Henderson).

Samuel Johnson never went to Iceland but was fond of saying that he could recite from memory a complete chapter of *The Natural History of Iceland*, written by a Dane named Niels Horrebow in 1752. According to Johnson, the text in its entirety was: "Chapter LXXII. Concerning snakes. There are no snakes to be met with throughout the whole island."

Jules Verne never visited Iceland, either. However, in writing his novel *Journey to the Center of the Earth* he did not shrink from introducing his adventurers into the bowels of the planet through a crack in the glacier on Snæfellsjökull.

"The men are generally ugly, the women less so." (Ida

Pfeiffer was a Viennese and the first female author-traveler to visit Iceland; she went there in 1845. She collected plants and insects, and wrote what a later traveler described as "a snarling, ill-tempered journal.")

"The women are really the only class of inhabitants, except the fleas, who possess any vitality. Rude, slatternly, and ignorant as they are, they still evince some sign of life and energy compared with the men" (Browne).

"Nature has made a mistake in forming Icelanders' faces; she should have inverted their noses, so as to facilitate their plugging them with tobacco" (Baring-Gould).

"Their predominant character is that of unsuspecting frankness, pious contentment, and a steady liveliness of temperament, combined with a strength of intellect and acuteness of mind seldom to be met with in other parts of the world" (Henderson).

"Not the least among the charms of Iceland is the slight impression that men have made upon it." (Frederick W.W. Howell. In 1901, at the age of forty-four, Howell, an Englishman, was crossing a river in northern Iceland on horseback when he was thrown from the saddle and drowned.)

In the workshop at Little Lava I found a box of old papers, including some farm records from the 1930s. There appeared to have been a total of three cows on the farm during that time. Oddný would confirm that fact when, in late August, before we left to go back to America, we sat in her clean, neatly appointed apartment in a suburb of Reykjavík.

Her daughter Anna, a handsome brown-eyed blonde, was present. Oddný was dark and thin, with a husky voice; forty years had put lines and wrinkles on the face of the young nurse who had smiled down on us all summer from the photograph in the parlor at Little Lava.

Oddný made us coffee and served a dessert like apple strudel. She reminisced in English while I jotted down notes; the following is my own rearrangement of her memories.

"At Litla Hraun, we were never hungry or cold," she said. "We always had plenty of warm clothes. My mother was a very good seamstress, and she made all our clothes. She made us shoes out of sealskin. Her name was Thóranna Guðmundsdóttir; she was born on a farm near Kolbeinsstaðir.

"My sister was born in 1930, and I in 1932.

"Our parents always had time for us. You forgot money at Litla Hraun. It was wonderful. I had a wonderful childhood there.

"We kept thirty to fifty sheep. We had four horses and three, sometimes only two, cows. From the cows we got milk. Mother made some of the milk into cream and butter. She packaged the butter and sold it in Borgarnes.

"Father netted seals and skinned them. We butchered the seals and ate the meat. The seal fat we melted and poured onto the hay that was given to the sheep; the fat had vitamins in it.

"Father wove horsehair into strings for tying the hay into bales. He sawed driftwood logs into boards at the seaside and used the wood to keep the house and the outbuildings in good repair. Some of the driftwood was bought by neighbors.

"You never threw anything away. If a dinner plate broke, it was fixed by sewing it. You drilled little holes in the edges and stitched the pieces back together again." (We had used one of those plates, repaired with thread, at Little Lava.)

"My mother lived to be ninety-two. She always rested every Saturday. She was a Seventh-Day Adventist, and she would not work on Saturday even if the hay was cut and drying and the sun was shining—she wouldn't pick up a rake, wouldn't touch it. That made Father very cross.

"We used kerosene lamps for light, although in the winter it was hard to get kerosene, so then we relied on seal oil with a *klófífa*—" She looked at her daughter.

"Cotton grass," Anna said.

"A wick made from cotton grass." Oddný sipped her coffee. She gazed out the window at the sky; the noise of traffic carried up from a highway several stories below. Oddný said, "My mother made a peat fire that would burn the whole night through; we used only one box of matches for the whole winter. We cut the peat in May and stacked it up so the wind could dry it and it could be burned the autumn after it was cut.

"My sister and I learned to read and write at home. Then we went to school at Snorrastaðir. We went there for a fortnight and stayed over. Haukur's father was the teacher. Ten children from the area went to school there. Two weeks of instruction, and then we would go home for two months. We went to school twice over the course of the winter. When we went home, we were expected to learn the new material the teacher had given us, and when we came back to school, we were tested on it."

She said, with some slight irritation, "I got lice at Snorrastaðir. We *never* had lice at our little home.

"At Christmas my mother and father would buy half a kilo of apples as a special treat.

"I remember my first pair of rubber boots. They were black, with yellow on the inside. I kept them by my bed so they would be the first thing I saw when I woke up in the morning.

"I remember the old whalebone stool very clearly; I remember it all my life. It was in the old house, and it was kept and moved into the new house because it was so special. Somebody found it on the seashore, I don't know when.

"In my grandmother's time two ships were wrecked on Gamlaeyri. They were French ships. The survivors came to Litla Hraun.

"One time I was picking berries on the edge of the lava between Stóra Hraun and Litla Hraun. It was in August. I looked up, and there was a lady in a long light-gray dress. As they wore in the old days. I only saw her in silhouette. She was about fifty meters away. I looked at her once, turned away, looked back at her again, and she was gone.

"Cars began showing up in the area around 1935; that was when they started building roads.

"I saw my first airplane during World War II.

"There was no radio or television then, just newspapers. My father loved to read the papers. Through them he saw the world, and it seemed to be passing him by. My mother said, 'Let them fight, out in the world. I will stay here and take care of my family and bake my bread.' Father was much more interested in the war and in current events. Mother wouldn't listen to him when he talked about such things, so he told them to his daughters and even to the cows when he was milking them.

"Father went to work in Reykjavík for the Americans, building the airbase in the city. There he could get a salary. With the money, he built the new house.

"The old turf house was warm and comfortable. The new concrete house was much colder. A neighbor helped Father build it. The wood came in as driftwood during the war. We borrowed a horse and wagon to get the sand and cement across at low tide. The new house was never finished; we only lived in it for two winters.

"Father did not want to stay at Litla Hraun. In 1946 we sold everything: cows, horses, and sheep. We moved to Reykjavík. I was fourteen years old at the time, and Ásta was sixteen. Mother always missed Litla Hraun and having that independence. People lived there because they were independent.

"When I go to Litla Hraun now, I see that the thúfur have greatly increased over the years. That is because no one is cutting the grass in the homefield anymore."

As writers, Nancy and I wondered whether anyone had ever written about Little Lava. I could not find any reference to the place in the journals of the English travelers who passed through western Iceland, although most of them commented on Eldborg and the volcanoes of Hnappadalur Valley.

A popular book in Iceland is *Ævisaga Árna Prófasts Thórarinssonar*, or *Biography of the Priest Árni Thórarinsson*, written by Thórbergur Thórðarson and published in 1969. Árni Thórarinsson was a priest in rural western Iceland in the late 1800s and early 1900s. He lived at Stóra Hraun and built the farmhouse that stands there today. In 1932, in the church at Kolbeinsstaðir where I attended Jón Thór Kristjánsson's confirmation, the Reverend Árni christened our neighbor Haukur of Snorrastaðir. According to Haukur, Árni was held in generally high esteem in the region during his lifetime, "but that changed a little when his biography came out."

The section detailing Árni's tenure on Snæfellsnes is entitled *"Hjá Vondu Fólki"*—"Among Bad People." Nancy translated several passages from it. She found that the Reverend Árni was highly critical of families in which infants died; he suspected them of killing their own children. He cautioned others never to believe a story told by a person from Snæfellsnes "before you have checked it out fully." He accused his neighbors of trying to infect his family with measles when a girl from Litla Hraun, who had the disease, chased after Árni's children. He had a feud going with a woman he identified only as "the mean widow of Litla Hraun," apparently Oddný's grandmother: he said she swiped horses from him; she said he filched driftwood from her.

Grétar, Thórður's father, may have been trying to put a

better spin on Árni's character when he translated "Hjá Vondu Fólki" as "How Wonderful with Bad People." He found for me a passage stating that whenever Árni needed to go to one of the three churches in his parish, he simply spoke the church's name to his horse, and without further instruction or guidance from its rider, the animal carried him to his destination.

One passage from the biography had Nancy and me laughing. It was entitled "Two Girls in the Dark."

According to the Reverend Árni, after New Year's Day in 1943 no one was at home at Little Lava except for two girls, around ten to twelve years old, their mother having gone to Reykjavík to meet her husband, who was working there. One evening, after the day's work was done, two farmhands from Stóra Hraun crossed the mudflats to see how the girls were faring. They found the pair sitting in the darkened house.

"Why is it that you're sitting in the dark?" the men asked. "Don't you have any lamp oil?"

"Yes, we have enough oil," one of the girls replied. "But we can see things more clearly in the dark." She pointed at the shadows behind one of the men. "For instance, that one, your fetch—he came here ahead of you." The girls turned to the other man. "And old Baldvin [a famous ghost of Hnappadalur], he came along with you, carrying his head dangling between his shoulders." The girls laughed lightly and said, "That and much more we wouldn't have seen if we had lighted the lamp." The men glanced about uneasily; they did not relish the long, dark walk back to Stóra Hraun.

At her apartment, we asked Oddný about the story from

"Hjá Vondu Fólki." It was true, she said. She and her sister, Ásta, had blown out the lamp when they heard the men coming. "We wanted to give them a scare."

One day at Little Lava, Nancy went outside to relieve herself. We were fairly informal about that sort of thing; Will and I would water down a handy thúfa, while Nancy generally selected a private spot in the homefield or went around to whichever was the leeward side of the house. As Nancy closed the door behind her, she happened to look up. On the edge of the lava, a dozen men and women were staring at her; they were seated on rocks, munching sandwiches.

We had gotten accustomed to our guests approaching across the lagoon or around the edge of the marsh, where we could see them a long time coming. This bunch had seemingly appeared out of nowhere. When we talked with them, we found that they had come across the lava from Snorrastaðir on Þrællyndisgata. The group were a hiking club from Reykjavík; they wanted to see the farm where Ásta Sigurðardóttir had been born.

Oddný's sister, Ásta, was herself a writer. She became known as Ásta Sig. Her short stories—many of which were illustrated with woodcuts that Ásta did herself—have been described as among the first examples of modernism in Icelandic literature. Most of them were existential in tone and were set in the city.

In an encyclopedia in Pétur's apartment I had found an

entry on Ásta Sig. (The book was an eclectic three-volume set, with passages describing "Astaire, Fred," "Barnes, Djuna," with a photograph of a beaming "Jassir Arafat" contrasting with pictures of Icelandic turf houses, beavers, famous waterfalls, the Statue of Liberty, Balzac.) The encyclopedia was in Icelandic, so unfortunately I couldn't read about Ásta. There was a photograph, a head-and-shoulders portrait showing a woman with thick dark hair, heavy arching eyebrows, strong cheekbones, and voluptuous lips. Ásta had a cigarette between her fingers, and she wore a necklace and maybe nothing else.

Anna told me that her aunt Ásta was the first "bohemian" in Iceland, the first woman to model in the nude for artists. Ásta had six children with two husbands. One of her husbands was a leading Icelandic poet. Ásta had a drinking problem; she may have been an alcoholic. She died in Reykjavík in 1971, of liver damage caused by tainted home-brewed whiskey that a lover had procured for her.

The hikers from Reykjavík were as surprised to see us living at Little Lava as we were to see them. Their leader had brought along an essay by Ásta Sig, *"Frá mýri, hrauni og fjörusandi"*—"Of Marsh, Lava, and Sandflats." He read some passages to the group. Before leaving Iceland, Nancy found the essay at a library and made a copy.

I wish I could have read it; Nancy told me it was a lovely, lyrical description of Little Lava. On the heath the *lóa*, the golden plover, called out *Dýrðin, dýrðin* ("Glory, glory"); when you slipped into a mire, the *jaðrakan*, or black-tailed godwit, advised *Vaddúti! Vaddúti!* ("Get out! Get out!") Ásta wrote about the marsh plants and their subtle colors, the fields of thúfur closing in. She told of hidden ponds in the lava that reflected the sky, mosses covering the rough rock, and the cave with the spring, the one that Guðmundur the Good had blessed. She said the water was so pure, it would have blessed Guðmundur himself had he drunk of it.

For Ásta, the shore had the greatest appeal. The first time she went to Gamlaeyri, it was on a horse, riding bareback behind her father. Later she walked there alone and wrote of resting between the ribs of a wrecked boat. She described the shining sea, and the seals with their human faces and knowing eyes, and the black-backed gulls and the eiders. On the seashore you learned to be alone, to work alone, think alone. If you did not become free while walking alone by the sea, wrote Ásta, then freedom had forever and always been drummed out of your soul.

11 | *In the Company of Birds*

The wind, out of the north, set the water in the tidal streams lapping against their banks. I was wearing a parka over my sweater and, by keeping up a brisk pace across the sand, could just stay warm. It was early in July. Clouds were thick in the sky, big gray ones proceeding southward like a herd of driven sheep, while above them, sailing in from the east, was a plane of paler clouds gilded by the morning sun.

Nearing the lagoon's far bank, I followed upon the many sets of our footprints that the rising tide had not erased— footprints that by now had become a trail across the flats. I stepped onto a grass-topped slab that had fallen away from the peaty bank. A few steps more and I mounted the table-top surface of the marsh. A gust almost bowled me over.

In the first days of summer, the skuas had been enraged

by our each and every transit. One day while Pétur was helping on the house, he had decided to go for a swim and a
beer at the regional school-cum-tourist hotel. (Three bucks
for the swim, eight for the bottle.) On his way to the car, he
strayed too close to the skuas' nest. The bird that was in-
cubating flew up in a panic, kicking one of the two eggs out
of the shallow cup. Under assault by both parents, Pétur did
not tarry to put the egg back. When he told me about it that
evening, the tide was already in and I was unwilling to walk
all the way around the marsh. I waited until morning. Early,
I crossed the flats, tramped through the marsh, and found
the nest.

The parents dived at me, hammering their gray wings at
my head. Then they changed tactics and set down on the
ground, where they thrashed about with their wings askew,
feigning injury in an attempt to distract me.

The eggs were exquisite, their olive shells overlain with
deep-brown blotches. I picked up the loose egg and tried to
warm it between my hands. The skuas were thrashing about
among the hummocks, crying shrilly. I set the errant egg
back next to its fellow, which I took the liberty of picking
up and examining. The undisturbed egg felt as warm as a
cup of tea.

Why hadn't the skuas nudged the egg back into the nest?
Were their brains not capable of imagining such a task?

At the time, I doubted that the chilled egg would hatch.

A week later, one chick and one egg were sitting side by
side in the nest. The chick was a lumpy, flaccid thing covered
with a dark fuzz that the wind ruffled. It had neatly pecked
through the eggshell around its circumference. From that

day on, I checked the nest each time I passed. The nestling grew and thrived; but the egg that had spent the night out of the nest failed to hatch. The egg remained there intact, more beautiful in its color and symmetry than the gawky gray nestling.

Over time, the chick became larger and more alert. It sat with its head up and watched us pass. Its parents' complaints had seemed to lessen somewhat in energy and volume; perhaps they'd grown tired of fighting off intruders who never actually bothered their nest.

On the cold day when I crossed the sand into the teeth of the north wind, I was wondering if the skua chick had started getting its feathers. I worked my way through the thúfur in the direction of the nest. But something was amiss. The adults did not fly up and scold me. I stopped and looked around, at the low cliffs near the car, at the rocks ribbing the side of the Stóra Hraun Peninsula. No sign of the vigilant gray pair.

Nor did I see the nest. Or, should I say, I did not lay eyes on the chick or the dud egg. Without them the nest reverted to what it had previously been, the top of a thúfa, of which there were many.

Casting about, I spotted a piece of splintered plywood, a scrap from the Stóra Hraun dump that had blown into the marsh and lodged between two thúfur. The nest had been only a few feet from the scrap.

The top of a large thúfa seemed slightly concave. I was

fairly sure the nest had been there—and confirmed it by finding a gray feather snagged in the grass. Other than the feather, nothing of the skuas remained. It was as if the birds had never nested at all, as if energy and will and the imperative to reproduce had not been concentrated on that one particular hummock in the marsh.

I imagined what had happened: A fox came loping past. It smelled the nest. It bolted the addled egg and appropriated the nestling to carry home to its pups.

I sat down on the thúfa. The wind was severe out of Hnappadalur Valley, where the red cones stood out sharply. A raven fought its way upwind, above the house and barn at Stóra Hraun, which were hidden from my view by a rocky rise.

What solace is there for birds that lose their young? Do birds grieve? Or do they cancel all thought of their vanished kin as easily as one might crumple a scrap of paper and toss it away on the wind? What adjustment would the skuas require to get back to the business of living? Perhaps they needed none. I supposed that the return to their own individuality happened with a wise and monstrous swiftness, and that now they were coursing across the landscape, looking for other birds to rob, other nests to plunder.

I thought about my mother. I knew, having lost my father, that life would go on for me. Over time, the pain of his loss had receded and I was left with good memories, of his lessons and his love. I wanted my life to become again a state of wonder and delight. I knew my mother would wish it so.

The death of a loved one is an ending, and it is not an

ending. In Iceland, between dark bouts of grief, in the summer of perpetual light, the world was slowly brightening.

Concerning the wagtail nest we'd been watching in the derelict summerhouse: Soon after Nancy and Will had joined me at Little Lava, we received a visit from Kristín and Jón Thór, the children at Stóra Hraun. They came puffing across the marsh, bundled up in snowmobile suits on a warmish drizzly day. These were the same stalwarts we would later observe swimming at high tide in the lagoon in front of their farmhouse. Nancy would call out to them in Icelandic: "Is it cold?" To which they would reply, *"Já, víst!"* Yes, of course!

They brought with them two puppies and a cat. We asked the children inside; the animals were left outdoors. Kristín and Jón Thór drank tea and ate cookies and looked all around, curious about how we'd fixed the old place up. They offered to leave the cat with us, to kill the mice. We thanked them but declined. After they left, I went into the summerhouse to get my kayak. A wagtail was flitting about, through the open doorway, to a weathered sill, onto a broken wall stud, out a window, back inside again. The bird had a moth in its beak and no begging scarlet mouth to plunk it into. The other wagtail fluttered around, cheeping. The nest was gone from the wall brace. It lay broken on the floor. All seven of the nestlings had been devoured. Fully feathered, they had been within a few days of leaving the nest.

.   .   .

On our first trip to Iceland, in 1986, I met with an ornithologist named Ævar Petersen at the Natural History Museum. At the time I was gathering information for an article
on ptarmigan. When the interview ended, Petersen had said,
"There's something I think you'd like to see."

He opened a file drawer. Inside were dozens of water-
colors of Icelandic birds by the American painter George
Miksch Sutton. According to Petersen, Sutton had donated
the paintings to the museum.

I looked at a redshank chick that seemed ready to ga-
lumph off the paper on its great ruddy feet. A golden plover
displayed its black belly and magnificent gold-mottled back,
the dorsal and ventral plumages separated by an S-shaped
swirl of white. A white wagtail perched on a mossy rock. An
Icelandic gyrfalcon, with its pale-gray back and yellow-
rimmed eye, stood on deadly taloned feet; its legs were
cloaked with white feathers fretted with comely dark markings that themselves resembled birds soaring on high.

I had seen the paintings reproduced in Sutton's book
Iceland Summer, published in 1961 by the University of
Oklahoma Press. Sutton had gone to Iceland in 1958 with
his friends Sewell and Eleanor Pettingill, who were photographing birds. Sutton wanted to make a series of drawings
directly from nature, showing the natal plumages of the
many waterbirds breeding in Iceland and the juvenal plumages of the half-dozen or so passerines, or perching birds,
that also nest there.

At Seltjarnarnes, near where Thórður's parents' house

now stands, Sutton observed a large breeding colony of Arctic terns, ducks, ringed plovers, and oystercatchers. I had been to the same colony several times over the years and had doubtless been attacked by the terns' descendants. Sutton very nearly failed to get out of Reykjavík alive. When checking on a wagtail nest in a marshy area near the city cemetery, he tumbled into a drainage ditch, and the ditch bank collapsed on top of him. A chunk of turf twenty feet long and three feet thick pinned down his legs, hips, back, and shoulders. The turf just missed covering up his head, and left his arms and hands free. Water was trickling through the ditch, and the turf dammed up the flow. Praying that the water would not deepen enough to drown him, Sutton began digging. As he worked, pressed down into the mud, he listened to the calls of redshanks, golden plovers, and meadow pipits. "A snipe was hooting loudly directly above me," he wrote. It took him an hour to get free. "The fingernails were wearing down by this time. The ends of the fingers were pale and wrinkled." He escaped, covered with mud and shivering uncontrollably, but with injuries no more severe than cuts and sprains.

Sutton was in Iceland for two months. While touring, he saw redshanks, which he described as "among the noisiest, most assertive birds I had ever observed." He watched fulmars on the clifftops, "like bits of light-struck dust floating against the darkness of the pinnacles." He was puzzled when he kept finding male phalaropes sitting on nests. Apparently ornithologists in the late 1950s had not yet realized that the female phalaropes depart soon after laying eggs, leaving their mates to hatch and rear the young.

Sutton described the cry of the Arctic skua as a shrill *error, error,* and saw one carrying off a meadow pipit in its beak. He wondered how the wren, with its stubby wings, could have flown across the oceans to colonize Iceland. He collected a chick from the nest of a great skua, declaring it "a droll, dumpy little creature, unable to move very fast and given to stepping on its own toes . . . As I picked it up," he reported, "I felt a rush of wind as one of the old birds barely missed me."

At the beginning of summer he stated: "How I longed for a glimpse—just a glimpse—of a white-tailed eagle, the majestic bird the Icelanders call the *örn.*" Almost forty years later, I wished I could somehow have given Sutton one of the many eagle sightings I made, for the bird painter's wish did not come true and he failed to see an eagle during his time in Iceland.

I had an advantage over Sutton. He spent his days rattling around the country in an old Chevrolet truck. I pretty much stayed in one place. I had ample time on my hands, and I always took my binoculars when I went out wandering.

Late one evening I was lazing with my back against a boulder, my binoculars trained on Snæfellsjökull. The sky was a glowing shade of amber. The peak was cerulean blue, lacking in definition, as if it had been cut out from colored paper. The mountain's horns jutted up from its summit. The map shows there are three outcroppings on top of Snæfellsjökull: Vesturthúfa, or "West Hummock"; Miðthúfa, "Middle Hummock"; and Norðurthúfa, "North Hummock"—although from Little Lava, and from every other direction from which I have viewed the volcano, I could distinguish only two.

Keeping my binoculars focused on the glacier, I strained for some detail: of crevasse or lava bulge or boulder field, or even the snowmobiles that take tourists up onto the ice. But Snæfellsjökull had no intention of assuming a third dimension or admitting that humans had tamed it.

Across my field of vision, across the blue cone, far away but distinct through the powers of magnification, passed the silhouette of an eagle.

Feathers drifted past the kayak's bow. One after another they rode the incoming tide and were urged along by the wind. The feathers were grayish-white, speckled, and curved at each end like tiny boats. Eider feathers. Out on the sandy reef, the males were molting.

The day was overcast, with fitful showers, chips of blue sky, an occasional shaft of straw-colored sunlight spearing a mountain's green flank. As often happened, a seal paralleled me at a cautious distance. My paddle circled, the blades splashing as they planted themselves in the bright water, the kayak moving forward in small surges. The seal's head submerged. It broke the surface a few yards farther on, glistening, drops falling from its whiskers.

I bent forward at the waist, working steadily. It seemed I was always battling the current, which was unsurprising, since in order to have the time to go somewhere and then get back again during a cycle of the tide, I had to launch against the incoming tide and return against water draining out of the lagoon.

Four broad-backed eider hens surrounded a pod of a dozen ducklings. As they urged the little ones away from me, they made a low nervous growling, *cor-or-or-or.*

The chop around the Stóra Hraun Islands overwashed the kayak with wavelets. I was always on my guard where the flow of the river interacted with that of the tide. Even though the water might look smooth, it could hide strong currents.

The water took the boat like a hidden hand. It held it for a while, then let go. Beyond the islands and out of the channel of the Haffjarðará River, the lagoon was peaceful. In many places it remained quite shallow even at high tide. Shadowed by the seal, I turned toward Suðurey, South Island. Soon my paddle was slicing the sand. The kayak ground to a halt twenty yards offshore. My seal companion did not like my looks when I stood and detached myself from the boat. It blew air out of its nose and dived.

I walked the kayak to shore. Patches of coarse grass grew on Suðurey. The wind pushed through the grass, rasping the blades together. I slogged up the sandy slope; at the top, I looked down on a broad bowl. On the far side of the bowl, a pair of graylag geese raised their heads and stood motionless while I studied them through the binoculars. I searched for the young birds that almost certainly were hiding in the tall grass, but I could not see any. The goose and gander had dark eyes and heavy pink bills. They remained standing.

I sat in the sand and watched them watching me as I drank from my water bottle and ate my lunch.

Suðurey was attached to the sandbar much favored by the eiders. I could see the bar, with crowds of black-and-white and brown ducks loafing on it; beyond the bar, the sea's rolling surface was scattered with rafts of eiders. Where the sandbar met the mainland, the farm Skógarnes occupied a height of land. We had introduced ourselves at Skógarnes. The farmer there was Trausti; his wife was Guðríður. Both spoke some English. They looked to be in their fifties or sixties. He was stocky and strong-looking; she was a tall woman with keen observant eyes. Also in residence at Skógarnes were a fat black cat, Jósafat, and an equally fat black Labrador retriever called President Clinton, whose name the couple pronounced "Clean Tone." Trausti and Guðríður invited us into their neat kitchen. Coffee, cake, crackers, and cheese were set on the table, and a pitcher of milk was fetched from the cooler in the milking parlor. As we chatted, Guðríður fed chunks of cake into the slobbering maw of President Clean Tone.

We told them we were living at Litla Hraun; from the way they nodded, I could tell they already knew. They told us we were welcome to drive onto the peninsula beyond their house to look at the birds nesting there—Trausti said that the sand at low tide was firm enough to support an automobile. So far, we had not made it back for any birdwatching; it always seemed there was more than enough to do at Little Lava.

As I sat on Suðurey, I was spotted by a pair of terns, who

came and bothered me dutifully for a few minutes before moving on. The *gowk, gowk, gowk* of a passing black-backed gull reached my ears. A redshank walked by me all hunched over, swiveled its head, regarded me for a moment, and ran off shrieking hysterically, *hee hee hee hee!* (Was it my purple dry suit?) The breeze brought to my ears a sonorous humming: the lowing of thousands of resting eiders.

The humming changed pitch slightly, intensified. I looked at the ducks, then looked skyward. High against the clouds was a black shadow. It flapped in level flight. The long, broad wings stopped moving, and the eagle soared.

What did the eagle see, there in the realm of the wind? The horizon dipping and teetering. The wrinkled sea and its half-hidden fish. The long, intricate coastline of Snæfellsnes. Eiders, in the water and on the sand. A red kayak and an islanded man.

The eagle flew off, between earth and heaven, like a soul on a long journey.

While walking on the flats, I saw a distant speck in fast level flight suggestive of a pursuit plane. The bird was out over Gamlaeyri. I swept the binoculars to my eyes. The bird was swifter than an eagle, more purposeful than a raven or a gull. I was certain it was a gyrfalcon, but it flew so fast that it was gone before I could get a good look at it. In times past, Icelandic gyrfalcons were much sought after as hunting birds. When Iceland was a colony of Denmark, the Danes exacted tribute in the form of falcons, which were given or sold to royalty in Europe and as far away as the sultans of North Africa.

At breakfast one morning a string of throaty *ronks* issued from the kitchen stove. We had no fire burning at the time. Curious, I eased out onto the front stoop. I stepped quickly into the grass and looked up at the chimney. A raven stared down at me. It was glossy and black, and its plumage gleamed in the strengthening light. I must have seemed as much an apparition to the raven as it did to me, for it gave out a squawk, abandoned its perch, and flew off muttering across the marsh.

Wood thrushes in the lava, like barely conceived thoughts flitting on the edge of one's imagination.

A gray-and-black wheatear acrobatically snatching moths out of the air.

A ptarmigan that landed on the roof of the ruined summerhouse. A male. Thus, incidental to the population. He croaked out a call, shuffled nervously, and hitched his head back and forth, watching me. We hadn't eaten fresh meat in a week. I had just picked up a stick when the ptarmigan gave a mad cackle and flew off in a rush of wings.

Snipe rummaging among the thúfur, hunting for worms, in workaday contrast to their songful sky dance, which continued on into July.

Mallard drakes flushed from pools in the marsh, their iridescent green heads catching the light, water falling from their bellies in crystalline drops.

From the heath, the *tloo-ee* of the golden plover, repeated so often that it sometimes grew wearisome.

Eagles on their rounds.

12 | *Under the Glacier*

We climbed through flowers, moss, and heather, the footing like a lumpy wet mattress thrown down on a flight of stairs. The wind tumbled a tuft of sheep's wool across the slope. From uphill came a fluty, trembling whistle. A bird ran off, hunched over, weaving between the thúfur. A large gray-brown sandpiper, with long sticklike legs and a curved bill: in Icelandic, a *spói*; what we call a whimbrel. Both names attempt to describe the bird's song, which Icelanders liken to porridge coming to a boil.

Gary and I stopped to catch our breath. Gary had just spent two weeks in France, touring caves in the Dordogne region, looking at the Pleistocene animal images painted on their walls (and, in the evenings, eating quantities of gourmet food, which, I had reminded him, he would not find at Little Lava); earlier in the year he had traveled to the Costa Rican rain forest and observed a volcano booming and sputtering. How a rural mail carrier from Pennsylvania could afford such exotic trips rather eluded me, but I was glad that my friend had planned a stop in Iceland on his way home from France.

After we picked Gary up in Reykjavík, he and I drove to Little Lava while Nancy and Will stayed on in the capital. As a birthday present for Will (we had celebrated his eighth birthday with a few small gifts and a cake smuggled in my backpack across the marsh), he would get to play on Thórður's computer and visit a children's park and the swimming pool he liked in the city. Nancy and Will would stay in Reykjavík for most of a week, while Gary and I hiked.

The climb up Kolbeinsstaðafjall was long and sweaty. We stopped to look back down into the volcanic chaos of Hnappadalur Valley. We slaked our thirst at springs trickling out of the mountain, whose flows commingled, hurried down the slope, blended with other streams, joined the salmon river, were carried in sweeping curves through its rock-walled channel to the lagoon and finally into the bay.

Another glorious summer day—the seventh in a row. I had read in a regional geography of Iceland that the number of overcast days per year on Snæfellsnes averages more than two hundred. So far, this had been anything but an average summer. Today there were a few clouds in the sky, but it didn't look like rain. I was half hoping for a several-day blow so that Gary could experience some real Icelandic weather of the sort I had often bragged of enduring. Also, I was worried about our water source at Little Lava: in spite of Bishop Guðmundur's blessing, the level of the spring was low and dropping further each day.

Gary and I looked at the topo map. We decided to aim for a saddle between Kolbeinsstaðafjall and a palisaded tower called Hrútaborg, "Ram's Fort." As we neared the ridge, the wind sounded like a waterfall. We eased out onto the saddle. One does not trifle with the wind in Iceland, which sometimes blows people off cliffs. Robert Jack was a Scottish parson who in the 1940s filled a Lutheran parish on Grímsey, an island off Iceland's north coast. The cliffs of Grímsey reach 300 feet above the ocean. To protect his children from summer gusts, Jack taught them to drop flat at the first breath of wind and hug the ground until the blow passed.

Today's wind was stiff and steady rather than blustery and malevolent. It chilled us after our climb. We found a rock outcropping and sat in its lee, where the sun warmed us again.

On the saddle's far side lay Hítardalur, "Hot River Valley," drained by the Hítará, or Hot River, so named because its flow is warmed by underground magma. The valley floor was a crazy quilt of tan, black, and terracotta lava flows. Toward the bay were the low-lying Mýrar, flat and green and mottled with cloud shadow. Much of the Mýrar had been drained for agriculture. Fields were studded with round bales of hay wrapped in white plastic; from our vantage point, they looked like mushrooms scattered across lawns.

Across the moors above Hnappadalur Valley we could see Breiðafjörður; beyond that many-islanded bay rose the mountainous West Fjords, topped with the white swatch of Drangajökull, "Glacier of the Lone Upstanding Rock." According to my map, the glacier was about eighty-five miles away, yet it looked as sharp as a chip of ice lying at my feet. I searched to the east for Langjökull, "Long Glacier," larger than Drangajökull and closer; however, tall mountains blocked the view.

The peaks of Snæfellsnes extended out to Snæfellsjökull. On this bright noon, the glacier sparkled in the sunlight, beneath an odd cloud formation like a stack of five white platters, slightly separated and floating one above another. Gary was taken with the mountain's beauty and made many photographs of it.

For centuries people assumed that Snæfellsjökull was the tallest peak in Iceland, because it rears up in solitary splendor. At 4,744 feet, it is hundreds of feet shorter than several other eminences. On top of the mountain, cupped within the hornlike prongs, is a crater filled with ice. The glacier, one of the smallest in Iceland, has been ablating, or shrinking, during recent warm decades; it is now about half the size it was a century ago.

Those who live near Snæfellsjökull are said to reside *undir jökli*—under the glacier, which also seems to imply: "under the glacier's spell." Iceland's foremost novelist is Halldór Laxness, who received a Nobel Prize in 1955 following the publication of his masterwork, *Independent People*. Another of his books is *Kristnihald Undir Jökli*, translated into English as *Christianity at Glacier*. Regarding Snæfellsjökull, Laxness wrote: "At night when the sun is off the mountains the glacier becomes a tranquil silhouette that rests in itself and breathes upon man and beast the word *never* which perhaps means *always*." And: "It is often said of people with second sight that their soul leaves the body. That doesn't happen to the glacier. But the next time one looks at it, the body has left the glacier, and nothing remains except the soul clad in air."

Snæfellsjökull is an awesome sight, whether viewed from the top of a mountain fifty miles distant, from across the bay in Reykjavík, or from the lonely fishing villages at its base. Snæfellsjökull is a mountain, and a glacier, and a volcano, and it commands awareness as each. It never grew stale to my eye. The mountain did indeed seem to have some force of life invigorating it, that force a potentially devastating one.

Among the first persons to successfully climb Snæfellsjökull were two Icelanders, Eggert Ólafsson and Bjarni Pálsson, pioneers in the natural sciences and the same duo who stretched a line across Eldborg's crater. In the mid-1700s they traveled all over Iceland, taking notes on everything from sea eagles to lugworms, from the uses of hot springs (for washing clothes, boiling milk, cooking vegetables, and steeping wood and bones to get them pliant enough to be worked into barrel hoops and other articles) to the shapes of saddles and panniers for horses as they varied from region to region. They noted the prevalence of sea winds on Snæfellsnes, judging them to be "very frequent and boisterous." Their book, *Travels in Iceland*, was translated from Danish into English in 1805.

Eggert and Bjarni undertook their ascent of Snæfellsjökull on July 1, 1753. Before setting off, they were warned by locals that the mountain was too steep to climb, that crevasses in the glacier were impassable, that sunlight glaring off the ice would blind them, that ghosts, trolls, or half-giants would surely ambush them. Undeterred, the scientists departed at one o'clock in the morning. They carried with them a compass, an altimeter, a barometer, a thermometer, climbing ropes, scarves of black crepe to tie over their eyes if the light became too harsh, and a sponge soaked in ammonia, to inhale as a reviving agent if the air proved too thin and dizzying. They rode horseback as far as the snow line, then went on foot. After climbing for eleven hours, the scientists gained the top of Miðthúfa, or Middle Hummock, the mountain's highest point. The temperature on top of the glacier was 24° Fahrenheit. The compass needle spun around erratically. From the summit, Eggert and Bjarni could see extensive scoria fields and deposits of pumice, ash, and rocks, which they correctly deduced had been cast forth by the volcano beneath their feet.

As we looked at the distant cone, I related to Gary a story the folk at Stóra Hraun had told us. Long ago, a male troll lived in a cave in Snæfellsjökull. He had a trollish lady friend who resided in Hnappadalur Valley. One day the troll woman decided to visit her lover at the end of the peninsula, taking along some skyr for him. Trolls turn to stone if the light of day catches them outside their caves, and the woman, bound for her swain's abode, realized that dawn was approaching. In her haste she dropped her skyr buckets and left her horse behind—lithified by the sun, the buckets became a pair of mountains each called Skyrtunna ("Skyr Bucket"), and the horse turned into a peak named Hestur ("Horse"). The troll woman got farther along. Today she

rests on one of the passes across Snæfellsnes, a stone spire
on Kerlingarfjall, "Old Woman's Mountain."

We worked along on the back side of the ridge toward the
formation known as Tröllakirkja, Troll's Church. Sheep trails
stitched the grass. The high-pitched bleating of a lamb, perhaps separated from its mother, came drifting up from
Hítardalur. On slopes across the valley, sheep grazed in what
seemed to be impossibly steep and stony situations. On our
right the cliffs were almost perpendicular, the rocks shattered by frost. We picked our way along the narrow trail.
We had hoped to climb Tröllakirkja, but its sides were too
steep and brittle. Scrambling through a notch between it and
another rocky turret, we made our way down to a ledge,
then to a tarn fed by melting snow.

We climbed down Kolbeinsstaðafjall following the same
route by which we had ascended. Along the road we met
some German tourists, two men and two women, who asked
whether we spoke any English. They requested directions to
a nearby farm, where there was supposed to be a lava cave
filled with formations. I spread my map on the hood of the
car and showed them how to get to the farm. I wondered if
they thought I was another bilingual Icelander.

Gary and I got back into our car and drove toward Little
Lava. My map showed a *hver* in the lava not far from the
Stóra Hraun road. We parked, and followed a well-worn path
through the heather. Hver means "kettle"; it signifies a hot
spring. This one looked as if it had been warming tired bod-

ies since the Age of Settlement. Had the old chieftain Sel-Thórir bathed here? Slabs of stone, their edges smoothed off, surrounded the steaming opening. Overflow from the spring drained into a sedge-grown pond. A low rock wall broke the north wind. At the base of the wall was a clay flowerpot containing a blue-flowering lupine and a small crucifix of tarnished metal. The hver was hotter than the hot pots at any of the municipal swimming pools I had been to in Iceland. Flat stones on the bottom let us sit with our chins above the water.

Wind in the birch brush. A snipe flighting. Our sighs of contentment. Blue razor-edged mountains peering down.

The old man stood bent over, trimming around the grave markers in the churchyard. His scythe bit through the grass in efficient, compact arcs. The tool's short blade was curved like a whimbrel's bill. The grave markers were stone slabs and iron crosses rusting in the salt air.

"If their meadows were smooth the product [of hay] would be much greater, and they would be able to introduce a much larger scythe than the little two-foot knife-blade used there at present." (Pliny Miles, journalist and traveler, born at Watertown, New York, visited Iceland in 1852. He died on the island of Malta at age forty-seven, on his way to Egypt to report on the opening of the Suez Canal.)

The old man stopped his cutting and straightened. In front of him the standing grass showed deep green and the scythed grass lay fanned out, catching the golden sunlight.

The old man stared at Gary and me. Actually, he stared mainly at Gary, who attracted a fair amount of attention; Gary had flowing gray hair and a vast beard, and Icelanders tend to wear their hair short and to be clean-shaven.

The old man was thin and stooped and had not bothered with shaving in a week of days. His eyeglasses tilted on the bridge of his nose. On his head was a billed cap in a wild pattern of colors, made from one of the new artificial fabrics, which I imagined to be the gift of a son or daughter moved away to the city. Ásmundur was the old man's name. Ásmundur of Akrar, or "Cornfields," one of the original farms named in the *Book of Settlements*.

"*Talar þú ensku?*" I asked the old man, suspecting that the answer would be *nei*, he did not know English.

He smiled mischievously. "*Talar þú íslensku?*"

I laughed and shook my head. I made a walking motion with a pair of fingers. I pointed at the low peninsula angling out into the bay beyond the church, then tapped the binoculars dangling at my chest. "*Fuglar*," I said, which meant "birds."

Ásmundur nodded and made some comment regarding our *bíll*, or automobile; I assumed he didn't want us driving it out on the peninsula. He lowered his grizzled face and went back to cutting. I was fairly certain we had been granted permission to hike out on Akranes, a three-mile sandspit where, we'd been told, many birds nested.

First we had to run the gauntlet of the terns.

They were nesting in a weedy pasture beyond the church. They rose in number from the ground and launched a determined assault upon our heads, an ongoing bombardment of droppings, and, even more unnerving, voices by the hundreds raised in a screeching chorus of alarm. The Reverend Robert Jack of Grímsey used to wear a cork table mat under his hat as protection against gashes from tern beaks. The terns drove us through a breach in the dune and down onto the beach, where, if we walked in the very wash of the waves, they let us proceed with only an occasional feint and imprecation.

Terns were making a circuit between the offshore shallows and their colony, bringing back fish for their nestlings. The surf was gentle. The sun warmed our faces. Black-walled islands rose out of a lapping sea that mirrored the turquoise sky. To the southwest lay the Hvalseyjar, or "Whale Islands," the largest of which was Húsey, "House Island," with a small square building for eggers and harvesters of down. I had been making plans, since before I came to Iceland, to kayak down the coast from Little Lava, about a dozen miles; I would stay for several days among the Hvalseyjar—sleeping in the eggers' hut or in a small tent that I'd brought—and then paddle back. It would be quite an adventure.

Shadows flashing past made us cringe. But it was not a flight of terns launching a sneak attack.

A gull raced by with a skua on its tail. When the white gull juked in one direction, the dusky skua followed instantly. As fast as the gull's wings flogged the air, the skua's were faster. The gull had probably picked up some item of food and bolted it; the skua was intent on harassing the gull into regurgitating the morsel. "Piratical" is an adjective that bird guides almost universally use in describing skuas.

The gull swung out over the bay, screaming as if it were

being killed, the skua right behind it. The birds were the same size, and the dark one might have been the pale one's shadow. The gull dived, and the skua plummeted after it. A foot above the water, the gull flared and sprinted for land. The skua executed the same maneuver.

The chase continued with the birds twisting and turning above ocean, beach, and dune. Abruptly the skua broke off contact: the gull swerved in one direction, the skua banked the other way. There seemed to be no particular reason for the skua to have stopped at that moment. The gull quit squawking. The skua flew off in a brisk, businesslike manner.

Gary and I strode along on the firm sand. Gary wore a pair of rubber barn boots, on loan from Kristján of Stóra Hraun. We didn't talk a lot, but it was still nice having someone to walk with.

The swash and hiss of the wavelets filled our ears. Long strands of kelp, olive-green and reddish-brown, lay twisted on the beach. Each rubbery blade had a stout stem attached to a rounded rock by means of a holdfast, a woody hand-shaped structure. Small slick stones, black with white blotches, tumbled in the wave wash like tiny orca whales.

The tide was falling. Each breaking wave would run up the slant of beach, stop and withdraw, and sink into the sand. Where it reached its farthest advance, the water dropped tiny black grains, apparently the densest of the particles it was carrying. Then, as the wave receded, it deposited the orange, mahogany, and white shell fragments that, taken together, gave Löngufjörur's beaches their characteristic golden hue. The result of all this washing and grading was that each wave left a distinct black band, no wider than an eighth of an inch, at the point of its greatest penetration. As the tide fell, black bands were scribed all down the fore-beach.

A perfume met us on the breeze. Curious, we trudged through a gap in the dune. The intensely sweet fragrance hit us in the face. It came from a dainty yellow flower growing profusely on the sandy ground. According to my plant book, it was lady's bedstraw, *Galium verum*; in Icelandic, *gulmaðra*, or gold madder.

Toward the end of Akranes the spit broadened and elbowed back toward the mainland. A formation of black rocks stood exposed by the tide. Dunlins, resting and sleeping on the rocks, made no move to fly as we passed among them. We splashed through clear pools, climbed over the algae-slick stone, and made our way to the end of the outcropping. On the sea floated hundreds of eiders, dark ducklings among the watchful adults. Guillemots, small black seabirds with white shoulder patches, swam farther offshore. A pair of puffins flew past on stubby blurring wings and lit on the water in a long white splash.

We sat in the sun. At that moment I would not have wanted to be on any tropical beach in the world. I considered, also, how inhospitable Akranes must become when a gale blows in off the Atlantic: the howling wind, onrushing waves with spindrift boiling off their tops, the waves smashing on the rocks, Faxaflói, the Bay of Manes, churning with white like the manes of a thousand horses fighting as they drowned.

.   .   .

Black-backed gulls stood paired, stock-still, magisterial, their dark wings folded against their white sides. Dozens of the great birds circled above us, calling out their displeasure in throaty tones.

Scores of nests were spread out before us. They were simple affairs, bowl-shaped depressions lined with moss. A rank chickenhouse smell blotted out the perfume of the flowering bedstraw.

The blackback lays its eggs in late April and early May. The eggs hatch in a month, and after another eight weeks the young fledge. Like the other birds, the gulls seemed to have gotten off to an early start this year. Today was the fifth of July and the young had already left the nests.

Gary waved me over to a clump of grass where a pair of young gulls cowered. They were coated with a pale-gray fuzz, dark spots on their heads and backs. Their bodies were bulky, although they still needed to grow into their immense webbed feet.

Black-backed gulls nest all over Iceland: on sandy deserts and fluvial plains, on mountains, skerries, islands in lakes and rivers, lava wastes and glacial moraines. They nest in oases in the moonscape of the interior highlands, and on rocky peaks called *nunatuks*—the word is Greenlandic—poking up through glaciers. The birds nest in such remote, inhospitable settings because they have been persecuted so heartily by Icelanders protecting their eider duck colonies.

I had been told that Ásmundur of Akrar was one of the few farmers in southwest Iceland who still suffered a colony of blackbacks to nest on his land. He exacted a fee, in the form of eggs harvested for the table and for sale in the markets.

Gary and I passed through a dense stand of arrow grass between the meadow and the beach. Along the beach were dozens of young oystercatchers. They looked much like their black-and-white parents, except that the juveniles had dark bills and feet, while the adults' were bright orange; also, the young birds' plumage was duller and scantier, giving them a smudgy aspect. Still flightless, they chirruped and ran away down the beach if we so much as took a step in their direction.

A half-dozen red-necked phalaropes floated a few yards offshore. The tiny phalarope has a brown back, a gray chest and head, and a brick-red neck with a white throat patch. The birds were feeding. They spun around on the still water, in tight circles, like children's tops. Now and then one would stab its needle bill to snatch up some minuscule scrap brought to the surface in the vortex of its whirling.

We started back. The lapping surf of the morning had become a booming three-foot swell. The tide had turned, narrowing the beach.

Ahead of us stood three young gulls, older and larger than the chicks we had found in the colony. Farther down the strand was a pair of adults. The young blackbacks would let us get within a few yards, then run off in a panic. Always they fled down the beach instead of up into the sand toward the dune. Tired after our long walk, we felt disinclined to slog up into the soft sand and circle around the frightened youngsters. Instead, we continued along on the beach, driving the flightless gulls before us. The young birds' parents would take to the air, scold us, soar a few yards farther on, and land. The little drama went on for almost a mile, until the young gulls had exhausted their strength. They stood and watched as we came up to them. Their beaks hung open; they panted.

One of the young birds finally lurched into the sugary sand, where it stood in glum indifference to what might befall it. The other two tried dodging around behind us through the surf. A wave sent them tumbling. One of the pair stopped at the tide line and crouched there forlornly. Its partner made for the sea; it was toppled by another breaker and sucked out in the backwash. The young gull popped up beyond the breakers, its plumage bedraggled, floating uncertainly. It seemed surprised that such a thing as floating could be accomplished. Then it swam away strongly. It was no less at home in the water than it would be in the air.

The next morning Gary and I packed food and raingear into our rucksacks. The day was breezy and overcast; it looked as if the weather might be changing.

In the homefield, a wheatear flitted from one pile of sheep dung to the next, snapping up the sluggish, mustard-colored flies that looped through the air above the excrement. The

Icelandic name for this nondescript bird, clothed in gray, white, and brown, is *steindepill*, "spot on a stone." The English name derives from "white arse."

We set off along Thrællyndisgata and soon turned south on a trail called Króksvegur.

Nancy and I had found out about Króksvegur in an unusual way. Nancy had been hiking by herself in the lava. She came around a bend and there stood a man, a rifle in his hands. He stood looking at her, as astonished to see her as she was to see him. She greeted him in Icelandic. The man was from Hnappadalur Valley; he and Kristján of Stóra Hraun were out hunting foxes, with Kristján elsewhere in the lava. The man showed Nancy a trail; Króksvegur, he called it. It was cairned, and we hiked it and learned it, and it proved useful in our explorations.

Gary and I followed Króksvegur for almost a mile before leaving it. Our destination was Selfit, "Seal Point." For the last hundred yards we went along in a crouch. We stopped behind a bulge of lava. A fissure led us toward the lagoon. The passageway was chest-deep, walled with fractured rock and carpeted with hawkweed, ferns, and wood geraniums whose bluish-purple flowers appeared incandescent in the soft light.

The crack brought us to a lava breastwork. We peered through chinks in the wall. Two dozen seals lay about sixty yards off, on a rock jutting out into the water. They were gray seals, also known as autumn seals, because that is when the females have their pups. The seals were thick and fat. They lay on their sides and bellies. The largest of them looked to be seven feet long. Their fur was light gray with dark spots; eyes and noses were black. At no time were all members of the group drowsing: at least one head was always raised, one nose checking the wind.

Ahead of us, the lava wall was low and gave little concealment. We crept past this gap on our hands and knees, but we were still observed. The seals snorted and grunted, arched their backs, and went belly-crawling off the rock. The sleek gray bodies flopped into the water. When the splashing had subsided, heads poked up from the bay like fenceposts set willy-nilly.

We kept still; the seals remained, watching. The curiosity of seals is legendary in Iceland. In times past, a method of capturing them was to lash a keg onto a rope and pull it back and forth across a narrow channel; seals coming to investigate would be caught in a hidden net. Hunters might fill a box with horn shavings, set the shavings on fire, and float the box near a net. Seals would be tolled in by the smoke and the strange, pungent smell.

People ate every particle of meat on the seals they caught. They singed the hair off the head and the flippers and pickled them, and considered the meat a great delicacy. The diaphragm of the seal was folded around pieces of the heart and strips cut from the flanks and wrapped in the scraped-clean guts to create the highly favored *selabaggi*, or "seal bag," eaten pickled or raw. People bound books in sealskin. They wore sealskin shoes. Seal oil mixed with tallow made a kind of butter. The best oil for frying bread and cakes was seal oil. Seal blood painted on buildings helped preserve the wood. Tarred seal stomachs were used as water wings by children learning to swim.

Icelanders still net seals for their hides and meat. Nancy and I once walked into a barnyard on an island farm and found the farmer and his wife skinning a seal on a trestle table. One day when we stopped in at Skógarnes, our neighbors Trausti and Guðríður proudly showed us a home video in which a relative of theirs shot a seal with a rifle, ran out into the water up to his neck, and hauled the seal ashore; it was then butchered expertly. Trausti said he used to hunt seals but had given it up because the price for their fur was so low—a development he credited to Brigitte Bardot, who has worked for animal rights since she retired from acting. Once, in the United States, I met a woman who mentioned that she had considered traveling to Iceland for a vacation. But she decided against it because, she said, she could not bear to be among people who killed seals and whales.

From Selfit Gary and I trekked through the lava to Snorrastaðir. On the way we saw the eagles' nest that Haukur had told us about, on the island in Kaldárós. Through our binoculars we spotted the brown lump of an eaglet.

Perhaps it was the only eaglet that would be raised near Little Lava this summer. When Nancy, Will, and I had gone back to check the nest along Þrællyndisgata, we found it had been abandoned. I climbed the lava precipice. The egg sat in the nest. I touched its smooth cold shell. From Stóra Hraun I rang up Kristinn Skarphéðinsson, the government ornithologist; he said I should collect the egg and he would pick it up later; but when I returned after a few days, the egg was gone. I assumed that a raven had made off with it, but later I learned that an associate of Kristinn's had gotten there before me.

At Snorrastaðir Gary and I were greeted by Haukur, who was about to depart for somewhere in his beat-up Volvo; nimbly we avoided an invitation to stay for coffee.

We took the trail up Eldborg. We climbed down into the crater on the steep path. Inside the cone, the air was still. The sun shone weakly through the clouds. The silence was complete. When we climbed back up, we kept to the rim, circling around to the north slope. We eased downhill toward the lava, our boots rolling in the gravel.

There was a trail on my map marked boldly across the lava, running east to west and passing the crater on the north. Once it had been clear and in frequent use, but now it was suspect. The map, published by the Icelandic geodetic survey, was based on a 1910 Danish chart. When Nancy had asked Haukur about the trail, he said it was grown over with woods.

We wandered among the low trees: birch intermixed with rowan, willow, and trailing juniper. Gray-green moss covered the slanting black slabs, hiding rocks that wobbled underfoot. In the 1860s an English traveler, Frederick Metcalfe, wrote of the Eldborg lava field: "Now and then the slag started up so abruptly, that I can compare it with nothing else than pulled bread for ruggedness." I did not know what pulled bread was, but I was certain that the lava field had grown no less rugged in the intervening 130 years.

Gary and I found what seemed to be the trail. We followed it until it vanished into a birch clump. We located it again; the track dwindled and died out after a dozen paces. We worked westward, going cautiously through the rough lava, moving more swiftly over the smooth. We watched out for pits and rifts, and swung wide around gullies. We saw no sign that sheep were grazing the heath; between the broken slabs, ferns and flowers grew abundantly.

A yellow dab on a rock: it was paint, not lichen. I called Gary over. We imagined that we could see a faint trail. We followed it and found another dab of paint, then another and another.

We had been walking for half an hour when two birds lifted from the lava field a quarter-mile away. They looked like chunks of lava that were levitated into the air and sent hurtling toward us in slow motion. The eagles uttered their hoarse grating *klee klee klee*. Swooping low, they filled our ears with their protests.

We abandoned the path. It took us half an hour to pick our way through the sharp rocks to the area from which the birds had flown. We stopped and scanned the lava with binoculars. I spotted some sticks near the top of a lava spire. A green beard of grass grew down below the sticks. As we closed in, the eagles landed and stopped calling. I climbed a fin of lava, looked across at the nest, and was staring at an eaglet.

The eaglet had a huge beak, dark and hooked, with a patch of yellow behind its gape. The bird appeared to be fully feathered. It crouched in the nest, wings held loosely at its sides. Its feathers gleamed. It might have been sculpted out of metal. It did not move a muscle, except for its eyelid, a cloudy flap that curtained down and up as it blinked.

. . .

The clouds had thickened and the wind grown cold as we worked our way through the lava. Late evening, nearly ten o'clock. We were ravenous. Our feet were sore. Our boots had fresh gouges in the soles and leather.

I looked forward to phoning Kristinn Skarphéðinsson. We had, I told Gary, confirmed Haukur of Snorrastaðir's claim: three pairs of sea eagles had nested near Little Lava.

We reached the power line that marched across the lava field, and I wrote down the number on the metal tag nailed to the nearest pole. With my binoculars I picked out the spire that held the eagles' nest; I memorized what it looked like and noted where it lay in relation to Eldborg and Stóra Hraun.

We turned south. Slate-colored clouds lay flattened over the bay. Snæfellsjökull floated at the peninsula's end, as gray and incorporeal as a ghost.

13 | *S a l m o n   R i v e r*

It was good having Gary at Little Lava. It was safer going with a companion into the mountains and the lava wastes. But sometimes, talking with him, I would freeze up. I would go away from Iceland. I would have to stop, look around, absorb the sight of the bare abrupt mountains and the limitless light, and work at filling my lungs with breath.

He reminded me of home. He reminded me of the fact that my mother had been murdered, that the man who had killed her had not yet come to trial and that at some point I would have to go back and confront again, in excruciating detail, the cruel, extraordinary thing that had happened to our family.

In Iceland I reveled in the emptiness of the land, which reflected the emptiness inside me. Any act, of work or leisure, any untroubled thought, was an achievement. Kayaking, fishing, gathering driftwood, drawing water, walking mile after mile—those things I could do. They helped draw me out of bleak and mindless lethargy. But summer, I knew, had to end. Already we were halfway through our Iceland sojourn.

The wind came gusting out of the southwest. To open the door, I had to push hard on it; it felt like I was pressing against a mass of sodden paper.

Outside, the rain slanted down. It fell on farms and lava, on mountains and the sea. On eagles' nests and foxes' dens and the roofs of houses.

In the homefield, sheep lay in sheltered places. Buttercups and hawkweed thrashed in the wind. I carried two large water jugs, empty, one in each hand, and a half-dozen smaller bottles in my rucksack. Between the thúfur and the old grass-blanketed foundations I walked, my head bowed against the elements.

A hen rjúpa clucked and took off practically at my feet. Her chicks went buzzing off in all directions, cheeping loudly, making short hopping flights on their stubby wings. They were half the size of bobwhite quail, tan with stripy markings. Their mother landed a few yards away. She ran along with a wing dangling. I did not honor her ruse but kept to the path. When I reached the lava, I looked back. She had jumped up onto a thúfa. She stood there in the blowing rain, her feathers rumpled. She would waste no time in gathering her brood.

The wind swirled inside the bowl in the lava. Ducking down, I entered the cave. The air was still. Water dripped. On the rocky wall, green fern fronds grew. A spider sat in its web.

Gvendarbrunnur was the lowest I'd seen it. Using one of the quart bottles, dipping carefully to avoid disturbing any sediment, I filled the four-gallon jugs. I filled all the small bottles and put them in the rucksack. When I was finished, the pool didn't look any lower than when I'd begun.

I stuck my hands in my pockets to warm them. I sat and looked out at the rain. The cave reminded me of the snow shelters my brother and I had built as children. We dug them on the edge of the driveway, in the pile of compacted snow that my father would heap up there when shoveling off the pavement. With our digging finished, Mike and I would sit inside, where it was quiet and oddly warm, and peer out the tunnel at the snowflakes whipping past. I always felt safe and secure inside the snow walls.

How strange to think that only a few feet from where we dug in the snow, a man would someday kill our mother.

I climbed out of the cave, picked up each heavy jug by its handle. Trudging back, I did not see the rjúpa or her brood.

Gary and Will were still asleep in the parlor, Will on the cot and Gary in his bag on a foam pad set on the floor. Nancy was up; she was in the kitchen making tea. I set one of the big jugs on the kitchen table, on its side so that its stop-cocked mouth projected over the sink that Pétur had rigged for us. I built a fire in the stove. Kindling crackled and caught. I added crumpled milk cartons, chunks of driftwood. The fire roared. I slid the big pot onto the stove lid above the firebox. The wind hummed in the chimney. Windows rattled. The view from the kitchen was of low gray clouds moving swiftly above the mudflats.

When Will and Gary got up, we made oatmeal garnished with dried cranberries brought from home. We washed and dried the dishes and put them away. Looking out the window, I said to Gary, "This is what summer can be like in Iceland."

"How long will it last?" he asked.

"No telling; a few days, a week, maybe the rest of the month."

Gary, Nancy, and Will settled in to read. I said I was going fishing. So far I'd had no luck. The folk at Stóra Hraun had not been encouraging; I might catch a sea trout, they said, or, later in the summer, a *bleikja*, an Arctic char, in one of the smaller streams. If I really wanted fish, they recommended a farmer with a lake in Hnappadalur Valley.

Salmon swam up the Haffjarðará, but the river was off limits unless I wanted to fork over 50,000 krónur a day, or $750. Along the river, on the other side of the highway near where the Stóra Hraun road intersected, stood the fishing lodge, a collection of neatly kept cottages with red walls and green roofs. Paying customers stayed there. A chef was on hand to prepare meals. A riverkeeper patrolled against poachers. When we drove out for supplies, we often saw the fishermen's trucks parked near the favored lays, shiny four-wheel-drive vehicles that must have cost in the millions of krónur. We saw the fishermen themselves, attended by guides, using long fly rods to flog the pools. We saw fish pulled out of the Haffjarðará: Atlantic salmon that were bright-sided and deep of draft, two and three feet in length. One of them would have fed us for days.

Closer to home, I had fished the winding stream near Krókar. I had cast from a point in front of the house at high tide when the lagoon became a bay. I had fished off the end of the Litla Hraun Peninsula and in the channel flowing past Seal Head. I had tried spoons and spinners, worms and clams. I had fished the incoming tide, the slack tide, the outgoing tide. I had slung my lures into the mouth of the Haffjarðará, where Haukur said I might fish. I knew he was using me as a cat's-paw to assert the rights he had won in court, and not wanting a confrontation, I kept an eye peeled for the river warden. Fortunately, he never came.

I was half afraid that I actually would hook a salmon and wondered if I could land such a huge, powerful fish. But all I caught were tough green waterweeds. I had not found any dead fish lying about at low tide, which suggested to me that fish seldom ventured into our side of the lagoon. Yet food was plentiful: lugworms, clams, and minnows in the fresh-water channels.

The main reason I kept fishing was that it got me out at all times and in all weathers. Now it goaded me into putting my boots back on and my damp raingear. I leaned against the door and opened it. Carrying shovel and bucket, I let the wind drive me down the hill and onto the flats. It was still raining heavily. Near Stakkholtssteinn I dug out a dozen lugworms and some clams. I headed back to Little Lava to drop off the shovel and get my rod.

The ewe lay flat on her back in a little ditch halfway to the house.

Her splayed legs fluttered feebly. A pile of droppings had collected beneath her nether end. Her eyes were half-open, and she breathed laboriously through her gaping mouth. I stepped closer. Noticing me, she struggled a bit before subsiding. Her two lambs, which had been lying nearby, got up and trotted off a few yards; they stood huddled together, staring at me. The rain pelted down. The ewe's breath steamed in the chilly air.

I was not a veterinarian, but it seemed obvious to me that this was a dying sheep. Some disease, most likely. I considered ending her sufferings with a rock, but that was too drastic a step. I shrugged and set off for home. Too bad for the sheep. I was less than sympathetic. From the house we would have a front-row seat to watch the scavengers. Ravens, gulls, foxes—would an eagle show itself? Back inside, I told Nancy, who went to the window.

"We have to tell the people at Stóra Hraun," she said.

"Why? I doubt there's anything that can be done. Anyway, I'm going fishing." The last thing I wanted was to walk all the way to the farmhouse and sit there drinking coffee and inhaling cigarette smoke while lamenting the loss of a grass-grubbing ewe.

"You won't catch anything," Nancy said. I knew from her tone that she would be taking the news to Stóra Hraun if I refused.

"Don't be so sure. I might bring back a salmon."

She looked down her nose at me. "That'll be the day."

I passed by the ewe, a gray lump in the grass, and turned west.

The firm sand gave the best footing anywhere about, better than the unstable lava, the gravel flats, or the mires. It was not surprising that early travelers had used Löngufjörur as a highway. About every third day we saw people on horseback crossing the sands, long strings of mounted riders accompanied by dozens of loose horses. Red horses, brown, black, dapple-gray, dun—colors that picked up the hues of the land. The horses flew along over the sand, tails and manes streaming.

On the flats, dunlins were feeding in small flocks. When I got close, the little sandpipers would take to the air, their white rumps and underwings showing like a burst of confetti. The color would shift back to grayish-brown as the group banked in unison and set down again on the sand.

Terns held position in the wind, poised above stream channels, their bodies jigging up and down as if suspended from an unseen puppeteer's crosspiece. Oystercatchers, great black-backed gulls, their slightly less nefarious cousins the lesser black-backed gulls, herring gulls, hooded gulls. Also what I believed were Iceland gulls, medium-sized gulls that were a uniform pale white, with pinkish legs.

I came to the stream near Seal Head. For the hundredth

time I wished for hip boots. I had brought an old pair, but they leaked like sieves, and new boots at Icelandic prices were out of the question. I pulled my feet out of the Wellingtons and rolled up my rain pants and trousers. The water was cold. It cut to the bone.

Wind blew the rain across the sand. The sky grew light, and the rain slackened. Then the sky darkened again and the rain came so hard I couldn't hear a thing above the drops pelting against my hood.

I reached the shelf of rocks extending out into the Haffjarðará near Barnasker. The rocks were skirted with wrack, which lifted and fell in the waves. I rigged up my rod. From the rocks I cast into the river. I let the spoon sink for a moment before reeling back in. I was wearing fingerless wool gloves, and my hands were numb. I cast again, but could not get the spoon as far out as I wanted.

I moved seaward along the river's edge, casting again and again. I assumed I was safe from the riverkeeper in this weather. I stopped and ate a sandwich, my back to the rain. I resumed my labors using a different lure. My casts hauled in heavy snarls of weed. The lure was being borne upriver. The tide had turned; the sea was pushing against the river, forcing it back into the bay.

I imagined the salmon that might be coming in with the tide.

Salmon can live in saltwater and freshwater. Biologists are divided on whether salmon are freshwater fish that have adapted to life in the ocean or maritime fish that have colonized rivers of the land. Salmon breed in gravelly, rock-strewn rivers whose bottoms offer nooks and crannies where the large salmon eggs can lie out of reach of fish that would eat them. Newly hatched salmon, called alevins, hide in the rocky bottoms. When they are a year old, most salmon swim down the rivers and into the sea. At that time they are called smolts. Of two fish from the same brood, one may spend its life in the upper reaches of a river and get as heavy as one or two pounds, while its sibling may travel thousands of miles through the open ocean, feeding on shrimp and fish and attaining a weight of twenty pounds.

Salmon spend up to five years at sea. Many Atlantic salmon, from European and North American rivers, gather off the coast of Greenland; a second major feeding ground is near the Faroe Islands. After they mature, salmon return to their home rivers to breed. They may find their way by using the earth's magnetic field. Since salmon swim near the water's surface, some scientists believe they navigate visually, looking up into the night sky and using the constellations to orient themselves—although that would not seem to be an option for salmon returning to Iceland beneath summer skies that never darken. It is thought that salmon can decipher ocean currents, subtle changes in temperature or salinity that have eluded our detection. Once a fish reaches coastal waters, its sense of smell—or perhaps the sense is better described as taste—guides it the rest of the way.

The Icelandic word for salmon is *lax*, pronounced "lox." There are numerous rivers in Iceland named Laxá, or "Salmon River." Salmon occur in more than eighty Icelandic waterways. Fishermen catch around 40,000 salmon a year. Icelandic rivers are short, swift, pure, and famous. There is a river within the city limits of Reykjavík, the Elliðaá, that flows past apartment buildings, shopping centers, and a power station; the Elliðaá yields 1,500 to 2,000 salmon per year.

Different people had told me that the Haffjarðará was the best salmon river on Snæfellsnes. It is a stable fishery, with little fluctuation in the annual catch. Most of the salmon in the river weigh from eight to twelve pounds, with some as heavy as twenty-five pounds. The Haffjarðará is the sole river in Iceland where fly fishing only is permitted—which, I supposed, transformed my futile incursions, using worms and flung metal, into sins of a doubly vile aspect.

I fished for another hour. The tide kept forcing me to back up, higher onto the rocks, then onto the sand. A seal surfaced in the steadily widening channel. A shag dived for fish. A line of geese went barreling past overhead, riding the wind.

The salmon were there, a hidden presence. I could feel them even if I couldn't catch them. Finally I picked up my bait bucket and headed back toward Little Lava.

The tide had risen so that I could not cross the Seal Head stream. I set the bucket down, baited with a hook and a lugworm, and tried a cast. The water was inscrutable, rain-rippled and flecked with foam. After a while I followed the bank toward Seal Head, a ten-minute walk. I climbed the hill-like island. In the grass on top I sat down out of the wind in a swale. The rain had slackened; it drifted down gently. The walking had warmed me. My eyelids were heavy. I leaned against the slope, my head cushioned on a clump of moss, my face turned away from the rain.

Under a hard shower, I came awake. One look at the flats half covered with water told me I'd better get moving. I grabbed the rod and bait bucket and stumbled down the slope, scaring a band of sheep, who raced off scattering sand with their hooves.

Between Seal Head and the mainland the channel was too deep. I followed the sheep's tracks. The stream was still too deep where it curled toward the grassy peninsula, Fitjar; so I headed farther south. Finally I was able to wade. I reached the low marshy land. There were ponds on Fitjar, black quagmires, and deep stream channels that had to be traced back inland until they grew narrow enough to jump across.

I saw a mink hunting in the rocks. Mink are not native to Iceland. They were imported and raised on fur farms; some of them got loose, and now the mink is a greatly resented predator of Iceland's ground-nesting birds.

I found a broad muddy path where the horseback tourists rode. I crossed the path and picked my way along the edge of the lava. I was in the vicinity of Stelpusteinn, the stone named for the girl who had drowned while herding sheep.

At Krókar another stream came curving out of the lava field. As I passed through a small cove, a redshank came screaming down out of the air. A pair of skuas tore along after it. It seemed the skuas were not simply trying to rob the redshank of food but were intent on killing it. Seeing me, they banked and flew off, dark shadowy reivers with knifing wings and hooked black bills and middle tailfeathers that were longer than the rest of the tail's fan, a feature heightening their sinister appearance.

The redshank tucked itself in under a ledge. I walked past, quite near it. It was the only redshank I had met that did not flee or rise up indignantly and denounce me.

Smoke streamed northward from the house chimney. I scanned the boggy pasture out in front of Little Lava and saw no overturned sheep. I went inside and found Nancy, Will, and Gary in the kitchen. Nancy put the kettle on for me. She informed me that we were now even more highly valued as neighbors by the family at Stóra Hraun.

Her announcement that a sheep was lying on its back had galvanized Veiga, the same woman who had presided over the rescue of the lamb from the water-filled ditch. She and Nancy rounded up two horses that some relatives had left there the day before. Nancy said it would have been quicker to have walked: they had to catch the horses, saddle them, ride down the lane, cross the bog, and urge their mounts through the streams in the mudflats. The horse that Veiga was riding turned out to be lame; it could not go with any speed.

When Veiga finally got across, she quickly found the ewe and got the creature to her feet. Nancy was trying to control her own horse, which was refusing to jump a stream, and did not see how the resurrection was effected. The ewe went wobbling off with her lambs. Veiga wanted to get back home before the tide cut her off, and the explanation she offered was in rapid-fire Icelandic: Sheep fall onto their backs all the time and can't get up again, and if somebody doesn't come along and right them, they die. Veiga seemed overjoyed at saving the ewe; she thanked Nancy lavishly. Nancy dismounted, and Veiga switched to Nancy's horse and rode off with the lame horse limping along behind.

How could the ewe, who had seemed on death's doorstep, have recovered so quickly? Later, we were able to ask our friend Hinrik, son of Hjörtur of Helgafell.

Sheep lie resting on their sides; sometimes they lean too far and tip over. "These Icelandic sheep," Hinrik said, "their backs are broad and flat, and they cannot shift their weight enough to roll onto their bellies again. Sometimes they get stuck between two thúfur." A sheep may lie on its back for days, becoming dehydrated and starving. "If the ravens find it, they peck out its eyes." If it has lain for too long, even getting the animal back on its feet may not save it.

It turns out that sheep in other lands get into the same predicament. In Scotland a sheep that has so upset is said to have "cowped." A passage describing the problem appears in *This House of Sky*, Ivan Doig's memoir about growing up in Montana. "When we spotted the telltale kick of hooves in the air," wrote Doig, "I would run to the ewe, grab deep into her fleece and heave her over." The Icelandic term for the condition is *afvelta*. It can be applied to horses, to cattle, and, derisively, to people. He is lying there afvelta. He is lying there intoxicated. Dead drunk.

On Gary's last day I walked him across the sands. We dropped off the rubber boots that Kristján had loaned him, drove to where the gravel met the blacktop, set Gary's backpack on the berm, and waited.

A tractor-trailer passed. A milk tanker. Beat-up cars driven by locals, shiny Japanese-built sedans carrying vacationers from the city. We talked idly. The bus came along, with a whippy radio antenna and big lugged tires typical for Iceland. The driver saw Gary's backpack and stopped. He put the pack in the luggage compartment, along with other brightly colored backpacks, probably belonging to young Europeans vagabonding in Iceland, and the battered suitcases of rural Icelanders going to visit relatives in the capital. Gary bought a ticket to Reykjavík. He shook my hand and boarded.

14 | The Confines of Hell

Fog swirled around the moss-covered lava. The landscape had a rosy tinge to it, from the flowers of thrift, thyme, and campion blooming among the rocks. In a deep crack next to the trail, I found what may have been the straightest rowan tree in all of Iceland: its trunk shot up twenty feet from the bottom of the crevice, as far as the ground's surface—but no farther, because the wind that normally swept the heath pruned back all additional growth. I supposed that, had I fallen into that particular crack, I could have escaped by shinnying up the rowan.

A bird came sailing across the lava. It spotted me and flared. Brown wings grabbing at the air, it lifted over a ridge and was gone. It was a merlin, hunter of redwings and meadow pipits, scourge of the young of plover and ptarmigan. The falcon's brown coloration meant that the bird was a female. The male of the species has a slate-blue back and wings: color of the sea on a gloomy day, color of the mountain Kolbeinsstaðafjall, now peering out of the mist ahead of me.

The trail I was following went north from Little Lava for most of a mile. It led to a tall cairn like a crooked finger, built on a high point in the lava field. Beyond the cairn, the trail died out among pockets of birch so thick that in places I had to proceed on my hands and knees. While casting about for the path, beneath the trees I found two eggshells. They were identical: two inches long, pointed at one end and rounded at the other, with an exit hole chipped in the side. The shells were the color of old ivory, blotched and dashed with brown. I supposed they were ptarmigan eggs.

I searched for the trail in the rough lava, the apalhraun, the aa lava. In Hawaiian, *aa* reputedly means "a surface on which one cannot walk barefoot." Smooth lava, or pahoehoe lava, is "a surface on which one *can* walk barefoot."

The rough lava was made up of clinker: thin-edged, broken rocks jumbled one against the next. Some of the larger slabs must have weighed half a ton. Coming down a slope, I stepped onto a slab like a tabletop. It tilted with a sudden clacking sound and came to rest at a new angle. I toed the next block of lava, then stepped onto it. The slab I had vacated shifted back to its original position with a grating *clunk*. Three steps farther on, I trusted a rock that swiveled beneath my boot and broke into two pieces, one of them sliding off into a pit, the other one buckling upward to scrape at my leg. I stabbed out with my walking stick and kept my balance.

After searching for most of an hour, I had to admit that the trail had vanished. The labyrinth of weird silent shapes had swallowed it up.

I sat on a boulder. The sky was clearing; a breeze had risen to disperse the mist. Kolbeinsstaðafjall stood out sharply. In Icelandic, a *fell* is a mountain and a *fjall* is a great mountain. Of the peaks one could see from Little Lava, Kolbeinssta-ðafjall showed best how the land had been built up—and was being torn down.

Visible on the mountainsides were bands delineating the many layers of lava that had accumulated over the ages; these strata ran across the entire massif, so that the same line carried on in different parts of the crag. At the bottom of the mountain, erosion fans spread out onto the plain. Some of the fans were naked rock, and some were covered with moss scarred with zigzag marks where streams ran out. I looked at the south wall where it rose above the gravel; I doubted if one could climb that face, so steep and broken was the slope. The erosion fans skirting the mountains in Iceland have built up since the last Ice Age ended 10,000 years ago. Wind, water, and ice, the staples of Icelandic weather, were at work on the sharp-edged bulk of Kolbeins-staðafjall.

Iceland sits astride the mid-Atlantic ridge, where the

North American and the Eurasian crustal plates pull away from each other. The mid-Atlantic ridge runs from the Arctic to the Antarctic. It is an underwater mountain range whose peaks jut above the ocean in the Azores and Tristan da Cunha in the South Atlantic, and in Iceland in the North Atlantic. A plume of superheated magma extends toward the earth's surface beneath Iceland. This plume, in tandem with the spreading of the mid-Atlantic ridge, sends forth stupendous volumes of lava.

During the Tertiary period, which ended 1.6 million years ago, Iceland was relatively flat: a pancake of lava with some soil on top. Following the Tertiary, ongoing volcanism built up the tall mountains. Then the climate cooled. During the last Ice Age, from 100,000 years until 10,000 years before the present, glaciers covered all of Iceland, except for the highest mountaintops. The glaciers honed the mountain edges. They gouged fjords out of the coastline.

When the glaciers withdrew and their great weight was taken away, the land rebounded upward. Volcanic activity increased. Magma surged out of the mid-Atlantic ridge. The ridge cuts across Iceland from Reykjanes ("Smoky Peninsula") in the southwest to Melrakkaslétta ("Fox Plain") in the northeast. Iceland is continually expanding, mainly on this southwest-to-northeast diagonal. Since the last Ice Age, the island has widened by six hundred feet. Since settlement began around a thousand years ago, Iceland has broadened by sixty-six feet. It spreads about six feet more every century.

Geologists believe that three million to six million volcanic eruptions have taken place in Iceland since the island emerged from the Atlantic. On average, a volcano erupts somewhere in Iceland every five years. There have been 220 to 440 major eruptions since the Age of Settlement. Of all the lava produced on the planet in the last five hundred years, a third has emerged in Iceland.

It is not possible to count the volcanoes in Iceland because of the way they blend into one another. Almost every significant landform seems to be a volcano, a remnant of a volcano, or the product of a volcano. Iceland has shield volcanoes. Spatter ring volcanoes. Scoria and cinder craters. Scoria and spatter crater rows. Classic stratovolcanoes. Linear stratovolcanoes. Tephra craters. Tephra crater rows. Explosion craters and explosion crater rows. Various classificatory schemes recognize up to twenty-five different types of volcanoes in Iceland. According to the textbook *Geology of Iceland*, by Thorleifur Einarsson, "volcanic activity has been more varied in Iceland than in any other area of equal size in the world."

From my seat in the Eldborg lava field I could see, in Hnappadalur Valley and on Snæfellsnes, a spatter ring crater (Eldborg), scoria craters (the red cones of Hnappadalur), and various cliffs, hills, and mountains created or shaped by volcanic activity, such as *stapi*, or table mountains; *móberg*, or palagonite, ridges; and rhyolitic domes. I could not now see the stratovolcano Snæfellsjökull, hidden in the clouds. Haukur Jóhannesson, the geologist I had interviewed in Reykjavík, characterized Snæfellsjökull as a very active volcano, even though it has not erupted for 3,500 years. Its last major event was a huge lava flow, combined with a violent ash fall to the north. Snæfellsjökull has been erupting on and off for 700,000 years, and, the geologist noted, Icelandic volcanoes tend to remain active for up to 2 million years.

The Eldborg lava field is considered to be a recent flow, having emerged since the last Ice Age. For me it was a visible demonstration of the powers lurking beneath the crust. I saw the lava field every day, and it never failed to impress me. It was Earth in the making. And already the forces of nature were breaking it down, just as they were gnawing away at Kolbeinsstaðafjall. The moss that covered the lava was feeding on the rock, consuming it molecule by molecule. Plant roots were insinuating themselves into cracks opened by freezing and thawing. Particles of lava were becoming soil and collecting in crevices and swales. The process was never-ending. It goes on everywhere on the planet, and it is boldly apparent in a place like Iceland.

Saint Brendan the Navigator, the seafaring Irish monk, may have visited Iceland in the sixth century, as suggested in the ninth-century manuscript *Navigatio Sancti Brendani Abbatis*, or *The Voyage of Saint Brendan the Abbot*. The saint, with a crew of seventeen other monks, set sail in a curragh, an open boat with a hull sheathed in oxhides. Brendan was looking for a "promised land" (ultimately he reached North America, some scholars believe). He took a northerly route, island-hopping as he went. The chronicle states that Brendan observed an island "very rough, rocky and full of slag, without trees or grass, full of smiths' forges. The venerable father said to his brothers: 'This island worries me. I do not want to go on to it nor even get near it. But the wind is driving us straight toward it.' " Brendan made the sign of the cross in four directions, and prayed, saying, " 'Lord Jesus Christ deliver us from this island.' "

An inhabitant of the island, "shaggy and full of fire and darkness," came down to the shore carrying a pair of tongs in which was held a great lump of burning slag. The shaggy man hurled the cinder at the servants of Christ, "but it did not harm them. It flew more than two hundred yards above them. The sea where it fell began to boil . . . and smoke rose from the sea as from a fiery furnace." More islanders appeared and began throwing flaming missiles as the monks rowed away in terror.

> It looked as if the whole island was on fire like a huge furnace, and the sea boiled as a cauldron of meat boils when it is thoroughly heated up. All day long they heard a great clamor from that island. And when they could no longer see it, the howls of the inhabitants still reached their ears, and a stench came to their nostrils. Then the holy father comforted his monks, saying "Oh soldiers of Christ, be strong in true faith and in spiritual weapons because we are in the confines of hell."

The account seems to describe the birth of a volcanic island. Since the days of Brendan, other seafarers have reported fires rising from the waters around Iceland. In November 1963, crew members on a fishing boat saw what appeared to be a ship ablaze twenty miles off Iceland's south coast. Coming closer, they realized an eruption was taking place. Over the next few days red-hot basalt lava issued from a seafloor vent. The lava made the ocean boil. The nascent volcano sent up columns of ash, which mingled with cauliflower puffs of steam. The eruption continued for three and a half years. The volcano rose 565 feet above the water. The island, about a square mile in area, became the southernmost part of Iceland. The quiescent heap of hardened lava was given the name Surtsey, after Surtur, a fire-giant in Norse mythology. Plants, insects, and birds began to colonize it. Surtsey's emergence let the ever-pragmatic Icelanders extend their international fishing boundary a few miles farther south.

Iceland's foremost volcano is Hekla, "the Hooded." It is a linear stratovolcano, with a cowled or hooded appearance; from the air it is said to resemble an overturned canoe. Hekla rears up on the northeast fringe of the southern lowlands, Iceland's most productive farming area. Its main fissure, Heklugjá, is three miles long. The mountain created by this infernal gullet is more than 4,900 feet tall and apt to grow taller with each eventual eruption.

Many centuries ago, an Icelandic priest is supposed to have traveled to Saxony, where he wooed and promised to marry a woman who was a witch. (I have noticed that the Icelanders always depict themselves as the seducers in such stories.) When the priest went back to Iceland, the witch realized she had been deceived. She sent the priest a golden chest, with instructions that no one but he should open it.

But the priest was nobody's fool; he rode with the chest to the top of Hekla and threw it into a gully. Since then, fire has burned inside the mountain.

But Hekla was exerting itself before the priest or anyone else lived in Iceland. According to the book *Hekla* by the volcanologist Sigurður Thorarinsson, after the glaciers melted and before settlers arrived, Hekla erupted with such force that it covered 80 percent of Iceland with ash. The ash remains today as a distinctive band in the country's soil profile.

Written records reveal that Hekla erupted in 1104, 1158, and 1206. An eruption that began in July 1300 lasted a year, with tephra covering a third of the country. Tephra is anything that comes out of a volcano other than gases and flowing lava: dust, ash, shards (lava spatters that solidify in midair), blocks, and bombs.

An eruption of Hekla in 1693 lasted seven months and was one of the most destructive in Icelandic history. Geologists estimate that 60,000 cubic yards of tephra were emitted per second during the eruption's first hour. Clouds of fluorine gas puffed from the vent. That day, the wind was out of the south. In northern Iceland, the leaves on the trees turned black, fish went belly-up in the rivers, ptarmigan fell over dead, and livestock perished after eating fluorine-poisoned grass.

In 1540 an Icelandic cleric, Gizur Einarsson, had an audience with Christian III, King of Denmark. According to a source from that era, "It seemed to Gizur that the King put to him many unneedful questions, especially regarding the mountain Hekla." Tales about Hekla had spread throughout

Christendom. People thought Hekla was the mouth of Hell, or perhaps Hell itself. Religious theorists suggested that Judas Iscariot was imprisoned inside Hekla. In 1675 a Frenchman who had traveled to Iceland wrote that the Devil liked to drag the souls of the damned out of Hekla's fires and cool them on the pack ice off the coast, in preparation for torments to come.

There are many notable Icelandic volcanoes. Eldgjá, "Fire Chasm," poured forth lava covering several hundred square miles in the year 930. In 1724 a steam eruption in the crater Víti, or "Hell," scattered mud and pumice over much of northern Iceland. Askja, a huge caldera cupping Víti within its depths, erupted in 1875; the tephra fall ruined so many farms in eastern Iceland that people emigrated in large numbers to North America.

The greatest lava flow anywhere on the planet in recorded history issued from Lakagígar, a 20-mile fissure in south-central Iceland. Between June 1783 and February 1784, some 135 craters disgorged 530 billion cubic feet of lava. The lava covered 174 square miles. It filled valleys up to 600 feet deep. On level ground it built up in thicknesses ranging from 20 to 100 feet. Enough lava, one geologist estimated, to cover England with a lava blanket 4 inches thick. Because the flow was so thick, it remained hot. Displaced rivers of glacial meltwater ran out onto the lava and danced and tossed about until they evaporated or cut new courses.

A haze of gaseous fluorine rose from the Lakagígar fissure and hung above Iceland. Where the haze was thick, the sun shone through it like a crimson fireball. People choked on the gas. Animals that grazed on contaminated plants developed strange growths on their teeth and bones, hindering them from feeding and walking. The grass ceased growing. The hay harvest was poor. The supply of fodder gave out. Even the fish disappeared from the coast.

By the time the 1780s had ended, a fourth of the people in Iceland had perished from hunger and disease, along with three-quarters of their livestock. At that time Iceland was a crown colony of Denmark. Today there exists in Iceland a popular conception that, following the vicissitudes of the eighteenth century, the Danish government sought to rescue its Icelandic charges by removing them all to the Jutland heath in northern Denmark. The surviving Icelanders, so the story goes, refused to leave their home.

Another illustrious volcano is Katla, "Kettle," hidden beneath Mýrdalsjökull, the country's fourth-largest glacier, in the highlands above the south coast. Mýrdalsjökull is a double hump of ice ranging in thickness from 600 to 1,200 feet. Katla has erupted at least sixteen times since the era of settlement, most recently in 1918. A river, the Jökulsá ("Glacier River"), flows south from Mýrdalsjökull. When Katla erupts, Jökulsá receives the outpouring of melted water from the glacier. The Icelanders have coined a word to describe this phenomenon: *jökulhlaup*, or "glacial burst."

A jökulhlaup occurs when magma beneath a glacier gradually melts enough ice so that the pressure lifts the glacier up and the water goes pouring out from under it. Or a subglacial volcano erupts, melting huge quantities of ice and causing a sudden flow laden with stones, mud, ash, and slabs of ice.

Landnámabók, the *Book of Settlements*, seemingly records

a jökulhlaup. Two old sorcerers, Loðmundur and Thrasi, were feuding with each other. One morning Thrasi beheld a great flood of water, which, by means of his witchcraft, he diverted onto Loðmundur's land. Loðmundur's slave informed his master that the sea had come in over the land, and Loðmundur, who was blind, asked to have a bowl of the water brought to him. He took a sip and noted that the water did not taste salty. He had his slave lead him to the stream. Putting the point of his staff into the water, he bit a metal ring on its end, whereupon the stream flowed westward onto Thrasi's land. The sorcerers sent the water back and forth between one another's farms until finally they agreed that the river should run where the distance to the sea was the shortest.

The discharge of Jökulsá during a typical jökulhlaup is 65,000 cubic yards per second. A bathtub holds roughly one cubic yard of water. Under normal conditions, the Mississippi River discharges about 18,000 bathtubsful of water per second. During a jökulhlaup the equivalent of three and a half Mississippis rush through one narrow valley south of Mýrdalsjökull.

In the eighteenth century a priest, Jón Thorláksson, made a written record of an eruption that took place beneath Öræfajökull, "Desert Glacier," in southeastern Iceland. The following is drawn from his account, as translated in Sir George S. Mackenzie's *Travels in Iceland* (1812):

> The Jökull itself exploded, and precipitated masses
> of ice, many of which were hurled out to the sea; but
> the thickest remained on the plain, at a short distance

from the foot of the mountain. The noise and reports continuing, the atmosphere was so completely filled with fire and ashes, that day could scarcely be distinguished from night, by reason of the darkness which followed, and which was barely rendered visible by the light of the fire that had broken through five or six cracks in the mountain. In this manner the parish of [Öræfi] was tormented for three days . . .

The surface of the ground was entirely covered with pumice-sand, and it was impossible to go out in the open air with safety, on account of the red-hot stones that fell from the atmosphere. Any who did venture out, had to cover their heads with buckets.

During the eruption, the priest rode to check on his parsonage. He and his companions could barely get their horses to swim the heated river. He found that his farm had been destroyed, including his tenant laborers' dwellings. When the jökulhlaup burst forth,

the people belonging to the parsonage were in four nearly-constructed sheep-cotes, where two women and a boy took refuge on the roof of the highest; but they had hardly reached it when, being unable to resist the force of the thick mud that was borne against it, it was carried away by the deluge of hot water and, as far as the eye could reach, the three unfortunate persons were seen clinging to the roof. One of the women was afterwards found among the substances that had proceeded from the Jökull, but burnt and, as it were, parboiled; her body was so soft that it could scarcely be touched . . . The sheep were lost; some of which were washed up dead from the sea in the third parish from [Öræfi]. The hay that was saved was found insufficient for the cows so that a fifth part of them had to be killed; and most of the horses which had not been swept into the ocean were afterwards found completely mangled.

The coast of southeastern Iceland has been scoured by one glacial burst after another. It is a bleak place, mile after mile of windblown sand with few farms and no towns. There are the Mýrdalssandur, the Meðallandssandur, the Brunasandur, and the vast, stream-veined Skeiðarásandur, 30 miles long and 15 miles wide. Skeiðarásandur lies on the plain below the Vatnajökull icecap, 3,000 feet deep at its thickest point.

Iceland is encircled by Highway 1, Hringvegur, the Ring Road. The Ring Road was completed in 1974, when a bridge system was built across Skeiðarásandur ("Sands of the River That Races"), the most extensive outwash area along the coast. Before the bridges went in, it was not possible to drive all the way around Iceland. The interior of the country is so volcanic, so carved with its own high-volume rivers, that only horse and jeep trails cross it. To get a sedan from Höfn in southeastern Iceland to Vík in southern Iceland, 120 air miles apart, required driving counterclockwise around the perimeter of Iceland, a two-day trip. Today the drive across the sands takes about three hours. (Don't try it on a windy day, our friend Thórður cautioned us, or the paint will be sandblasted off your car.)

The Ring Road does not resemble a modern highway. It has two lanes. Most of it remains unpaved; most of the bridges have only one lane. Yet the Ring Road seems to represent in the Icelandic consciousness an emergence from the old days of privation and severity, when the only way to travel was on foot or by horseback. The Ring Road is a lifeline to the present. It is thin and brittle, subject to breaching by jökulhlaup.

In October 1996, just over a month after we had returned home from Iceland, a volcano erupted beneath Vatnajökull. There are many volcanoes under the icecap; this was a previously unknown one, which was given the name Gjálp, after a troll woman in an old legend. Gjálp remained active for a month. Where the ice melted, the glacier slumped in on itself. A large basin beneath Vatnajökull began filling with meltwater. Above the basin, the ice was 800 feet thick. Slowly, like a lid on a boiling pot, Vatnajökull was lifted.

When the jökulhlaup came in early November, it released a flood of 45,000 cubic yards per second. The leading wave was fifteen feet tall. It washed away seven miles of the Ring Road, destroying one concrete-and-steel bridge and badly harming another. Damage to roads, bridges, and utility lines was estimated at 1.1 billion krónur, or about $16 million. No lives were lost. The Icelanders went to work repairing the roadway, and in three weeks the Ring Road was open to traffic again.

Because the Gjálp eruption took place in a sparsely settled area, and the volcano released little ash, the eruption became more of a media event than a catastrophe. Radio and television crews came from around the world to report on the situation. Icelanders sold T-shirts adorned with images of the steam cloud puffing above the glacier. New videos started showing up in the gift shops in Reykjavík, with footage taken from the airplanes that circled above Vatnajökull. Iceland's trademark phrase, "Fire and Ice," was trotted out again and again by the media.

The settlers of Iceland did not know what to make of the volcanoes that periodically laid waste to their adopted land. They shoveled the ash off their homefields. They buried their dead. They attributed the eruptions to the whims of the gods, to a witch's vengeance and sorcerers' stratagems and trolls' tricks. As the centuries passed, they suffered severely during times of intense volcanic activity.

Today's Icelanders reside on top of live magma and either realize it, when their houses go up and down as the magma moves within its chamber, or remain unaware. Active volcanic zones, including the one extending along Snæfellsnes, cover a third of Iceland. Not only in Reykjavík but in many parts of the country people warm their houses using geothermal heat. The earth-borne energy is piped to greenhouses and swimming pools.

I asked the geologist Haukur Jóhannesson what would happen if a big eruption took place in Iceland today. He said it depended on where the volcano was situated. An eruption in the interior, where no one lives, might not cause too much damage. An eruption near Reykjavík could disrupt power installations and freshwater pumping stations. An eruption that spread a lot of ash could cause agriculture to collapse all over Iceland. Or, if the wind was favorable, it might turn out to be just another tourist attraction.

Where we lived at Little Lava we were not susceptible to a jökulhlaup—although the folk directly *undir jökli*, in the farms and the few small towns at the end of Snæfellsnes, would have been. Still, a fissure could have opened in the lava field in our back yard. Or in Hnappadalur Valley, or in equally volcanic Hítardalur Valley one mountain range to the south. A new fiery schism could have appeared anywhere on Snæfellsnes, where the results of eons of volcanism rear their craggy heads above Faxaflói. If Snæfellsjökull had chosen the summer of 1996 to end its slumber, and if the wind had been out of the west, we could have been in trouble. There were times when I saw some real advantages to having an asbestos roof.

Two small eruptions did take place in Iceland during our summer at Little Lava. Each resulted in a brief jökulhlaup on the southern coast. Lacking a radio or a television, we never knew about them.

When someone I know has died and is gone from the
earth, I find that I look more carefully at the sky. At its color.
At the intensity of its light, at the zenith and on the horizon.
I look at clouds moving across the firmament, changing as
they travel. The sky is always different than before, and
never different, and the same can be said about life.

A sea mist pushed in over the mudflats, and clouds hung
low, masking the mountaintops. The sun pierced the overcast to spotlight various peaks: Skarðsheiði near Borgarnes,
Skyrtunna on Snæfellsnes, and a scarred crag whose name I
didn't know farther out on the peninsula.

It rained. It ceased raining. The tide fell, and birds arrived to feed on the flats.

In the afternoon Nancy, Will, and I walked across to Stóra Hraun. Parked in the farmyard was a blue Toyota pickup truck with an extended cab and a cap over the bed. Inside the house, drinking coffee at the kitchen table, were Kristinn Skarphéðinsson and his colleague, another ornithologist, whom Kristinn introduced to us as Arnór. (The name concatenates "Eagle" and "Thór.") Arnór was a burly man with a heavy brow and thick features. He and Kristinn were talking with Kristján of Stóra Hraun. They seemed to be discussing the local birdlife. I heard *stokkönd* (mallard), *urtönd* (teal), *fálki* (falcon), and *örn* (eagle).

Will would be staying the night at Stóra Hraun, since he was not capable of making the arduous trek that we were planning, across the lava to the eagles' nest. Margrét had been to Borgarnes and rented some videos of American movies; I asked her not to let him watch the more gruesome ones (the family's taste seemed to run toward vampires and ax murders). Nancy and I hugged Will goodbye and climbed into the Toyota.

Kristinn drove to where the power line crossed the road. We got out, and the two ornithologists debated whether or not to wear their waterproofs. "Will it rain?" Kristinn asked, looking at the sky. "Are we in Iceland?" I answered. Smiling, Kristinn donned his rain parka. He also put on an orange stocking cap, a souvenir from his graduate-school days in Wisconsin, where orange stocking caps blossom on the heads of thousands of deer hunters each autumn.

We followed the power line across a hayfield. Both Kristinn and Arnór were troll-like fellows, tall and broad; they advanced with long, ground-gobbling steps, and Nancy and I had to scramble to keep up. Arnór had brought along his Irish setter Snót (it means "girl" and is often used in romantic poetry), a sweet-tempered bitch who made me think of my spaniel back home. She coursed back and forth in front of us. Arnór said he used her to hunt ptarmigan.

The clouds lowered, and the sky got dark and gloomy. We splashed through a bog, jumped across a drainage ditch. The power line climbed into the lava field, where the footing became dry rubble. On both sides, the lava field spread out jagged and black. Rain began falling; we'd had enough rain in the last week that the spring in the cave was back to its normal level.

When we reached the correct power pole, I turned toward Eldborg. I found the eagles' spire and pointed it out to Kristinn. We left the power line and, trying to avoid the worst of the lava, worked our way toward the nest. We all split up—though we remained within sight of one another—each thinking he or she could find the smoothest route. I thought of my own personal Icelandic proverb: Through rough lava, each walker picks his own path.

The wind whistled through the angular slabs. Boulders groaned and shifted beneath our boots. Kristinn said the Icelanders have a name for such treacherous, unstable rocks: "Judas stones."

The eagles were perched separately. I was certain they had seen us the moment we entered the lava. One of the birds lifted off with a few economical wingbeats and glided toward us; then the other one took to the air. As the eagles circled above us, Kristinn pointed with his chin. "The female is bigger than the male, and her voice is lower." He said the eagles were old birds, evidenced by how pale their necks and heads were.

Arnór called Snót in and leashed her to a rock; he didn't want to whip the eagles into a greater fury by taking a foxlike creature near their nest. We crossed a low ridge of lava, and I pointed out the nest again. I hoped the eaglet would still be there.

When I had telephoned Kristinn and told him about the nest, he was elated. No one had known of any eagles nesting in that part of the Eldborg field since 1914, when the famous local priest, the Reverend Árni Thórarinsson of Stóra Hraun, had ordered a pair killed illegally and their nest destroyed. "What were you doing wandering around in there, anyway?" Kristinn had asked me. He chuckled. "No Icelander would have gone through that lava."

The eagles landed and quit scolding, as they had done when Gary and I got near their nest. Using my binoculars, I spotted the eaglet's round eye, which contrasted with the blotchy lichens on the rocks and the angular sticks that made up the nest. After I located its eye, the rest of the eaglet snapped into focus.

Nancy and I climbed onto the nearby fin of lava and settled in to watch. Taking careful handholds, Kristinn ascended the spire. I was surprised that the adult birds didn't attack him. They sat where they were, black gargoyles on the tilted slabs.

Kristinn edged around the rock to the nest. The eaglet hissed at him. It was fully feathered and looked like an adult bird, except for its black beak, which would turn yellow as the bird matured. The eaglet spread its wings. It opened its mouth menacingly. It reared back and presented its talons. Kristinn reached out and dropped his stocking cap over the eaglet's head. Gently he tipped the bird onto its side; it seemed to relax.

He got out a pair of pliers and the biggest bird band I had ever seen. He had a hard time getting the band to close satisfactorily around the eaglet's leg. "Some minor technical difficulties," he called over to us, flashing a smile. Meanwhile, Arnór was clambering over the rain-slick parapet, looking for prey remains and collecting shed feathers. Kristinn pried the steel band apart with the pliers and closed it again, seeking an exact fit. "This is the only time the eagle will have this experience," he said, "so it might as well enjoy it."

Finally he stood. "A nice, healthy bird. In a week or so, it should fly."

The scene was otherworldly: the mist-shrouded mountains, the black lava field, the light shifting erratically in the distance, rain coming in sideways, the tooth of rock with the two big men standing above the eaglet. Kristinn pushed buttons on a handheld Global Positioning System device that beeped as it communicated with satellites tracking invisibly across the heavens.

On our way back we picked up the whining, tail-wagging setter. We stopped on the power line right-of-way and had a bite to eat. Arnór put his sandwich down and raised his binoculars. Over the lagoon—which by now had half filled with the tide—was a small cloud, slightly darker than the overcast sky. The cloud resembled a dust devil. It expanded, contracted, vanished for a moment, then reappeared and went whirling off toward the north.

"Waders," Arnór said. "Dunlins, most likely."

"Arnór is studying the wading birds," Kristinn said. "Those are probably females. They tend to bail out early and leave their mates to finish up with the nestlings. They're not like the red-necked phalarope, where the female flies away right after the eggs are laid. The female dunlins just depart a little bit early in the fall."

We said goodbye. Kristinn and Arnór headed down the power line to their truck, and Nancy and I turned south toward Little Lava. The wind blew the rain in our faces. A long stretch of smooth lava snaked between areas of rough lava; we kept to the smooth as long as we could, then slowed as we entered the rough terrain. I watched for the fingerlike cairn and hoped that the mist would not thicken. We both stumbled along on leaden legs. Golden plovers flitted away from us over the heath. In Icelandic, the golden plover is the *heiðlóa*. The much smaller dunlin, which often feeds alongside the golden plover, is the *lóuthræll*, "the lóa's slave."

We found the tall cairn that leaned like a crooked finger. From there we had a trail. Finally we saw the chimney of Little Lava. The house came into view, as gray and subtle as the rest of the landscape. We went inside and took off our raingear. We were both shivering. I built a fire in the stove. We drank hot tea laced with whiskey and went to bed.

I woke in the middle of the night. From the kitchen window I looked out across the marsh. The outdoor electric lights had come on at the regional school. It was the first I'd seen them all summer. I remembered looking at the lights through the same window when Pétur and I had visited Little Lava the previous December. I remembered how the lights had glittered in the black night and the iron cold.

Now they shone against the deep gray mass of Hafursfell, whose upper half was lost in the clouds. The light of day was still present in the sky, but it was subdued and dingy. I felt a momentary unease, a vague dread. I wondered at the almost-physical sensation brought on, I was certain, by the intimation of night. It was the first real sign that summer was beginning to wind down. The dunlins had sensed it; so had the other birds, whose eyes and brains were calibrated to detect the shortening of the days. There is no reason to believe that our eyes and brains were insensitive to the waxing and waning of seasonal light. Summer was finite. Winter was stirring itself, a mute beast in the north. I checked my watch. It was 1:30 on the morning of July 18.

About an hour earlier, in the United States, where it was still the evening of July 17, a Trans World Airlines passenger jet had taken off from New York, headed for Paris.

The next afternoon we picked Will up at Stóra Hraun. Another cool, drizzling day. We drove to the school. I took a long shower, scrubbing off a week's worth of grime. I swam a few laps, from one end of the small pool to the other. I roughhoused in the water with Will, feeling his ribs and skinny arms and elbows and warm, slippery flesh. Nancy and I lingered in the hot pot, trying to banish the previous night's chill. Driving back to Little Lava, I turned on the car radio, set to a station in Reykjavík that could occasionally be picked up from the higher elevations; the station played classical music. We had listened to it perhaps three or four times all summer. By chance, we came in on a BBC report in English. It told of a Paris-bound jetliner that had exploded above the Atlantic off the coast of Long Island.

Nancy and I found the news more than usually disturbing. We hadn't read a newspaper in almost two months. We had isolated ourselves from knowledge of what was going on in the world: the ferry sinkings, tribal wars, epidemics, starvation, terrorist bombings, assassinations, murders—the innumerable sad events that, when you hear of them day in and day out, when they do not affect you directly, become numbingly routine. Living at Little Lava, we were absorbed in the land. We knew only its comprehensible tragedies: the sheep trapped in the lava, the skua chick vanished, the redshank in the fox's mouth. In those cyclings of life, death was transformed into survival and reproduction. Cloistered at Little Lava, we found the falling of a jetliner a stark reminder that we would have to leave this simple, basic place and return to a human world complicated with strife and pain.

On the way back we stopped at Stóra Hraun to pick up the wash that Margrét had done for us. Because of the rain, she had not hung it outside but had dried it in the warmth of the laundry room. She gave it to us folded neatly inside plastic grocery bags.

As usual, we were invited in for coffee. Margrét asked if we had heard about the American airplane. "It is so sad," she said, her face downcast. Then she brightened. A package had just come in the mail for William—she called him by the Icelandic "Vilhjálmur." I opened the cardboard box, and Will tore the wrapping paper off the presents inside: late-arriving birthday gifts from his cousins, Nancy's sister's children. A book. A board game. A card from his cousin Claire, a watercolor painting she had done of a blue heron in a marsh. Claire, age fifteen, had also sent a T-shirt with a design she had created herself, in which different kinds of insects depicted the letters of the alphabet.

Two days had passed when next we hiked across the flats from Little Lava. Nancy drove off in the car for a few days' travel on her own, to look around in an area fifty miles north, where she intended to set a historical novel. Will and I stayed for a while at Stóra Hraun. I talked to Margrét's son Alli, short for Arilíus. He was a tall, thin young man, shy but friendly, at home recuperating from an injury: he had almost severed his ring finger in an accident in the fish factory where he worked, farther out on Snæfellsnes. He had been flown in an airplane to Reykjavík, where the finger was surgically reattached; Kristinn Skarphéðinsson had told me that the event made the televised evening news.

Alli and I talked about trout fishing, which he very much liked to do. I made two telephone calls to the United States, to a man who was painting our house and to friends taking care of our dog. I timed the calls and kept them short; I would pay the folk at Stóra Hraun using the easily calculated overseas rate.

The moment I finished my second call and placed the receiver in its cradle, the telephone rang. Instinctively I picked up. I was surprised to hear English being spoken instead of Icelandic. Someone was asking for Nancy. I recognized my father-in-law's voice. He and our nephew Patrick were scheduled to join us in Iceland for ten days later in the month, and I assumed he was calling in regard to their trip. My father-in-law was confused for a moment by my answering the phone. Then I realized that his voice was freighted with something in addition to puzzlement. He asked if I had heard about the TWA jetliner. Our niece Claire had been a passenger on the plane.

I broke the news to Will as we sat on a rock next to the tidal lagoon. My heart ached for Claire, for her parents and grandparents and brothers, for all of us who had known and loved her. I felt sorry for my son. He was eight years old. How hard it must be, how threatening it must feel, when the world turns malign. It had been a grievous year for us in the wake of my mother's death. I had not told our new friends here at Stóra Hraun what had happened to my mother; it didn't seem they needed to know, and I didn't want them to think I came from a place where such things could happen. They knew about the plane crash, though, and about Claire, and had clearly been moved by our loss. For some reason I resolved to tell them now about Mom.

"Dad," Will asked, "what happened to the plane?"

"It blew up."

"Why did it blow up?"

"We don't know." I paused. "It could have been a bomb."

His face was twisted. "Somebody laid a bomb in the plane?"

"Will, honey, we just don't know."

He buried his face against my chest. I held him tight, and we cried together. Beside us the lagoon lay drained by the tide. Dunlins fed near the shore. Redshanks ran along on their lanky orange legs and halted suddenly to thrust their bills into the sand. Gulls flickered like falling snowflakes, landing far out on the glistening expanse.

I thought of the days we had spent at Little Lava. I had found solace in the sea, the birds, the mountains, the unsparing light, the blue vistas opening in all directions. Iceland did not lack for dangers. A volcano could erupt. There were perilous currents in the waters, and the implacable tide. Holes and cracks in the lava. Falling rocks. Winds to blow a hiker off a cliff. One could prepare for such dangers. One could not always avoid them, but precautions could be taken.

Nature was indifferent to the fate of a wagtail, an eagle, a human. I found no evil in that indifference.

A call had been placed to the hotel where Nancy would be staying. I needed to go back to Stóra Hraun and wait for her to telephone me. Nancy's father had said that the family wanted us home in Pennsylvania. We would try to go there, and we would come back to Little Lava as soon as we could.

Almost two weeks had passed.

I sat on the edge of the lava field looking down at the house at Little Lava. While we were in Pennsylvania, the grass had ripened. It lay like a lavender haze covering the thúfur and the turf-covered ruins and lapping against the house. The grass shushed in the wind. The lagoon was a shimmering silver. Across the bay stood the mountain Halldór Laxness called "the soul clad in air." On this cloudless night in early August, Snæfellsjökull had a cerulean base that graded up into a pinkish-blue apex, set against a sky awash in spectral colors: cantaloupe fading upward into lemon, the lemon darkening to a delicate blue-green, then marine blue, then purple blue.

At first America had been foreign, dreamlike. We were met at the airport in Baltimore by the driver of a van dispatched by a friend who owns a small company near our home. The van carried us northward into night. The darkness was palpable, like a thick black veil. I had not seen darkness for two months. In Pennsylvania the summer had been rainy, the driver said; it had rained that day, and as the van eased down our driveway around midnight, it seemed we were descending into a well. The branches of trees hung down over the road and pushed out into the house clearing. Water dripped from the green, full leaves.

In the morning we drove the seventy miles to Montoursville for Claire's memorial service and funeral. Her body had been one of the first recovered from the sea. Other families grieved for children who were still missing. I felt like an empty vessel that the wind blew into and out of again. They asked me to read from the Bible at Claire's service, and I was glad to do so. I don't remember now what I read. There were many mourners in the church. As we rode to the cemetery, we passed a church where another child was being lamented. We stayed for several days in that town where people mourned with great dignity and strength the lives that had been lost: twenty-one students and chaperons with the high-school French club.

Nancy, Will, and I went home to our house in the woods. We had to camp out in one end of the house because of the painting being done in the other end. My friend brought our dog to us. I tried to make myself avoid anything having to do with my mother and her death and found I could not. I called up the people I had rented the house to. I checked in with the prosecutor and found out the status of the criminal investigation; the trial would not be held for months yet. I talked over the phone with both my brothers. The best thing Nancy and I did was to put the canoe on the truck and drive to a lake and paddle through the water weeds into the hazy distance and beach on a point of land and pick blueberries in a bog.

We returned to Iceland on the same flight as Nancy's father and our nephew Patrick. Thirteen days had passed since the explosion, which was now being referred to as the TWA Flight 800 disaster. Patrick, age thirteen, was Claire's younger brother. I was surprised that their parents would let him fly so soon after Claire's death. I was touched that they would entrust him to us, and I was proud of him for deciding to go ahead with the trip that he had been looking forward to. Neither Nancy nor I spoke of the fact that we had asked Claire to be with us all summer.

In Iceland we were met with deep and sincere sympathy: from Pétur and Anna; from Thórður and his parents, who put me up in their home; from other friends who took in the rest of our party; from the employees at Icelandair, the national airline, who had arranged our travel on such short notice and had even flown us first class. Our neighbors at Stóra Hraun were waiting for us with fresh bread and rhubarb jam.

Claire was Nancy's *systurdóttir*. The Icelanders place a great value on kinship ties. The fabric of Icelandic society has depended on such linkages since the time of settlement. In Iceland any male relative, no matter how distant, is your *frændi*, your kinsman; any female relative is your *frænka*, your kinswoman. The Icelandic language includes terms for one's brother's wife's sister, one's grandfather's brother's son. And Icelanders—living in a rugged land, where many are engaged in dangerous work, where the trials of the past remain vivid in the national mind—are not strangers to the emotions wrought by untimely death.

The logistics of getting back to Little Lava had been complicated by the fact that all of us plus our luggage could not fit in the Mitsubishi sedan. So Nancy had driven north, with her father, Will, and Patrick, while I had taken the bus. I got off in Borgarnes at about the same time that Nancy was depositing her father, the boys, and the luggage at Little Lava. She made one trip across the mudflats, escorting her father and the boys (Patrick carrying his Boy Scout pack, Will a rucksack) and leaving her pack and a couple of bags on the far shore. She and her father hiked back to the car, he to make a second haul on his own, she to fetch me. Time was of the essence; it was stórstreymi, the spring tide, and we wanted to make our crossings before the tide rose.

As Nancy was passing Stóra Hraun, Veiga flagged her down and asked if she would buy her a pair of shoes. Nancy did not know how to explain in Icelandic that we were in a hurry and this was not an ideal time for a shopping trip— worse yet, she couldn't understand what kind of shoes Veiga wanted, what size, or where to get them. Nancy told Veiga to come along. She waited while Veiga went back inside to wash up and change into clean clothes for the trip into town.

In the meantime, I was sitting alongside the road with my back against a signpost. It was a warm sunny day, August 1. Highway 1, the Ring Road, went through Borgarnes. The traffic was steady.

Across the street stood a two-story stucco building. I think it was a doctor's office. A door opened in the building. A woman, short of stature and gray-haired, came out.

It was my mother. It was not simply a woman who looked like my mother, for one brief moment, it was my mother in actuality. My heart filled with love, which slowly turned to pain. The woman had come onto the sidewalk, turned, and walked toward the center of town. She took short, toed-out steps. She was Icelandic, of course, and I had never seen her before.

Many cars had passed before I finally spotted the Mitsubishi; Nancy beeped the horn. While Veiga headed for a nearby sporting-goods shop, Nancy and I filled a cart with food at the truck stop's small grocery. Then we had to find Veiga again. We finally located her inside the truck stop, wearing new white-and-purple running shoes and licking an ice-cream cone. We got her into the sedan and flew back to Little Lava. We practically shoved her out of the car at Stóra Hraun, stuffed the groceries into our backpacks, and hoofed it onto the mudflats. The tide had turned two hours earlier and was rising quickly to the flood. It came skating in across the sun-warmed flats. We could see the stream channels broaden as we walked. We took off our boots, rolled up our pants, and sloshed across.

At the house we roared with laughter when Nancy's father described how he had sunk into the sucky mud, stood there trapped, almost fell over while trying to pull loose, and nearly left his boots embedded in Löngufjörur.

We already knew that others had been to Little Lava in our absence. Oddný and her daughter Síf had arrived to pick berries—we had invited them to come while we were in residence and were sorry to have missed them—and Pétur and his brother Gunnar had shown up the same day. The mice, which we'd gotten under control with traps and by securing the food inside lidded buckets and in the cupboard, had been encouraged by opened packages left on tables and shelves and uneaten food scraps dumped in the trash can. Cigarette ashes smudged the floor. A handful of coins had been left strewn on the table. Nothing to do but laugh some more—at least partially at our own heightened sense of propriety toward Little Lava—and get out the broom and dustpan.

Now, three days after our return, I sat on the edge of the lava field, soaking up the magic of the Iceland summer, the dwindling Iceland summer, and of the lonely farm, Little Lava.

The sun had gone behind the mountains. The air was tranquil. Snæfellsjökull had turned a deep blue, and the colors had cooled in the sky. The breeze pushed through the grass, the ripe full grass of the homefield. I realized I was not hearing something that had been with us all summer: snipe in their territorial flight, the tremulous, ascending tune that Nancy said sounded like elves laughing.

I could see Claire's face more clearly than I could see my mother's: there had been pictures of her displayed throughout Nancy's sister's house. Claire was tall and pretty, with fair skin and a splash of freckles across her nose. I remembered her coming to Nancy's and my wedding, a perky little girl in a dress. I remembered a recent outing that she and I had taken together in my canoe, on the same lake where we picked the berries, and I remembered thinking, as I looked at her in the bow, that Claire was a woman now, that her life lay before her like the lake opening up before the canoe's prow.

I felt tired and still empty and, in some confusing way, closer to a state of acceptance. I was not alone in my pain —which had been added to so recently. Of course, I had known that fact intellectually. But to see others grieving as desperately as I had grieved for my mother brought the message home. I was not the only person in the world with a broken heart, I was not even the only one in my immediate family. I hoped that Little Lava would prove a healing place for Nancy's father and Patrick, as it had for me.

In the marsh, the bog cotton glowed in the pale, clear light. Sheep moved about grazing, the lambs almost as large now as their mothers. The tide had filled the lagoon and swallowed up Stakkholtssteinn; the water had begun fanning out across the land.

I looked at the soul clad in air. It had grown cold and distant. I raised my eyes in the direction the summit pointed. In the sky, straight overhead, a pinprick of light. A star twinkled, the first star I had seen in Iceland all summer.

16 | *Windland*

The days were growing shorter. At night, when the sky was clear, we could see more stars. Cassiopeia's wobbly W, the Big and Little Dippers. On cloudy nights Snæfellsnes faded into the gloom; on the peninsula farm lights twinkled like stars that had fallen to earth. Indoors we lit candles and lamps; no longer could we read in bed much past ten o'clock.

By day, Will and Patrick ranged over the homefield and explored the fringe of the lava. Will seemed to have finally accepted Little Lava as home. His favorite pastime was keeping the sheep away, so that they wouldn't leave their droppings all around the house for us to track inside; Thórður had suggested that Will take on this chore. Pretending his broomstick was a spear, he stalked the sheep, then went charging at them, hurling his weapon and sending them pounding off through the grass. He earned himself a nick-name: "Vilhjálmur Sheep-Bane."

One evening a fox showed up at our food dump. It was a pup, newly out on its own. When Will and Patrick approached, the fox slunk off a short distance into the lava and stood with its ears pricked; later it returned to feeding on scraps. It showed so little fear of humans that I ran at it, gave a yell, and chased it off. It needed educating, otherwise it wouldn't last long among the watchful farmers.

Grasses in the marsh changed color, from the spectrum of greens to orange and cinnamon and bronze. Wind attacked the cotton grass, stripping away the seedheads and sending the white fluff skittering across the bog. Golden plovers had begun flocking; bands of twenty and thirty fed in concert on the mudflats, then flew into the heath to rest.

In the lava, the heather bloomed purple. Leaves of blue-berry and crowberry turned a rich mauve; we picked the berries and ate them on the spot, or took them home and mixed them with skyr, the Icelandic yogurt. The berries were small and seedy, neither as sweet nor as abundant as the blueberries we had picked in the bog back in Pennsylvania, which seemed so far away in time and distance.

I wondered how Patrick and my father-in-law were coping with Claire's death. We had talked about it so much back in America; now it seemed there wasn't much left to say. She was my father-in-law's first grandchild. Gone. Like my mother, she had left a hole in our world so vast that the wind moaned through it.

We took our guests to favorite spots. We crept the Mitsu-bishi up Hítardalur Valley on a red-gravel road that wound surreally between tan, chocolate, and black lava flows. The valley was a lonely place, with a few farms and trout-fishing huts. At the lake at the head of the valley the midges were fierce, flying with persistence into our faces. We ate lunch on the windiest point we could find, then bundled ourselves back into the car and left.

We went to Akrar, where Gary and I had chivvied the young gulls down the beach ahead of us. It was a rainy, blowy morning; kelp lay in windrows on the sand. The young of the black-backed gulls were completely aerial and capable. Arctic terns, which a month before had pressed home their attacks so vigorously, remained irascible, but were not so aggressive. Their young sat at the foot of the dunes and lifted into the wind, trying out their wings; then they set down clumsily on the sand. The tails of the juvenile birds were shorter and less prominently forked than the magnificent V's of the adults. Along the beach, parents were landing with minnows in their beaks; the young terns would crouch, gape their bills, bob their black-capped heads, and beg in mewling tones.

At Skógarnes, the farm of Trausti, Guðríður, and President Clean Tone, we walked the golden beach. In pebbly stretches, bright stones shifted and tinkled in the waves' wash. On down the peninsula, Snæfellsjökull glistened; one of the mountain's horns showed up black, melted free of snow.

Turnstones were working the tide line, stocky sandpipers whose pale faces were overlain with dark bars like the visor of a knight's helmet. The turnstones used their faintly up-turned bills to flip over small stones and pieces of seaweed, searching for food. Turnstones do not breed in Iceland. The birds nest in Greenland and on the wilderness islands of northern Canada; they winter in western Europe and stop off in Iceland on their way there. Their presence on Löngu-fjörur was another sign that summer was drawing to a close.

Nancy took Will, Patrick, and her father on a trip to Breiðafjörður, on the north side of Snæfellsnes. I stayed behind. In the morning I fished, with the usual results. I walked the sands, watching the birds that were gathering. I made oatmeal for supper. I drank a cup of coffee, sitting on the stoop. I lit a candle and read a chapter in *Njál's Saga*, often described as the greatest of the classical Icelandic sagas. The sagas are full of strife and feuding and loyalty and faith; many scholars consider them the finest literature of the Middle Ages. But the words slipped through my mind like dust.

I thought of Mom and Claire. Which was the more tragic death? Was it possible or even profitable to compare them? My mother had lived seventy-three years. She had married and raised a family and watched her sons go on to have families of their own; she had held her grandchildren in her arms. Claire had died before her life ever bloomed.

The world was an uncertain place. If fate could emerge and wipe out my mother and my niece, it could do the same, at any moment, to my wife, my son, or me. All my life I had known that evil existed and had power; one had only to pick up a newspaper, open a book. I had respected it chiefly by acknowledging it. I had never thought it would strike so close to me.

. . .

Little Lava was such a windy place that only twice all summer did I see a millpond reflection on the waters of the
lagoon. Those waters were far from smooth one evening
when, for the first time since we'd returned from the United
States, I got out my kayak and carried it down to the bight
near the house.

Late evening, the rising tide. Nancy, her father, and the
boys came to see me off. I put Will in the kayak and walked it
a few feet out into the lagoon. I let him paddle back to shore.

I fitted myself into the hull. The kayak felt tricky and
strange for a few minutes; then it was familiar again. My
paddle circled and dipped, slit the water and dug into it. A
tern greeted me by fluttering above my head, opening its
blood-red mouth, and screeching. Gray clouds held low in
the north. On the great bay Faxaflói, out beyond Barnasker,
gulls were hovering and diving into the water; they looked
like grains of salt and pepper. Beyond lay the flat gray line
of the horizon. The world looked as if it ended there.

I had to work to make headway against the wind, which
was blowing in conjunction with the tide. I quit paddling,
and the kayak stopped dead. The wind pushed the bow
around. I let the wind turn the boat in a half circle.

The beach was empty; everyone had gone back to the
house. Just like that, I was alone. From where I floated I
could not see a person or a farm or a road. Lined up with
Eldborg's crater was the house at Little Lava, the only man-
made structure in view: the house that had held us, kept us
together, provided shelter and a focal point on the land-

scape. I had come to love that austere dwelling. How fine it would be, I thought, if we could slow time down; if we could linger here, drawing out the days. But time works in an opposite manner. As the summer passed, the days shortened and came faster, today on the heels of yesterday, tomorrow crowding in. As a middle-aged man, I was starting to feel the same way about life.

Turning the boat back around, I applied myself to my paddling. I was a long time traveling down the lagoon. I wanted to cruise around the Stóra Hraun Islands, slip between them or between the larger island and the end of the peninsula, and paddle into the far side of the lagoon. But I did not like what was happening on the water.

The swell continued to build the farther I went. The wind pushed the tide against the boat's left bow. Waves washed over the bow and ran down the length of the deck. I could feel the thump as each wave hit, then the kayak rising and flexing as the wave passed over and around it. The kayak bucked up and down, up and down. At the bottom of each trough I would find myself looking at a foam-flecked green wall. As I paddled, the kayak would start to climb the wall and punch through the wave about halfway up; then it would plummet again.

From a crest I noticed that some waves were breaking before they reached me. Most of the waves were quartering toward me on the port side, at about ten o'clock, while others came slanting in from starboard. Where the two trains of waves collided, the water frothed. I concluded that I was in the salmon river's flow—among the straumur, or currents, that people had warned me about.

Between the peninsula and the island, waves were breaking on partly submerged rocks. I decided not to try threading that needle. In the stream farther along, eiders were bobbing about, scarcely paying attention to my boat. Or so it seemed: I didn't have time to give them more than a quick glance. I had to gauge each wave as it raced toward the bow, knife the bow through the wave, paddle hard to make a little headway, and position the bow to deal with the next roller. When I read a wave incorrectly, it would crash down onto the deck—then I had to brace with my paddle to keep the boat upright.

On this one evening I had not worn my dry suit. I hadn't wanted to fight my way into the thing (the gaskets that fit around my neck, wrists, and ankles were more than tight), hadn't wanted to get all sweated up. Now I cursed my laziness.

I kept paddling. I drew near the opening between the two islands. I dropped my guard for a moment and the swell shoved me sideways. I felt the kayak tip and trimmed it by shifting my weight. The boat was lifted up and hurled back by the combined forces of the wave and a gust of wind. I drew the stern around quickly to get the bow pointed at the next roller. Next and next and next.

I did not want to swamp. I admitted to myself that I was afraid. The water was cold. The current was stealthy and powerful. Tide, wind, and river flow: I could not make sense of those forces.

In the back of my mind lay the old superstition that bad things happen in threes. I did not want a third bad thing to befall my family. I thought of Nancy and Will. I knew now that I would not kayak out on Faxaflói. I would not run the millrace past Barnasker; I would not try launching through the surf from Gamlaeyri. I would not venture down the coast to explore the Hvalseyjar. My kayaking teacher, Nigel Foster, would be disappointed in me. But I sensed my limitations, both physical and mental, and did not want to take a chance.

My trip to the far side of the lagoon could wait. I let the next wave sweep past me, then quickly turned the boat 180 degrees. I pointed the bow toward Little Lava. I had to paddle harder on my left side than on my right, to keep the kayak aimed for the house. The wind plastered my jacket against my back. It tried to blow the paddle out of my hands. With each wave I would feel the boat shoot forward, riding on the crest; I would hear the gurgle as the moving water carried me. Then the kayak's momentum would slacken when the wave surged on ahead.

A big wave struck as I planted the paddle. The gunwale dipped. I lifted my right leg and straightened my left leg and swung my torso away from the water. The kayak righted. I pressed the paddle blade onto the water to steady myself. I started watching each wave out of the tail of my eye. I ruddered with the paddle and quit trying to propel the boat.

I let the tide carry me home.

There was an old saying that Icelanders lived with one foot on the land and the other in the sea. It meant that people depended equally on farming and fishing for their livelihood. Both were risky enough, although the chances for dying were greater when fishing. I can hardly imagine rowing out onto the ocean in the open boats that fishermen used until well into this century. Today the Icelanders have larger and more modern vessels, but men are still lost at sea. Storms blow up quickly, and predicting the weather is difficult: there are no weather stations immediately west of Iceland, where most of the storms originate.

The strongest blow I ever encountered in Iceland reached Force 8 on the Beaufort scale—gale force, with winds that were sustained at between 39 and 46 miles an hour, and with even more powerful gusts. The storm occurred while I was hunting ptarmigan during my visit to the West Fjords in November 1988. The evening of the storm coincided with the presidential election in the United States. The Icelanders with whom I was staying were more interested in the election results than I was. Late into the evening they sat around the television, eating and drinking and watching the early returns. The storm screamed around the eaves. I went to sleep in an upstairs room with wind ruckus filling my ears. In the morning my friends told me that George Bush had defeated Michael Dukakis, which is what I had told them was going to happen. Outside, the wind still shrieked and battered.

I went out to see what was happening. It was hard just staying on my feet. The wind cut through my clothing and chilled me. It wrapped my coat around me and threatened to blow me across the garden and into the fjord.

The gulls seemed to be at ease in the storm; when one of them wanted to get somewhere, it would face into the wind and let itself be blown backward, peeking over its shoulder and making adjustments with its wings until it reached its destination. The man who lived at the farm, Einar, said that this was a mild storm compared to some he had seen.

The farm's name was Botn, which meant "Bottom" and referred to its location at the bottom, or the extreme end, of a fjord. The valley that ascended from the fjord was narrow at first; then it widened as it mounted to the highlands. If the wind came from the highlands, Einar told me, the valley funneled it down so that it blew past the house with a greatly increased force. Sometimes Einar would get home in his truck and have to crawl to the front door on hands and knees to avoid being rolled away. Once, he claimed, a gust picked up a shed that was full of old cast-iron radiators, carried the building and its contents over a waist-high fence, and deposited them in the fjord.

Later we learned that, in the night, the storm had torn the roofs off several buildings in a nearby town. At a local salmon-raising operation, the wind was strong enough to blow fish out of the tanks in which they were swimming; employees spent the night crouched in the lee of the tanks, scooping up the salmon and putting them back in the water. Power was lost throughout the region, although not at Botn, which had its own water-powered generator emplaced in the stream that came tumbling down the valley.

Recently I read of a storm hitting the West Fjords with gusts recorded at 107 knots, or 123 miles an hour; sustained winds were in the neighborhood of 90 miles an hour. A wind is considered to have achieved hurricane force when it reaches 74 miles an hour. The wind peeled the pavement off streets. It pushed the sea into fishing villages, wrecking docks and houses. Grétar, Thórður's father, once told me that his forebears should not have called their home "Iceland." "Windland would have been a better name," he said.

The French explorer and oceanographer Jean Baptiste Étienne Auguste Charcot lived from 1867 to 1936. He carried out extensive charting around the Antarctic Peninsula, where an island is named for him; he studied plankton in the English Channel and conducted oceanographic inquiries in the Hebrides, the Arctic, and off the coast of Greenland. His ship was named *Pourquoi Pas?* In French. *Pourquoi pas?* means "Why not?"

The *Pourquoi Pas?* weighed 449 tons. A steamship, it was also equipped with sails. It was 140 feet long and had a beam of 31 feet, a polar vessel stoutly built to withstand the pressure of pack ice. In August 1936 it had picked up four members of a Franco-Swiss expedition that had crossed the Greenland ice cap. *Pourquoi Pas?* put into Reykjavík for minor repairs. While the ship was in port, the polar explorer and ethnologist Vilhjálmur Stefánsson, a friend of Dr. Charcot, spent a day on board the vessel. It was fortunate for the Greenland explorers that they hitched a ride back to Europe on a Danish mail steamer.

On the afternoon of September 15, the *Pourquoi Pas?* left Reykjavík and steamed northwest through Faxaflói Bay. The ship was bound for France. That night a storm came, with winds estimated at 70 miles an hour. The captain of *Pourquoi Pas?*, whose name was Le Conniac, decided to turn back to the harbor. But the wind and a strong current had forced the vessel so far off course that the captain mistook one lighthouse for another. The ship ran onto a reef. The engine stopped. The captain tried to set the sails to get away from the rocks, but the maneuver failed. The *Pourquoi Pas?* was blown onto another rock, called Hnokki, which means "Urchin."

In the dark, *Pourquoi Pas?* broke apart and began sinking. Waves swept over the decks, snapping masts and carrying sailors into the sea. Crew members tried to launch lifeboats, but these overturned or were dashed against the side of the ship. In the morning, the inhabitants of farms and hamlets along the coast found wreckage floating in the water and a life preserver bearing the ship's name. A little later they spied a man holding on to a piece of wood—or perhaps he had lashed himself to the wood—which was variously described in newspaper articles as a cabin door and a gangplank. The Icelanders brought the man ashore, wrapped him in blankets, and got some hot coffee into him; according to an account published in *The New York Times*, the sailor murmured his name, Eugène Gouidec, "and fell into a deathlike sleep."

A Danish sloop and an Icelandic gunboat picked twenty-four bodies out of Faxaflói, all of them wearing lifebelts. Six other bodies washed ashore. The men had not drowned; they had died of exposure in the frigid water. Corpses were laid in a row on a grassy slope in front of the farmhouse where Eugène Gouidec was sleeping. Dr. Charcot, the *Times* reported, was still "in a blue travel suit and his characteristic black collar and tie." Photographs show a line of men apparently sleeping peacefully. Gouidec was the only survivor. He had spent five hours in the sea. He woke up the next day; with his eyes so swollen by the salt water that they would hardly open, he told what had happened. As *Pourquoi Pas?* began breaking up, Charcot stood on the bridge alongside Captain Le Conniac. Charcot had a pet, a gull which he kept in a cage. The bird had flown aboard the ship off Greenland; exhausted, it refused to leave. Charcot kept the gull as a bird of good omen, letting it fly around the ship during the day and confining it at night. According to Gouidec, Charcot went below and brought the bird's cage on deck, opened the door, and let the gull fly away. Then he resumed his position on the bridge of the sinking ship.

The bodies were brought to Reykjavík aboard an Icelandic fishing vessel. As the boat docked, bells tolled throughout the city and two thousand citizens stood silently at quayside. On a farm fifty miles north of the capital, near where *Pourquoi Pas?* had wrecked, a six-year-old girl named Ásta, who would someday become a writer, learned about the sinking of the ship. And a part of the ship, a beautiful piece of reddish wood painted blue, came drifting into the lagoon next to the farm called Litla Hraun.

Icelanders are accustomed to saving foreigners from their country's inhospitable land and waters. In 1947 a British fishing trawler, the *Dhoon*, foundered off Látrabjarg, a cliff wrapping around the westernmost jut of the West Fjords, eight miles of basaltic ramparts upon which millions of sea-birds nest. The local people make a practice of lowering themselves on ropes to gather eggs from the nests. When the trawler slammed into Látrabjarg, residents of a nearby village roped down to the wreck and hauled twelve crew members to safety. Halfway up the cliff, they stopped on a ledge and fed the sailors hot soup before drawing them the rest of the way up.

One often hears of English, French, and German tourists being helicoptered to safety, generally off Iceland's glaciers. One Norwegian in particular needed a lot of rescuing. First he tried to kayak from Greenland to Iceland and was caught in drift ice. A polar bear, out wandering on the floes, watched him for a while, sizing him up. The Norwegian activated a rescue signal in a radio set he was carrying, and an Icelandic helicopter came and picked him up. To his dismay, they would not take along his kayak. Six months later the same chap, whom my friends uniformly referred to as "that stupid Norwegian," dropped his Global Positioning System device overboard while paddling his (new) kayak off Iceland's south coast. At the time, the swells were so deep that his radio would not transmit when his kayak was in the bottom of a trough. The Norwegian was not shy about sending out another Mayday.

As I was writing this book, I learned that, within a period of six days, storms around Iceland had sunk a fishing trawler off the Reykjanes Peninsula, a container vessel off eastern Iceland, and another container ship on the sands of the south coast. In those six days, one sailor and one rescuer drowned.

The Icelandic Coast Guard helicopter *Líf*, or *"Life,"* rescued thirty-nine seamen, lifting them off the decks of the disabled boats or plucking them out of the water. In one instance ten sailors wearing inflatable cold-water suits had linked their arms together and stayed afloat for two hours as thirty-foot waves washed oil and debris over them.

For three days it rained and blew. Mostly we stayed indoors, playing cards, reading, talking, eating. Soon Nancy's father and Patrick would go home. Nancy, Will, and I would be leaving Little Lava in just over two weeks. It made me sad, knowing we had to go. I was also starting to look forward to our home in Pennsylvania—our house, our dog, our friends. I had kept notes on things that had happened in Iceland, bird sightings and weather and occurrences on the heath, the beach, and the marsh. I wanted to start writing again; I wanted to try to resume my life.

When the storm ended and the clouds broke up, a peak on Snæfellsnes was dusted with new snow. With the kayak beneath my arm, and sheep scattering in front of me, I splashed through the bog to the launching bay. I packed food and water in the kayak. The tide, as usual, was opposed to my plans, although the wind was agreeable, coming down Hnappadalur Valley and pushing at my back.

I paddled down the lagoon and entered the river's current, where the chop today was not severe. Eiders floated in the channel. Included in the black-and-white throng—there must have been a thousand ducks—was a single white swan. As I drew close to them, the eiders growled and dived, or went flailing off across the water: maybe they were still molting and could not fly. The flock parted for me. On both sides, frantic wings sounded like concert-hall applause.

Beyond the Stóra Hraun Peninsula was a low island edged with tan boulders and covered with grass and with figures that, from a distance, resembled people.

I beached the boat. Pieces of driftwood stuck up all over the island, leaning at crazy angles. Clothing scraps hanging from the driftwood flapped in the wind. Wooden uprights were encircled by rusty zippers, all that remained of clothes that had disintegrated in the salt air. One scarecrow had an orange trawler buoy for a head. A plastic pipe sticking up from the ground gave voice to the wind.

At the scarecrows' feet were eider nests beneath crude shelters made of boards, flat stones, and plastic scraps. Pale olive-colored eggshells lay in and around the nests. The down had not yet been harvested from the nests: property of the farm Hausthús.

On a distant beach, seals lay like bright metal shavings. No sounds but the lapping of water, wind lamenting through the pipe, and gulls screaming. Oystercatchers and redshanks peered around rocks at me. Black-headed gulls with their half-black pates and pert pointed tails floated in the water. It was not absolutely clear from my map, but I believed I was on Bæjarey, the site of the old church whose parishioners had drowned at Christmastime in 1562, when their boat was sunk by the current. Depressions in the grass and swatches of darker green implied building foundations. No sign of any graves. The church had been known as Haffjarðareyjarkirkja, "Church of the Islands of the Sea-Fjord River."

According to the biography of the Reverend Árni Thórarinsson, after the drowning took place the church was relocated to a farm, Hrossholt, and from there it was moved to Rauðamel in Hnappadalur Valley, where it remains today. The Reverend Árni said that the graveyard on Bæjarey became eroded by the waves, and that he reinterred many bones, with sermons and psalms. At one point Vilhjálmur Stefánsson came to the island and, with Church permission, collected some of the bones for Harvard University. Árni helped the noted explorer, who, to the good Reverend's chagrin, proved to be an unbeliever. ("They are all unbelievers, and godless, these bone-diggers," the Reverend Árni opined.)

Árni noted that the teeth in the skulls were unusually sound and healthy-looking. Two of the skulls were odd, in that they lacked sutures, the jagged lines where the bones knit together: skulls as smooth as billiard balls. Árni asked the archaeologist about them.

Stefánsson examined the skulls. "They are from the Anglo-Saxon race," he replied. "Most likely seafaring men who washed up here on land."

The tide was ebbing. Paddling back from Bæjarey, I troubled the eiders again. A dozen geese flew overhead; they circled, locked their wings, and descended like falling leaves to land upon the draining lagoon.

River, tide, and wind were urging me toward the channel mouth. However, there was no turbulence, since the forces were acting in unison. All it took was hard paddling to free myself from their grip.

17 | *Leaving the North*

One morning I went out on the sands and found that the
terns had gone. The flats were crowded with gulls and shorebirds, loose groupings of mixed species, and not a tern
among them. Not one, to hold above a stream peering down
for its prey, to come at me on graceful wings, and dart and
stoop, and float above and fill the air with invective.

The terns had gone, and with them the summer. On the
days that the sun shone, the air was warm enough; but when
clouds filled the sky and the wind blew, there was a chill
that had not been present in July or the first half of August.
The nights grew longer and darker. There was a somberness
to the landscape. One had the sense that change had slowly
and imperceptibly taken place and that greater, swifter
change was coming.

With their departure, the terns had resumed their wandering. As well as in Iceland, Arctic terns breed in Greenland, northern Canada, Alaska, Siberia, on Spitzbergen and the rest of the Svalbard Islands, in Finland, Sweden, and Norway—all the lands ringing the north. As summer ebbs, the terns are a white wave that will wash its way to the Antarctic.

Terns from Iceland fly southeast to Britain; they join with others of their kind from Scandinavia and Russia, then head south past the Iberian Peninsula and the bulge of West Africa. Off Cape Verde, it is thought that the wave divides. Most of the terns curve back along the African continent, while a lesser number of them veer off to the west, fly across the Atlantic, and resume their southerly course along the coast of Brazil.

The prevailing winds push the greater company of the terns eastward until they are in the southern Indian Ocean. They find good feeding along the edge of the pack ice as it retreats with the Antarctic summer. Terns enjoy two summers a year, one in the north and the other in the south. A tern sees more daylight than any other living creature. When it is time to head north again, the birds have worked their way south of the Atlantic. In a year, a tern may travel 25,000 miles, a distance equal to the circumference of the earth.

On the flats near Stakkholtssteinn I counted fifty-six golden plovers. Feeding steadily, they paid no attention to me, other than to shuffle aside as I moved among them.

Hiking seaward, I came upon long tongues of weed lying oriented with the retreating tide. The weed looked like green paint strokes on a canvas.

Six riders and a strong dozen of loose horses passed between me and the salmon river. The horses looked the size of ants. But even at that distance I could see them lining out in the *tölt*, the signature ground-gobbling gait of the Icelandic horse. At the tölt, the horse lets its feet fly and arches its neck while its back remains level—riding on a tölting horse, you can carry a stein of beer at arm's length and not spill a drop. Nancy had twice gone out with Haukur when he guided tourist groups across the sand; Haukur gave her his mare Elfa, or "Elf," a good tölter. Nancy described the tölt as the most comfortable, least-jarring riding rhythm she had ever experienced.

The horses crossed the stream channel with a noise that sounded more like crackling than splashing. They traveled up the Stóra Hraun Peninsula, past where we parked our car. Now, though, the parking spot was vacant: Nancy, along with Will, had driven her father and Patrick back to Reykjavík for their flight home. I was on my own for several days. Solitude, which had been torture three months ago, I could now endure. Still, I wanted to keep myself busy.

I tramped across the tide-scoured flats. A band of gulls let me get to within a hundred yards; I stopped and stood still, and they went back to feeding. They lined the freshwater stream like hogs at a trough. Occasionally one would strike out with its beak when another gull got too close. The birds lifted up clots of seaweed, shook them, and snatched up any food that was dislodged.

A redshank flopped around in a stream channel. At first I thought it was wounded and writhing in extremis; when it lifted its head and started preening, I realized it was just cleaning itself. It splashed and tumbled so violently that it caused a gull to walk away and then stop and look back over its shoulder.

Rain started falling. I shook out my parka, which was enough to send the redshank fleeing, the gulls flapping into the air. The gulls circled and set down near a group of wading birds all huddled together, each with its head held tight against its body, many of them standing on one leg.

The waders, numbering at least a hundred, seemed communally skittish and lifted off in unison before I could get close. They wheeled past me in a tight formation, showing flashes of white and giving an overall impression of a rust color—not the brick-red plumage they had worn in the spring, but ruddy enough to let me make an identification. They were the red knots Kristinn Skarphéðinsson had told me about, the shorebirds that staged on the flats of Löngufjörur in such great numbers in the spring. Now they, too, were on the move, faring south.

The rain beat on the sand. It ran in rivulets on the gentle slopes of the flats. I reached the mouth of the salmon river. An oystercatcher stood bobbing nervously, then went winging off as I drew near, its shrill *beek-beek-beek* swallowed in the rain. A band of purple sandpipers seemed as composed as the oystercatcher had been panicky; I sat down less than twenty feet from one of the trusting creatures, who, when it closed its eyes, blended perfectly with the rain-washed rocks.

In the channel a seal went past, moving seaward. The

seal's head cut through the water, and the water healed it-self. The seal looked like a wraith, like someone's fetch.

The fetch—*fylgja* in Icelandic—was a powerful omen to the Norse people. It could be a close relative, no longer living, who followed you around and watched over you. Or an apparition in animal form, a ghostly double of its fleshly counterpart. If you saw this second type of specter, you were fated to soon die. In *Njál's Saga*, a man named Thórður sees, within the bounds of Njál's homefield, a startling symbol: "The goat seems to be lying in the hollow there, drenched in blood," he says to his friend Njál. Njál replies that he sees no goat, or anything else. "Then what is it?" Thórður asks. "It means you are a doomed man," Njál says. "That was your fetch you have seen. Be on your guard." To which Thórður replies resignedly, "That will not help me much if that is to be my fate."

Fylgja is also the Icelandic word for the placenta, source of sustenance in the womb, and, when finally exposed, evoc-ative of the weltered mysteriousness of birth, the first step in life's fateful march.

I started off again. To sit was to grow cold in the gloomy air. In the sand-bottomed streams, long strands of electric-green grass flared and twisted. The mountains drifted in and out of the uncertain light.

I found myself at Toppar once again. The place was like a magnet for me; I always seemed to have it in mind as a destination. From there, I could gather each aspect of the environment to the senses: sands, bay, salmon river, rocky islets and skerries, even the mountains and volcanoes and lava wastes, all no farther off than a swivel of the head.

Among the rocks, dunlins were resting: soon they would depart and go as far south as Morocco. Harlequin ducks were buoyant swimmers at ease among the waves that came crashing into Barnasker. The harlequins, like the eiders they fed alongside, would cleave to the rocky Icelandic coast all winter.

A red-throated diver—the Icelanders' *lómur*, a type of loon—cruised in the channel, its body low like a submarine, its dirklike beak angled upward. The diver might stay the winter in Iceland, or it might go south.

A skua winged past, and I wondered if it was one of the pair whose nest had failed on the marsh. The skuas that breed in Iceland spend the winter far out on the Atlantic. They fly south of the equator. No one knows precisely where they go.

The seal lay like a gunny sack stuffed to the limits. Its head was battered, and black with blood; scavengers had opened it at the eyes and nostrils. There still remained an impression of life in the creature's form: the clean, perfectly curved black claws on its front flippers, the back flippers tucked up neatly behind the body.

Webbed gull tracks marked the sand all about. White splashes dappled the seal's back.

Not a fetch. Most definitely a seal, and dead for some time, my nose told me.

The gulls would enjoy more meals. It was a week until stórstreymi, when the tide would rise this high once again, perhaps to float the seal off the sandbar and give it back to the ocean.

Looking at the carcass, I felt no particular emotion. A sack of bones and rotting flesh. No clue as to how it had died: perhaps of nothing more than old age. I wondered if I would look at death for the rest of my life and never again feel the fear it had once inspired in me. Was this attitude in some strange way a gift? Death was an aspect of life I had gotten well acquainted with. The grief and fear that had gripped me for almost a year were showing signs of melting. In their place was a void that nothing could ever quite fill.

The ocean breathed upon the sand. The rain fell. I gazed steadily out to sea, where the water grew dark and deep. I rested for an hour on Toppar. There was no place in the world I would rather have been. But the tide would not let me stay.

Another day, and I was still alone at Little Lava; alone and liking it.

I set out through a breach in the homefield wall and headed north. Since no one knew where I was going, I traveled with an extra measure of caution, moving slowly, testing with my stick, watching for holes and Judas stones.

I spotted movement. A fox. It saw me at the same moment, and when it froze, it disappeared against the charcoal-colored slabs. Then it ran, dodging between boulders with a speed I could scarcely comprehend.

When I reached the spire I climbed it and stood in the

eagles' nest. The nest was made of birch branches and stalks of dried heather. The central cup was lined with moss and grass. On the rocks below lay the curved, naked backbone of a fish; also a pile of gray feathers with some flesh still attached, dark and swarming with flies.

An Englishman, John Wooley, indulged himself in the Victorian pastime of collecting birds' eggs. Wooley was especially keen on accumulating the eggs of the white-tailed sea eagle, many of which he got in Scotland during the mid-1800s, contributing to the eagle's demise in that place. Wooley once wrote: "To enjoy the beauties of a wild coast to perfection, let me recommend to any man to seat himself in an Eagle's nest."

I seated myself in the nest. The light was gray and flat. The coast of Snæfellsnes stretched westward; to the north and east were volcanoes and mountains.

I remembered how I had planned on coming to Iceland and the book I'd intended to write. I envisioned a time of exploration, of immersion in an exotic, out-of-the-way place. I would learn about nature along the coast. I would get to know Iceland and Icelanders.

Well, my summer hadn't quite gone the way I'd envisioned it. I hadn't studied nature. I had simply been present in it and to it.

When Nancy, Will, and I crossed the sands and drove to town for supplies, or went to Stóra Hraun, or visited at Snorrastaðir, it had often surprised me to hear Icelandic being spoken. I hadn't made any effort to learn Icelandic myself.

It had been a saving thing, having the house and the land

waiting. What began as an expedition became a seeking after refuge.

Henry Beston withdrew to his house on Cape Cod not long after the First World War. Beston was a soldier in France. He had seen and participated in carnage and ruin. What demons did he carry with him to his cottage on the shore? He never wrote of those things in his book *The Outermost House*.

He wrote instead about "the turn of the sun's wheel, always the imperative, bright sun," and how all of life followed the sun's cycle. He wrote of storms and wind and waves. He wrote of human life, noting that "the ancient values of dignity, beauty, and poetry which sustain it are of Nature's inspiration; they are born of the mystery and beauty of the world."

His book now seems almost ancient in its own lyricism and elegiac wisdom, although it was written only seventy years ago.

Beston wrote often and beautifully about birds. About shorebirds, "the thin-footed, light-winged peoples, the industrious waders, the busy pickup, runabout, and scurry-along folk." He wrote about terns—"mackerel gulls," as they are known on Cape Cod—and how they assailed any and all intruders near their nests, and fed their fledglings, and flew along above the breakers before sunrise "like spiritual creatures in the dusk."

He wrote of watching a band of gulls on a mild September morning as they sat resting on a sandbar. Something panicked the gulls, which rose quickly and streamed away southward "in a long, fugitive storm of wings." Beston looked up.

"I saw far above the birds, and well behind them, an eagle advancing through the heavens."

Sitting in the eagles' nest, looking out on the lava field and the dark cone of Eldborg, I heard a grating cackle. I lifted my eyes. It was the female eagle, recognizable by her great size. She swooped down and circled above me, making a scolding circuit. Then she flew into the lava and landed far off on a jagged hump. The male rose from where she had landed; he came and circled and scolded me before returning to the same spot. It was there, I assumed, that the eaglet had flown.

The way back to Little Lava was cold and hard. The clouds had settled over western Iceland. The wind was blustery and raw. There were showers over the lava field, gray shifting walls of rain. Snæfellsnes looked like a long, low slab of stone, the tops of its peaks and the glacier hidden.

The house came into view. It was good to get off the lava and onto the yielding soil. The homefield flowers had all faded, save for a few yellow hawkweed blooms scattered through the grass. Picking a path among the thúfur, as I had done so many times that summer I flushed out a snipe. It gave its raspy cry as it curved down into the marsh. I hadn't seen a snipe in several days and was wondering if they, too, had gone. The snipe of Iceland fly south to the bogs and fens of Ireland.

I went into the house. I built up the fire. I wasn't kidding myself, I knew how cold this house and this land would become in winter.

Like the snipe, I was almost ready to go. I could afford to love Little Lava because I could leave it.

18 | A Visitor from the Heath

The kayak glided past Seal Head. The water reflected rocks and islands, with just enough of a breeze to riffle the surface and break up the details.

Four whimbrels flew over, trailing their long legs. Higher up, a line of geese wavered across the sky. Six swans—the white parents and four dusky young—swam up the lagoon, waddled ashore in the saltmarsh meadows, and began grazing.

I slipped between the Stóra Hraun Islands. Crowds of eiders rested on the sandbar. For once, I did not have to fight the wind. The kayak moved easily across Löngufjörur. I had no destination in mind. With Nancy and Will still in the city, I did not have to be back at any set time, had no one to worry if I stayed away too long.

I stopped paddling. The boat coasted, then slowly came to rest. Gently it rocked on the water. The water was the same pearly color as the sky. Sitting in the boat, I was suspended between earth and air.

That evening as the tide ebbed, a truck drove to our parking place. I noticed it as I sat at the kitchen table writing in my notebook. The truck maneuvered so that it was facing across the lagoon. Its headlights flashed twice.

I walked down through the homefield. The man who was coming toward me negotiated the far bog at a brisk pace. We both entered the flats at the same time and met near Stakkholtssteinn.

Heiðar grinned broadly. He opened his arms and bear-hugged me. Rather demonstrative behavior for an Icelander, but then Heiðar was no ordinary Icelander.

"Hello, my friend," he said. He pulled back to arm's length and looked me up and down. "You're looking well."

"You, too," I said, and indeed it did look as if things were going well for Heiðar. It was still officially summer, so he was a salmon guide. In another month he would become a market hunter, the occupation in which he was engaged when I had met him in the West Fjords eight years earlier. Right now he wore shiny chest-high fishing waders made by an upscale American company. A tan many-pocketed vest over a wool sweater with leather patches at the elbows. A long-billed cap. Eyeglasses, tinted ones which I'd never seen on him before. "These?" he said. "Polarized. For seeing the fish in the water." He took them off and folded them into a case. "Very useful, and very expensive." He looked toward Little Lava. "I had no idea the place was this remote."

We started walking.

I had visited Heiðar the previous December, when I was in Iceland to check out Little Lava for the first time; Pétur had dropped me off at his house in the suburbs of Reykjavík. We sat in Heiðar's living room drinking coffee. It was dark outside and raining steadily. His wife was in the kitchen but did not come out and meet me; I wondered if that meant that Heiðar often had guests and they had little in common with his wife. In the background a radio was tuned to a station playing American country-Western music. An announcer said something in Icelandic, and then a song came on, with the twangy repetitive phrase: ". . . there's somethin' women like about a *pickup* man."

That evening Heiðar offered to loan me a .22 rifle for the summer. With it I could shoot seals for meat ("Just eat the backstrap," he advised, "don't bother with the rest") and pick off the occasional ptarmigan, or even a big meaty oystercatcher. I decided not to borrow the gun, however, and hadn't found the time to contact Heiðar later, when I returned to Iceland at the beginning of summer. But I remembered that he was scheduled to guide on the Haffjarðará in late August, and I had driven to the fishing lodge and left a message for him.

"Did you have any trouble finding the place?"

"I stopped at the farmhouse and asked," Heiðar said. "Actually, I came yesterday, but it was high tide." He found the cut in the bog bank and climbed swiftly through it. "Have you caught any fish?"

"Not a one."

He stopped and gave me an astonished look.

I shrugged and made some excuses. Then I told him about the kayak and how it was showing me an entirely different face of Löngufjörur. About the eagles, and finding the nest. We climbed through the homefield. At the house we stood on the stoop. The sky was darkening; a line of clouds was shifting in from the southwest.

I offered Heiðar supper, but he wasn't hungry. "You wouldn't believe how much they feed you at the lodge," he said, lowering himself onto the whalebone stool. "Gourmet food. The best. They have a chef, an Icelander—the guy you left the message with. You'll have to come over for dinner, I can arrange it. Tomorrow, after I'm off the river—I'll pick you up then.

"In the meantime," he said, flashing a grin, "if you have that whiskey . . ." At Heiðar's house last December he had asked that I keep on hand a bottle of his favorite Scotch, Johnnie Walker Black. Coming through the airport's duty-free shop, I had forgotten about his request. However, I did have some Scotch on the shelf, an excellent single malt from the Orkney Islands. I set the bottle on the table and got out two glasses.

"A pity," Heiðar chuckled, unbuttoning one of the pockets in his vest and taking out a can of Coca-Cola, "to waste such good whiskey on me." He poured a generous amount of the whiskey into a glass and added a trickle of cola.

"You have had a fine summer," he said. "So warm and fair." Outside, the light was failing, the clouds covering the mountains. Heiðar lit a cigarette, the flare from the match accenting his cheekbones. On the windowsill was a dish with a candle set upright in it. I lit the candle.

He told me about the anglers he'd been guiding: a Hungarian baroness, a vice president of a Manhattan bank, a consortium of gold prospectors from the United States, Scotland, and South Africa. The prospectors were planning to look for gold in Iceland, a place where the metal has never been mined on a commercial basis. "They say that Iceland is the new frontier," Heiðar said. "I was driving them around, and we stopped, and on the edge of the road they picked up a rock—it had been dumped there by the highway department as fill. And they said, 'Jesus Christ, Heiðar, where did *this* come from?'"

"You really get the high rollers," I said.

Heiðar replied, very seriously, "That's because I'm the best salmon guide in Iceland."

"Who's the most famous person you've ever guided?"

"Well," Heiðar blew cigarette smoke from his nostrils, "I would have to say . . ." He paused. "Ted Turner and Jane Fonda. That was a couple of years ago. Except, unfortunately, their plane could not take off from Atlanta, because there was some kind of an electrical storm." He shrugged. "So they canceled their fishing trip." He poured himself another drink.

"How's the ptarmigan hunting?"

"It's going *great*. I still have Nóra, of course. She is such an excellent dog. And the pointer is working out very well

—this is the dog I got from Sweden. You know, hunting rjúpa used to be a job for me. I needed the money, so I had to get up and go hunting even if the weather was bad, even if the snow was deep or it was very frosty or raining. Now I hunt mainly for pleasure. The salmon guiding is going so well that I can afford to hunt when I want to."

"How many birds are you getting?"

"I used to kill around six hundred a year. Now it's more like two hundred. I'm selling them to friends and other people, I'm not bothering with the restaurants anymore."

"That was a fine time, when you and I and Venni and Einar went hunting in the West Fjords."

He nodded. "It was a good place to hunt." He ground out his cigarette and took another out of the pack. "Tell me, are you seeing any *tóur*?"

Tóur, pronounced toe-er, was the plural for fox.

"When I got here in May, they were doing a lot of barking," I said. "Nancy found a den in the lava with two pups playing out in front of it. Sometimes we see them hunting. They come and eat the food we throw out."

Heiðar screwed up his face, lifted his chin, and let out a long, mournful howl with a guttural undertone. He looked at me and grinned. He leaned back on the stool and howled again. It sounded just like the fox I had heard in early summer, whose calling seemed to move about in the lava heath.

"Heiðar" means heath. It is his middle name. His given name is Ásgeir. Most people know him as Ásgeir Heiðar, although he permits his friends to call him simply Heiðar, and that was how he was introduced to me. His father, he told me once, is a Dane who never married his mother, never recognized his son. In return Heiðar sees no reason to acknowledge his father by using his name. Thus he is one of a few male Icelanders who is not a "-sson"—a Jónsson, a Magnússon, a Snorrason, a Hjartarson.

"You know, the foxes really do kill sheep," Heiðar said. He poured another shot of whiskey, another slosh of Coke. "Once a fox learns to kill sheep, either by watching another fox do it or by experimenting, he becomes a sheep killer for life. That's why the farmers shoot them."

I said I found it hard to imagine a slender, wraithlike fox of ten pounds or so killing a stout Icelandic sheep weighing nearly a hundred pounds.

"What they do is bite the face, again and again." Heiðar made a fast snapping motion with one hand. "The sheep bleeds to death. Once, I saw a fox circling and circling around a sheep, wondering how to kill it. I don't know if he ever figured it out.

"They eat a lot of birds. A fox can carry six birds in his mouth all at the same time, so he can take them home to his children." He took the cigarette from between his lips, lifted his face, and barked again. He barked five or six times. The mournful howling filled the darkened house. He took a drink, set the glass down. "One time in the middle of the night, my fishermen were all asleep in the hut. I was still out on the river. I heard a fox calling on the other side. I called back to him. He was in love with me. We talked back and forth for hours."

I poured us each another drink. The Scotch had a smoky, peaty taste; I drank mine neat. After each swallow, my throat burned and I was seized with a little shudder. I understood that I was getting drunk. I hadn't been drunk in years. My face was warm and my lips were numb, and my hand moved with a stately slowness as it delivered the glass to my mouth. My mind was clear and racing.

I remembered a story Heiðar had told me. "Tell me again about the eagle you caught."

Heiðar grinned. "I took pictures of that eagle, I'll show them to you someday."

It was summer. He was climbing on the mountain above the farm where we had hunted ptarmigan together. Heiðar's wife, and Einar and his wife and their two daughters, were all fishing in the stream that flowed down the valley. Heiðar's Labrador, Nóra, was with them.

The eagle was soaring above the mountain. It got too close to a falcons' nest. The falcons flew up, rose above the eagle, and stooped on the larger bird. With their knouted feet, the faster, more maneuverable falcons struck at the eagle again and again. They drove it to the ground. The eagle crashed onto a ledge on the mountain and crouched there, stunned and panting.

Heiðar approached the eagle. He took its picture. He kept expecting it to fly off. The eagle was huge, with a great pale head. Heiðar took off his sweater and threw it over the eagle. He tied its feet together with one of his bootlaces. He picked the eagle up. It did not resist. He descended the mountain, carrying the eagle in his arms. When he got near to his wife and friends, he called down to them, but they did not hear him above the rushing of the stream. Heiðar had a silent dog whistle in his pocket. He blew on it. Nóra looked up, then ran toward her master; her sudden departure caught the attention of Heiðar's wife and friends.

When they were all looking, Heiðar took his knife and cut the eagle's bonds. He threw the eagle into the air. The huge bird swooped low over his friends' heads. It caught the air with its wings and soared.

"Before I let it go," Heiðar told me, "the eagle looked at me. It stared into my eyes. It seemed to say: 'How dare you touch me.'"

The candle, my face, and Heiðar's face were mirrored in the window. Heiðar drained his glass, placed it emphatically on the table. He recited a poem he had composed in Icelandic, a verse full of alliteration and internal rhyming that compared his enemies to the worms found in the flesh of codfish. Then another poem, which he said dealt with sluttish country women. He told me that the syndicate of gold prospectors were planning to lease a salmon river and wanted him to be the riverkeeper. They would pay him a princely sum to watch over the river and guide them when they came to fish. Heiðar again declared, "I am the best salmon guide in Iceland." He said, "I am the only hunter left in Iceland."

We passed the bottle until it was empty. Heiðar told me I should move to Iceland permanently. He offered to teach me the country. He would take me to the best places to hunt rjúpa and geese. He would teach me how to catch fish. We would go into the deserts of the interior, and he would reveal to me where the hot springs were, the trails and the oases and the caves. "I will show it all to you," he said.

I was certain he meant it. I weighed the offer in my mind. Nancy would no doubt agree to such a move—she might even urge that we do it. Will was young enough to learn Icelandic, although I had no confidence in my own ability to do so. Mom was gone—that wasn't a factor any longer. Iceland was a beautiful, beckoning place. But it would be hard, maybe even impossible, for me to earn a living there as a writer. Maybe I could make it as a hunter and a gillie, in partnership with Heiðar. But my roots were deep in Pennsylvania. And winter in the north was a long, fearsome tunnel that the light of summer could not quite make amends for.

When I told Heiðar I would walk him back across the marsh, he said I needn't bother. "No," I said, "you don't know the way. You might fall in and get wet." This was a teasing insult to an Icelander with Heiðar's outdoor savvy. Also, I didn't want this apparently lucky man taking the luck away from Little Lava.

Outside, we urinated on the edge of a grass-covered mound. The homefield looked like a lumpy blanket. The breeze brought the smell of the sea. The sky had clouded over. It was after midnight, and the light was dim.

"Now we will go *að thúfuganga*," Heiðar announced. He took off at a dead run. His legs churned, and his feet darted this way and that as he planted them between the humps. "Come on!" he yelled back over his shoulder. I started running.

We raced down the hill. It was crazy. A wrong step and I could have wrecked a knee or snapped an ankle.

I followed Heiðar as he dashed through a gap in the barbed-wire fence. Across the bog we ran, startling sheep whose hooves thumped the wet land. We jumped across the winding stream cuts. The heads of the bog cotton were stars suspended above the black abyss of the ground; we soared above them.

We leaped down onto the flats, kicked free of the sucky mud, and churned toward Stakkholtssteinn. We slowed to a walk, breathing hard, laughing. The tidal streams coiled like liquid silver. A faint light limned the horizon. On the far side we commenced running among the thúfur again, until we came up to Heiðar's truck. Neither of us had fallen, although I had stumbled twice and caught myself, palms down in the muck and the grass.

Heiðar was still laughing as he opened the cap on the back of his pickup. His dogs jumped out. Wagging her thick tail, Nóra nuzzled my hand with her wet nose; the pointer, Nella, came up to be petted. I felt their velvety ears and the ripples of their ribs and their panting breath and the hot licks from their tongues. The dogs, too, seemed to be laughing.

I shook hands with Heiðar. Again we embraced. We set a time for me to have dinner at the lodge. He got in the truck and started the engine.

Walking, I smelled the myriad rich scents of the marsh. A redshank rose into the night, crying out with a voice so pure and wild and unknowing that it made my heart soar. Across the flats, I saw a tiny point of light, the candle burning on the windowsill at Little Lava. It guided me back.

19 | *Crossings*

Nancy and Will had been back from Reykjavík for a week. We worked at closing up the house. I took down the geologic map of Snæfellsnes that had been pinned to the wall, folded it, and put it in my pack. I looked in my pocket calendar and counted the hash marks in the upper right corners of the days. They added up to 102: over the summer, I had made 102 trips across the marsh and the flats. This seemed to me to be a lot of comings and goings, when the main impression I had was of staying in one place, being grounded, at home. Our next-to-last day at Little Lava: the walk out in the morning would be my last.

I wondered how long it would be until there was no trace of our presence on the land. How many months for the spoiled skyr and the tags on the teabags to rot in the garbage midden? How many times for the grass to push up until the path we had beaten to the spring was erased? How many tides to smooth away our footprints in the sand?

I would miss Little Lava. And I looked forward to going back to the wooded hills, my real home. Time was gliding on, like a kayak borne by tide and wind. I was ready to face whatever I needed to struggle against.

Will and I took his kite outside; it climbed into the crisp, perfect blue. He sat in my lap and held on to the string. Sunlight streamed down and glinted off the flats. The marsh was bright with autumnal colors. Snæfellsjökull stood pure and white at the end of the peninsula, its summit the sky's only cloud. The day was a going-away present. I was starting to remember that each day is a going-away present.

"Someone's coming," Nancy called. She got out her binoculars. "It's Pétur."

Pack on his back, he came across the sands. We met him at the homefield edge.

He was planning on staying for a few days, to do some photographing and sketching. He had brought lamb steaks and a bottle of wine for our last dinner at Little Lava.

In the morning we said our goodbyes. Nancy, Will, and I trudged down into the marsh. Nancy was crying. We walked out on the sand. When we got to the car, we took a last look back. The house blended with the lava. A tall figure crossed the homefield, headed toward the house.

I took off my pack.

A Note on Icelandic

The following Icelandic letters do not occur in English, although they were part of the alphabet of Old English, spoken from the fifth to the twelfth century. The thorn, Þ (lower case þ), is pronounced like the *th* in "think." The eth, Ð, (ð), is similar to the *th* in "the." The ash, Æ (æ), is like the *i* in "time."

Since the thorn transliterates into an English *th*, I have spelled it that way: Thór rather than Þór, thúfa instead of þúfa. The eth defies exact transliteration, and I have kept it. I have also retained the ash.

In Icelandic, an accent mark above a vowel does not indicate stress (Icelandic words almost invariably receive the stress on the first syllable) but rather that the vowel has a different pronunciation than the unaccented form. The vowels are pronounced roughly like this:

a as in *father*
á as in *cow*
e as in *met*
é is like the *ye* in the Russian *nyet*
i as in *hid*
í as in *deed*
o as in *cot*
ó as in *vote*
u as in *wood*
ú as in *moon*
y as in *rhythm*
ý as in *deed*
ö as in the French *fleur*
au is similar to the vowel sound in *buoy*
ei and *ey* as in *day*
The consonant *j* is always pronounced like the *y* in *yes*.

Acknowledgments

M any people helped in the making of this book. First and foremost, my wife, Nancy Marie Brown, supported me throughout the disruptive, draining months that followed my mother's death; instinctively and wisely, she kept me moving toward Iceland. She translated passages and conversations, helped me remember things and events that I had forgotten, and read the manuscript several times and offered criticism. I value her skills and her steadfast loyalty better than I sometimes remember to say.

Leonard Rubinstein read an early draft, got to the heart of what was wrong with it, and told me how to fix it. He was my writing teacher and remains my friend; he is the most perceptive person I know when it comes to evaluating a piece of writing.

My editor, Paul Elie, knew when to call and check on the book's progress, and when to leave me alone. He, too, helped me understand what it was that I wished and needed to tell.

In Iceland, two friends were indispensable: Thórður Grétarson helped me buy a car (and then sold it after we left) and generally navigated me through modern Icelandic society. He also found and translated information from old books and documents and read a draft of the manuscript. Pétur Baldvinsson helped me fix up the house at Little Lava and was a good compatriot in many other ways. His drawing of the house begins each chapter.

Thórður's parents, Grétar Guðbergsson and Gúðný Thórðardóttir, graciously opened their home to us when we were in Reykjavík. They were extremely kind, especially to our son, William.

Anna Gyða Gylfadóttir and her mother Oddný gave us permission to stay at Litla Hraun. They have a deep feeling for this seat of their family, and I am grateful that they would let us use it for the summer. Thanks are also due their relatives Haukur Sveinbjörnsson and Ingibjörg Jónsdóttir of Snorrastaðir, who allowed us to range across their land and who showed us many other kindnesses.

Finally, I offer special thanks to the family at Stóra Hraun: Kristján, Margrét, Arilíus, Kristín, Jón Thór, Guðlaug, Sigurveig, and Thóra (who rescued Will from the manure pit, an adventure that does not show up in these pages). They were good neighbors.

These others also helped (and I list them in no particular order and apologize to any I may have inadvertently forgotten): Kristinn Skarphéðinsson and Haukur Jóhannesson at Náttúrufræðistofnun Íslands, Hjörtur Hinriksson and the family at Helgafell, Sólveig Gunnarsdóttir, Vésteinn Jónsson, Magnús Jóhannsson and Anna María Ágústsdóttir, Ástfríður Sigurðardóttir, Kristín Vogfjörð, Guðrún Bjarnadóttir, Guðmundur Páll Ólafsson, Bernard Scudder, Patrick J. Stevens at Cornell University's Fiske Icelandic Collection, Matthew Driscoll, Nigel Foster, Larry Edwards, Ralph Diaz, Richard Fortmann and Anne Crowley, Bob Montler, Dale Gericke and Elizabeth Llewellyn, John and Amy Bravis, Margaret Brittingham, Upton Brady, Lynn Warshow, Icelandair, and Feathercraft Kayaks.